START YOUR OWN COLD STORAGE UNIT

OTHER RELATED BOOKS

- Fruits & Vegetables Processing Hand Book
- Fruit Beverages & Processing With Mango Products
- Food Processing & Agro Based Industries
- Manufacturing Technology of Snacks Food, Namkeen, Pappad & Potato Products
- Preservation & Canning of Fruits and Vegetables
- Hand Book of Food Dehydration & Drying
- Meat Processing & Meat Products Hand Book
- Technology of Food Preservation & Processing
- Hand Book of Food Packaging Technology
- Agro Based & Processed Food Products
- Potato & Potato Processing Technology
- Technology of Maize & Allied Corn. Products
- Technology of Food Processing Industries
- Technology of Sweets (Mithai) with Formulae
- Hand Book of Organic Farming And Organic Foods With Vermi-Composting and Neem Products
- Hand Book of Fish Farming And Fishery Products
- Hand Book of Mushroom Cultivation, Processing And Packaging
- Hand Book of Spices & Packaging With Formulaes
- Start Your Own Cold Storage Unit
- Hand Book of Bakery Industries
- Hand Book of Confectionery With Formulations
- Breakfast, Dietary Food, Pasta & Cereal Products Technology
- Hand Book of Modern Bakery Products
- Modern Bakery Technology & Fermented Cereal Products With Formulae
- Technology of Confectionery, Chocolates, Toffee, Candy, Chew-ing & Bubble Gums, Lollipop and Jelly Products with Formulations
- Hand Book of Poultry Farming & Feed Formulations
- Hand Book of Pig Farming
- Agro Based Hand Book of Plantation, Cultivation & Farming
- Agro Based Plantation Cultivation & Farming
- Agro Chemical Industries (Insecticide & Pesticides)
- Modern Bee Keeping & Honey Processing
- Technology of Modern Rice Milling And Basmati Rice
- Hand Book of Goat Farming
- Floriculture Hand Book (Flowers Growing Technology)
- Aloe Vera Cultivation, Processings, Formulations And Manufacturing Technology
- Hand Book of Dairy Formulations, Processes & Milk Processing Industries
- Milk Processing And Dairy Products Industries
- Hand Book of Dairy Farming to Produce Milk with Packaging
- Hand Book of Ice Cream Technology And Formulae
- Hand Book of Milk Processing Dairy Products And Packaging Technology
- Dairy Farming for Milk Production Technology
- Ayurvedic & Herbal Medicines With Formulaes
- Hand Book of Ayurvedic Medicines With Formulations (A Complete Hand Book of Ayurvedic & Herbal Medicines)

* E-Mail: eiribooks@yahoo.com & eiriprojects@gmail.com
*Website: www.eiriindia.org & www.industrialprojectreports.com

START YOUR OWN COLD STORAGE UNIT

Written By

EIRI BOARD OF CONSULTANTS & ENGINEERS

ENGINEERS INDIA RESEARCH INSTITUTE

4449, Nai Sarak, Main Road, Delhi - 110006 (India)
Ph: +91-11-23918117, 23916431, 45120361, 23947058, 64727385
* E-Mail: eiribooks@yahoo.com & eiriprojects@gmail.com
*Website: www.eiriindia.org & www.industrialprojectreports.com

PRINTED & PUBLISHED BY

ENGINEERS INDIA RESEARCH INSTITUTE

4449, Nai Sarak, Main Road, Delhi - 110006 (India)
Ph: +91-11-23918117, 23916431, 45120361, 23947058, 64727385
* E-Mail: eiribooks@yahoo.com & eiriprojects@gmail.com
*Website: www.eiriindia.org & www.industrialprojectreports.com

Sole Distributor:

EIRI PROJECT CONSULTANTS AND PUBLISHERS
4/54 Roop Nagar, Delhi-110007

3rd Edition

ISBN: 9788186732205

Printed in New Delhi (INDIA)

₹ 900/-

Printed & Published by Sudhir Gupta for "Engineers India Research Institute", 4449 Nai Sarak, Main Road, New Delhi -110006

PREFACE

Cold Storage is a special kind of room, the temperature of, which is kept very low with the help of machines and precision instruments. India is having a unique geographical position and a wide range of soil thus producing variety of fruits and vegetables like apples, grapes, oranges, potatoes, chillies, ginger, etc. Marine products are also being produced in large quantities due to large coastal areas. The present production level of fruits and vegetables is more than 100 million MT and keeping in view the growth rate of population and demand, the production of perishable commodities is increasing every year. The cold storage facilities are the prime infrastructural component for such perishable commodities. Besides the role of stabilizing market prices and evenly distributing both on demand basis and time basis, the cold storage industry renders other advantages and benefits to both the farmers and the consumers.

The farmers get opportunity of producing cash crops to get remunerative prices. The consumers get the supply of perishable commodities with lower fluctuation of prices. Commercially apples, potatoes, oranges are stored on large scale in the cold storages. Other important costly raw materials like dry fruits, chemicals, essences and processed foods like fruit juice/pulp, concentrate dairy products, frozen meat, fish and eggs are being stored in cold storages to regulate marketing channels of these products.

Cold storages are essential for extending the shelf life, period of marketing, avoiding glut, reducing transport bottlnecks during peak period of production and maintenance of quality of produce. The development of cold storage industry has therefore an important role to play in reducing the wastages of the perishable commodities and thus providing remunerative prices to the growers.

There are no harmful effluents in the process. However, NOC may be taken from the concerned State Pollution Control Baord.

Proper insulation should be given to avoid loss of heat/temperature. Quality Control and Standards The Directorates of Agricultural Marketing and Inspection in State Governments and Govt., of India are regulating cold storage industry under Cold Storage Order, 1980, promulgated under Essential Commodities Act, 1955 all over India except in the States of UP, West Bengal, Punjab and Haryana and provisionally in Bihar. State Governments are regulating the industry in their respective States under their respective Acts/Orders. The Ministry of Agriculture has now repealed the Cold Storage Order and advised the State Governments also to repeal it totally. With the repeal of this Order, the cold storage industry will now be able to enter the market free from all kinds of administrative interference.

The book **Start Your Own Cold Storage Unit** contains 23 chapters, i.e, *Special Features of Cold Storage Project, Brief About Refrigerated Cold Storage, B.IS. Specification,Selection of the Location for the Cold Storage, Production Details and Process of Manufacture, Operating Conditions, Principles of Fresh Food Storage, Refrigeration, Technical and Design Section, Main Features of Ammonia Compressors, Refrigerated Cold Storage Design, Quotation for 50,000 Bags Cold Storage Plant, Quotation for 1,00,000 Bags Cold Storage Plant, Quotation for 1,50,000 Bags Cold Storage Plant, Details of Equipments Machineries, Project Profiles, Vaccine Cold Chain, Controlled Atmosphere Storage, Cold Storage (Controlled Atmosphere, Apple), Cold Storage of Pears, Cold Storage for Potato and Other Horticulture Products, Plant Rconomics of Cold Storage (Controlled Atmosphere or CA), Refrigerated Cold Storage Equipments & Allied Equipment Suppliers.*

EIRI Board of Consultants & Engineers

Contents-cum-Index

Chapter 6

Operating Conditions .. 21-24

Chapter 7

Principles of Fresh Food Storage 25-48

Chapter 8

Chapter 9

Technical and Design Section 86-103

Chapter 10

Main Features of Ammonia Compressors 104-130

Chapter 11

1

SPECIAL FEATURES OF COLD STORAGE PROJECT

1. Priority Sector as per Govt. Policy :

Today, we have a very weak post-harvested storage and marketing infrastructure. This causes tremendous national loss. To overcome this problem, in the recent Union budget it has been proposed to introduce a new creditlinked capital subsidy scheme for construction of cold storages and godowns. This scheme, which will be implemented by the ministry of Agriculture with the help of NABARD, will help create additional cold storage capacity of 12 lakh Tonnes and will rehabilitate and modernise 8 lakh Tonnes of existing units over the next few years. Further proposed to create an additional 4.5 lakh Tonnes of onion storage capacity. Govt. will provide many other facilities for setting up a new cold storage project.

2. Easy Financing Facilities :

Finance may be taken from various National/State level Financial Institutions such as IDBI, SIDBI, IFCI, NCDC, HFC, HSIDC, DFC, UPFC, PICUP, RFC, RIICO, PFC, PSIDC, etc. The terms and conditions of these FI's are very reasonable and affordable, such as lower rate of Interest, easy repayment schedule, fast processing of the loan case, etc.

3. Easy to Manage :

A cold storage project is very ease tō manage and operate. It does not require a very high technology & know-how to be employed. Simple qualified staff are sufficient to operate the plant. A promoter without having any previous knowledge and experience of this project can also set up a new cold storage plant easily and run the same smoothly.

4. Only Fixed Assets Investment :

All the investment to be made will be towards Fixed Assets only such as Land, Civil Construction, Plant & Machinery. There is no requirement of Working Capital Investment. Only **Term Loan** is required to finance this **Cold Storage Project**. The Fixed Assets will provide a good security to the Lenders.

5. High Rate of Return :

There is a very high rate of return in this project. The occupancy rate of cold storage is very high due to lack of these facilities. The charges generally taken by the cold storage owners are far higher, sometimes more than 4 times, than the Govt. fixed charges due to big Demand-Supply Gap. The chances of failure of a cold storage plant is very minimal since there is no problem of marketing.

6. High Demand of Cold Storage Facility :

There is very high demand of cold storage facilities in all the agricultural dominated areas specially in the potato growing regions. Every year the marketing of Potato, Tomato, Onions gets a very adverse setback due to non availability of Cold storage facility to store these agricultural produce in time.

7. Tax Benifits :

The Union Budget has announced a few very strong tax benefits to the cold storage project to be set up newly.

Where a cold storage plant begins to operate at any time during the period begining on the 1st day of April,1995 and ending on the 31st day of March 2000 shall be entitled for a deduction of 25% or 30% where the assessee is a company of the profits and gains for a period of 10 Consecutive Assessment Years. (12 years in case of a Co-operative Society).

Where the cold storage plant begins to operate at any time during the period begining on the 1st day of Oct. 1994 and ending on the 31st day of March 2000 shall be entitled for a deduction of 100% of the profits and gains located in a backward district of Category 'A' (for 5 assessment years) and of category 'B' (for 3 assessment years) begining with the initial assessment years and thereafter 25% or 30% where the assessee is a company of the profits and gains for a period of total 10 Consecutive Assessment Years. (12 years in case of a Co-Operative Society).

8. Financial Incentive :

The ministry of Agriculture, the department of Horticulture has proposed to introduce capital subsidy scheme for the new cold storage project to be set up in the backward areas and other areas. It has been recommended the subsidy may be available to the new entrepreneur upto 25% of the investment in fixed assets in the project. It will prove to be a good amount of incentive to boost up the courage for the potential investors/ entrepreneurs who are willing to venture for this cold storage unit.

Brief Analysis of a Model Cold Storage Project

Cost of Project	:		Rs. 450.00	Lacs
Means of Finance	:	Capital :	Rs. 180.00	Lacs
		Term Loan :	Rs. 270.00	Lacs
			Rs. 450.00	Lacs

Rate of Return on Investment	:	60%
DSCR	:	3.50
B.E.P.	:	30%
Repayment of Term Loan	:	8 Years
Occupancy rate of the unit	:	80%

Courtesy : Mr. Ramesh Kumar Aggarwal, (C.A.)

Note : Patrons may also approach 'EIRI' for getting Project Finance of Cold Storage.

2

BRIEF ABOUT REFRIGERATED COLD STORAGE

Refrigerated Cold Storage is any building or section which control storage condition using refrigeration.

Cold storage industry is a very important and essential industry. In India, fruits and vegetables are produced in plenty. A large number of fruits and vegetables are exported to other countries and even in India itself fruits and vegetables are transported from one place to another. This transportation business takes some time. So, it is desirable that fruits should be kept at a place where they can remain safe, otherwise lots of its will be wasted. For this purpose, Cold Storage is used.

Cold Storage is a special kind of room the temperature of which is kept very cold with the help of machines and instruments. The temperature is maintained low with the help of precision instruments. In deciding the scale of a cold storage plant, all the external condition locational conditions stored, object etc. must be considered. When the scale of plant is larger however running costs would generally be less and automation would become more exact.

Cold storage is used to preserve fruits, vegetables, medicines, dairy products, dry fruits etc. Once they are kept in the cold storage, they do not get spoiled even after many months. Some times, in production season of certain vegetable or fruit crop, the demand for that thing decreases, which in turn decreases the consumption in surplus amount of that particular item is kept in a cold storage.

The conditions within a closed Refrigerated chamber must be maintained to preserve the stored commodities. This refers particularly to seasonal, self life and long-term storage. Specific items for consideration as under :

1. Uniform Temperatures.
2. Length of Air blow and impingement on stored product.
3. Effect of Relative Humidity.
4. Effect of Air Movement.
5. Controlling Ventilation Systems, if necessary.
6. Product Entering Temperature.
7. Expected Duration of Storage.
8. Required Product outdoor Temperature.
9. Transportation in and out of Storage Area.

3

B I S SPECIFICATIONS

A number of Indian Standard Specifications have been formulated for the refrigeration industry, they include performance standards, safety standards, basic standard and glossary of terms.

The Indian standards are listed below:-

Indian Standards on Refrigeration & Air Conditioning Industry

IS :	659-1964	Safety code for air-conditioning.
IS :	660-1963	Safety code for mechanical refrigeration.
IS :	661-1964	Code of practice for insulation and safe operation of cold storages.
IS :	1391-1960	Room air-conditioners.
IS :	1474-1959	Commercial refrigerators.
IS :	1475-1959	Self-contained water-coolers.
IS :	1476-1959	Domestic refrigerators (mechanically operated)
IS :	2143-1962	Open surface milk-coolers with tinned copper tubes.
IS :	2167-1962	Bottle-coolers.
IS :	2370-1963	Sectional cold rooms (walk-in type).
IS :	2372-1963	Timber for cooling towers.
IS :	3615-1967	Glossary of terms used in refrigeration and air-conditioning.
IS :	3621-1966	Domestic refrigerator (absorption type).

IS :	3661-1966	Farm milk cooling tanks.
IS :	3719-1966	Open surface milk-coolers with aluminium tubes.
IS :	4192-1967	Aluminium farm milk cooling tanks.

Above Specifications may be obtained from

Bureau of Indian Standards,

9, B.S. Zafar Marg,

New Delhi - 110 002.

NOTE :- The use of the ISI Certification Mark is governed by the provisions of the Indian Standards Institution (Certification Marks) Act and the Rules and Regulations made there under. The ISI Mark on products covered by an Indian Standard conveys the assurance that they have been produced to comply with the requirements of that standard under a well-defined system of inspection, testing and quality control which is devised and supervised by ISI and operated by the producer. ISI marked products are also continuously checked by ISI for conformity to that standard as a further safeguard. Details of conditions under which a licence for the use of the ISI Certification

4

SELECTION OF THE LOCATION FOR THE COLD STORAGE

Mark may be granted to manufacturers or processors, may be obtained from the Indian Standards Institution.

Important locations for Cold Storage, Public or Private are :

1. Point of Processing
2. Intermediate Points for General Commodities
3. Final Distribution Point

Selection of location for the cold storage is a very important task. So, this should be done very carefully. While selecting a location for the cold storage the following factors should be accounted for:-

1. Market and production field should be near the cold storage so that the expenditure incurred in to and for transportation is less and it is convenient also.

2. Cold storage should be near a highway so that the transportation to other cities is not difficult.

3. At the site of the cold storage, the cost of the land should be less.

4. There should be a convenient arrangement of water and electricity at the location, where cold storage is to be established.

Taking these factors into account, the suitable site for cold storage is chosed and then building is constructed after that machines and instruments are installed to keep the building cold.

REFRIGERANTS :

The following compounds are used in refrigeration systems:

i. Ammonia
ii. Sulphuric acid
iii. Carbonic acid
iv. Sulphuric ether
v. Methyl ether
vi. Freon

Ammonia and freon are utilized for commercial refrigeration as refrigerants because they have good refrigerating properties. For Ice Plants only Ammonia is used being cheap and less hazardous.

Refrigerant	Pressure in psi at 0°C	Evaporating heat per pound at 0°C	Specific heat of liquid	Required compress on density	Liquid loss during cooling
Sulphuric Acid	10	171.2	0.41	61.7	0.24
Carbonic Acid	310	123.2	1.00	32.4	0.81
Ammonia	30	555.5	1.02	23.3	0.18

From the above comparative chart we predict that carbonic acid has the highest pressure hence very rugged and strong machinery equipments are needed. Sulphuric acid has the least and ammonia medium. Sulphuric acid handling requires special material of construction for machinery. So only ammonia is the only choice left.

Column No.2 and 3 of the chart show that ammonia has the highest heat of evaporation and liquid specific heat. The heat of evaporation and liquid specific heat. The heat of evaporation is defined as the amount of heat required in order to evaporate one pound of liquid into vapour 0°C. The liquid specific heat is defined as the amount of heat required to increase the temperature of 1.0 gram at the substance by 1°C in liquid phase. Since ammonia has the highest heat of evaporation and liquid specific heat it is the best refrigerant out of the three. So the total refrigerant required for achieving a given refrigeration capacity is the least in the case of ammonia and hence of our choice.

Column No. 4 indicates the size of compressor needed for different refrigerants. Sulphuric acid requires compressor of very big size, carbonic acid of very smaller size and ammonia of medium and moderate size column No. 5 allows the loss of refrigerants during cooling step. Carbonic acid has the biggest loss and ammonia has the least. so the recharging amount of refrigerant required is very little for ammonia and hence the least expensive.

Thus we conclude that ammonia is the best refrigerant for an ice plant technically as well as economically hence ammonia is employed in the ice plant.

Name of Liquid or Gas	Water	Ammonia	Sulphur-Methyl ice ether ether		Sulphur Dioxide
Specific gravity when Air's specific gravity is one	0.622	0.59	2.24	1.61	2.29
Boiling temperature at atmospheric pressure	212	-37.3^{0}	96^{0}	-10.5	14^{0}
Latent Heat	966	900	165	473	132

The above chart gives properties of ammonia in comparison to other refrigerants. From the above chart we infer that specific gravity of ammonia is the less implying that total refrigerants weight during handling is less and hence easy and economical operation. The boiling point is also the least, namely -37.3° meaning most potent evaporating refrigerant. Hence very quick in heat removal so efficient in working. The latent heat is defined as the amount of heat required to evaporate one kg. of the substance at its boiling temperature. The latent heat from the above charts of ammonia is the highest next to water. The means amount has a larger heat removing capacity than others.

In view of the above said advantages ammonia is the final choice as a refrigerant in the ice plant.

PROPERTIES OF AMMONIA :

Having selected ammonia as the final refrigerant in the ice plant we should have a look at its various properties of our use. Pure ammonia is never used but a mixture. Ammonia is prepared in order to improve upon its thermodynamic properties, making it the most efficient and economics. The folloiwng charts give properties at various physical conditions.

Ammonia Mixture

Beaumi	Specific	% of Ammonia in the Mixture	Beaumi	Specific Gravity	% of Ammonia in the Mixture
10	1.00	0.0	21	0.927	19.4
11	0.99	1.8	22	0.921	21.4
12	0.98	1.8	23	0.915	23.4
13	0.979	5.0	24	0.909	25.3
14	0.872	6.7	25	0.903	27.7
15	0.965	8.4	26	0.897	30.1
16	0.958	10.4	27	0.891	32.5
17	0.952	11.9	28	0.886	35.2
18	0.945	13.7	29	0.880	——
19	0.939	15.5	30	0.875	——
20	0.933	17.4	——	——	——

The above chart gives an idea about ammonia mixture being good or bad. Pure ammonia has a specific gravity of 0.623 and use of pure ammonia is very hazardous from the health point of view of workers and the neighbourhood. So the general practice of using ammonia is in mixture ammonia form. So from the above chart we conclude that generally 29.5% or in its vicinity of ammonia mixture is used.

Having looked at the nature of mixture ammonia with respect to its purity and specific gravity at various degrees, Beaumi, we should now consider its various thermodynamic properties of our interest. The following chart gives its thermodynamic properties.

TEMPERATURE OF AMMONIA AT VARIOUS SECTIONS TEMPERATURE

Temp. of Section	Condenser Absolute Pressure	Section pressure in Absolute					
		20	25	30	35	40	50
0	90	199	165	138	116	98	83
0	130	261	222	193	169	150	132
0	160	296	257	226	202	181	163
10	130	275	237	217	183	163	145
10	90	213	110	151	129	110	96
10	160	313	273	241	216	195	176
20	90	228	192	164	141	123	106
20	130	291	152	222	197	176	158
20	160	329	228	256	230	209	190
25	90	235	199	171	148	129	111
25	130	299	259	229	204	183	165
25	160	338	296	264	237	216	197
30	90	242	206	177	154	134	118
30	130	307	267	236	211	190	171
30	160	346	304	271	245	223	203
32	90	245	209	179	157	137	121
32	130	310	270	239	213	192	174
32	160	350	317	274	248	226	206

In the above chart it is shown how compressed ammonia temperature varies after compressed into the compressor. In the chart ammonia gas pressure is in psi absolute. The following example clarifies the charts understanding and practical use of it.

According to chart 32° is the temperature of section or tank and condenser pressure is absolute is 160, that means the gauge pressurize 145. IN the chart 50 pound section pressure absolute or 35 pound pressure gauge shown ammonia gas temperature at 206 degree which is the highest. This implies about compressed gas that the more it is hot the more heat is removed hence early cooling.

The above chart shows that as we increase section pressure

condenser pressure and section temperature there will be a corresponding increase in the heat of the compressed gas. The following chart is about refrigerating power of ammonia at various section temperature.

Section Ammonia Temperature	Section Pressure (Gauge)	Liquid Temperature in °F				
		Condenser Pressure at the Temperature Gauge Corresponding				
		103	115	127	139	168
0	16	54.8	54.3	53.7	53.2	52.0
5	20	61.5	60.8	60.2	59.6	58.3
10	24	68.6	67.9	67.2	66.5	65.1
15	28	75.8	75.1	73.3	72.5	72.0
20	33	85.1	83.3	83.4	82.5	80.8
25	39	95.5	94.5	93.5	92.6	90.7
30	45	106.2	105.1	104.0	103.0	100.9
35	51	115.2	114.5	113.0	111.2	109.9

The chart shows a relationship between various section or condenser pressure, and heat removal by one cubic foot of ammonia. The heat removed is in B.T. U (British Thermal Unit). For examples table the last line of chart. The section temperature is 35°F. corresponding to the section pressure is 51.

At this condition if condenser pressure is 103 pounds then the heat removed by one cubic foot of ammonia is 115.2 B.T.U., and if the condenser pressure is 168 pounds the heat removed will be 109.9 B.T.U. for the same amount of ammonia. So the best results are obtained at condenser pressure of 103 pounds.

5

PRODUCTION DETAILS AND PROCESS OF MANUFACTURE

There are two popular refrigerants in the market present one is Freon and other is Ammonia. Ammonia and Freon compressors are being manufactured indigenously. Ammonia Refrigerant is cheap, easily available and is of high latent that of evaporation but has various disadvantages like highly toxic in nature and also forms explosive mixture when it is mixed with oil containing high percentage of carbon.

Rooms of different temperatures must be separated by insulation and should be protected from moisture.

Whenever possible, one coating of foam glass with vapour proof material should be used against the outside wall.

While fixing the insulation, the points taken are:-

a) The surface to be insulated should be completely moisture proof and be reasonably even, free of lump or hole plaster on the walls and ceiling must be before surface is insulated.

b) Precautions may be taken to ensure that the moisture from outside can not penetrate through the wall ceiling floor.

The fruits and vegetables which are to be kept in cold storage are sorted out and blemished cones are to be removed. The sorted material is packed in boxes or in the jute bags and are kept in cold chambers of the storage. The temperature and R.M. is to be maintain depending upon the fruit and vegetables kept in it. The requirements for successful storage of some of fruits and vegetables are given in the following table:

Name of fruit	Storage Temp. (FO)	Cold Storage Life (Weeks)	Remarks
1	2	3	4
1. Apples	32-35	7-26	Small fruits keep better than large ones.
2. Berry Fruits	30-32	2-3	
3. Bananas	55-60	2-3	
4. Cherries	30-32	2-3	
5. Guavas	47-50	3-4	
6. Grapes	30-32	4-6	Furigation with 1.2% sulphur dioxide before storage reduccs decay. Storage life can be increased to 8-12 weeks
7. Lemons	50-55	9-13	Lemons for Storage should be picked at the greenish yellow colour.
8. Mandarin Orange (Loose Skinned)	45-50	4-6	
9. Oranges (Tight Skinned)			Tight-Skinned Oranges can also be kept at over temperature if to be stored for less than 8 weeks.
i Malta (Punjab)	36-39	13-17	
ii Sathguli (Madras)	39-42	13-17	
iii Mussambi (Bombay)	42-45	43-47	
10. Pears	30-32	2-4	
11. 50-55	50-55	3-4	

OPTIMUM STORAGE CONDITIONS FOR VEGETABLE R.H. 85-90 EXCEPT FOR (*) 90-95%

Name of vegetable	Storage Temp. (FO)	Cold Storage Life (Weeks)	Remarks
1	2	3	4
1. Beans	32-35	2-3	Beans are liable to sweet in storage. Need more ventilation should be in crate & not in bags
2. Beetroot	32-35	6-8	
3. Brinjals	47-50	3-4	Big brinjals keep better than small ones
4. Carrot	32-35	13-17	
5. Cauliflowers	32-35	4-6	Only firm and compact heads should be stored as loose heads ahrivel badly
6. Cabbage	32-35	9-13	Only firm and compact heads should be stored
7. Onions	32-35	17-26	
8. Potatoes	37-38	25-35	In cold storage potatoes become sweet due to accumulation of sugars. This defect can be removed by keeping potatoesof ordinary room temp. for 1-2 weeks before they are processed.

PROCESS DESCRIPTION (COLD STORAGE)
ARRANGEMENT OF COLD STORAGES :

The cold storage described in this book will be used for variuous fruits & vegetables including medicines, dry fruits, potatoes etc. So keeping this in mind, there should be two rooms in the cold storage. One room is meant for potato seeds and other room is meant for potato vegetables. Potato seeds are kept in the cold storage for almost six months i.e., till the season for seeding comes. But the storage of potato vegetables depends upon the consumption of potatoes. There should be a pre-cooling chamber between these two rooms. Fruits and other vegetable and other vegetable can be kept in this precooling chamber.

Usually, potatoes are kept in large packets made of jute which in turn, are kept in the cold storage. This practice should be discontinued because it is not useful. These jute contains are bad conductors of heat and act as heat insulator. Due to this, effect cold atmosphere decrease on the potatoes and in turn the potatoes do not get cold fully.

While installing a cold storage, it should be planned in a way so that the capacity of cold storage can be increased in future. It is desirable to have a high plant room with some space left in it. This empty space can be utilized to install the plant & machineries in the future. The floor of the plant room should never be permanent because, this floor may create problems while attempts are made to increase the capacity.

It is recommended that two compressors should be used. In this, both will have 50% load each for keeping the potatoes cold. This is very useful in one respect that when both the chambers have potatoes in them then both the compressors are used. While, only one chamber has potatoes in it, only one compressor will be used.

This economies the cost of operation. Another important equipment used in a cold storage is a condenser. There are three types of condensers available in the market.

1. Shell & tube condenser.
2. Atmospheric type condenser.
3. Other type condenser.

Out of these three, atmospheric type condenser is used in most of the cases.

Atmospheric type condenser has one distinct advantage over the other condensers that even hard water does not effect this condenser. Because, in this case water is sprayed over the condenser coil only. In case of hard water, some impurities are deposited over the upper portion of coil which can be cleaned with the help of a brush.

Usually two types of refrigerants are used in the condenser.

1. Freon Refrigerant.
2. Ammonia Refrigerant.

Both of these refrigerants are manufactured in India. Ammonia refrigerant is easily available in the market and is very useful also. It has got high latent heat of evaporation. It is a cheap refrigerent and its odour can be tolerated. But it has got one big draw back that when it is mixed with an oil containing carbon, it firms an explosive.

Freon is free from such draw backs but it is a costly refregerent .

INSULATING OF WALLS :-

It is very necessary to insulate the cold storage walls other side the heat from outside will come into the room which will result in extra expenditure into maintain the specified temperature. So it is desirable that both the sides of the walls should be insulated. At the same time, the walls in the middle of cold chambers should also be insulated because some times only one cold chamber is needed e.g. when the season for seeding comes, the seeds are taken out or the one chamber and only potatoes are left in the other chamber. So, that time, this insulation will help. The thickness of the insulation should be half of the insulation thickness of the outer walls.

The insulation layer should be kept protect from humidity and water because of two reasons first it is easy to keep dry the wet layer.

Secondly, if this layer gets humid or wet its insulation power decrease to a large extent. To protect the insulation layer from water and humidity, outside layer has to be protected from air because in summer, humidity of the air increases. The humid air which comes in contact with the insulating layer, some amount of water is transferred to the layer, and it becomes humid. It is suggested that the insulations should be converted by a layer of a water proof substances such as foam glass.

The insulation layer on the roof should be thicker by 10% as compared to the normal thickness because the sun rays fall on the roof without any obstacle. There is a more chance of heat escaping from outside in this case.

The following materials can be used for insulation :-

1. Thermocole
2. Thermofoam
3. Thermolloyed
4. Cellotherm
5. Expanded Polystrene.

The thickness of insulation varies with the temperature required in the cold storage.

Room Temperature	Thickness of insulation
32 - 35°F	4"
35 - 50°F	3"
50 - 60°F	2½"

CONTROL :

For the temperature controls in cold storage, the machinery & equipments are controlled with the automatic control. The liquid refrigerent is controlled in the coil. An expansion valve can also be used to control the flow of refrigerent. This valve is a automatic ore & results in a heater control.

Vegetable	Temperature	Relative Humidity	Approximate. Storage Life
Potatoes	Early Crop 50°F	85 - 90	
	Late Crop 40°F	85 - 90	5 - 8 months
Tomato	Green 14 - 21°C	85 - 90	2 - 4 weeks
	Ripe 7 - 10°C	85 - 90	2 - 7 days

For cost estimation, we must keep in mind the following points. The cold storage can be economically lower by minimising the cost at insulation, refrigeration & building construction.

The insulation material should have low thermal conductivity then smaller in the thickness of insulation and force a give exterios dimension more space is available for storing. By comparative study it is shown that even the use of costly insulating material is found cheaper in all aspects than to use a cheaper insulating material. The economic thickness of insulation is obtained (Graph -1) after optimizing cost of insulation and running cost of refrigeration. We must also note that larger thickness of insulation yields higher cost of insulation but lesser like refrigeration running period.

GRAPH

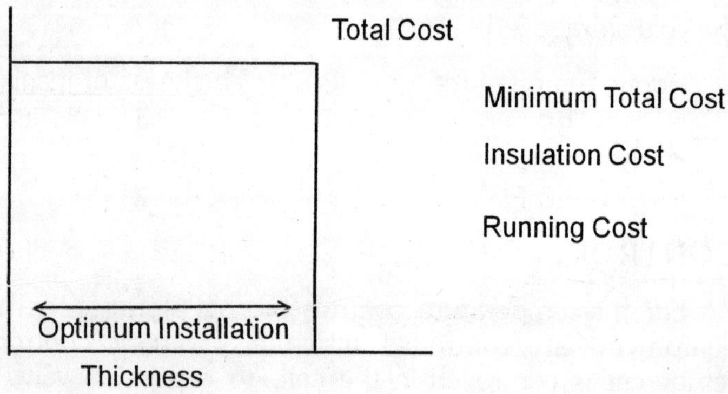

Insulation Thickness

6

OPERATING CONDITIONS

ONION :

Optimum storage condition : Temperature 0°C.
Relative humidity
95 - 98 per cent.

Salad onions should preferably be stored in units no larger than 5-7 Kg. After storage at 0°C and at a relative humidity 98 per cent a shelf life of three days can be expected. For successful storage it is essential for the filled heat to be removed quickly, certainly within 3-4 hours. For this purpose hydrocooling is recommended.

BRUSSELS SPROUTS :

Optimum storage conditions : Temperature 0°C.
Relative humiduty 95-98 per cent.

Brussels sprouts detereorate very rapidly at temperatures above 10°, loss of quality is characterised by yellowing of the outer leaves, loss of turgidity and browning of the cut ends. Generally under commercial conditions storage life will not extend beyond seven days; however, maximum storage life depends to a large extent on the rapdity of cooling and if fast effective cooling can be achieved storage life can be extended. Good air circulation through the container is essential if rapid cooling is to be achieved. The ice bank cooling system with positive ventialation is ideally suited for this. In a conventional store the smaller the container the faster generally the cooling rate.

High humidities are essential for the successful storage of this crop but a loss of moisture through transpiration tends to be high even if the relative humidity is kept at the recommended level.

LETTUCE :

Optimum storage conditions : Temperature 0.5 - 1°C
Relative humidity 95 per cent.

Lettuces are highly perishable and should therefore be stored only in periods of surplus and over weekends or holidays. Deterioration shows as wilting, yellowing of the outer leaves and discolouration of but ends.Generally, storage beyond seven days cannot be recommended.

Successful storage largely depends on prompt cooling after harvest. For this season vaccum cooling has been found to be the most effective method available for precooling lettuce. So that in the USA, where greater distances and temperatures are involved, the majority of lettuce is packed into cartons and is vacuum cooled immediately before shipment in refrigerated transport.

Storage at 0.5-1°C greatly retards deterioration, but as lettuce is easily damaged by freezing, it is important that all parts of the storage room be kept above freezing, it is important that all parts of the storage room be kept above freezing point.

High humidity is essential to maintain lettuce in a fresh turgid condition. For this reason individual head wraps using perforated plastic bags help to reduce weight loss during storage.

Optimum storage conditions : Temperature 0°C.
Relative humidity 95-98 per cent.

Salad onion should preferably be stored in units no larger than 5-7 kg. After storage at 0°C and at a relative humidity of 98 per cent a shelf life of three days can be expected. For successful storage it is essential for the field heat to be removed quickly, certainly within 3-4 hours. For this purpose hydro-cooling is recommended.

ASPARAGUS:-

Optimum storage conditions : Temperature 7.5 - 8.0°C
Relative humidity 85 per cent.

Asparagus can be held in store for short periods of up to ten days. Even at 0°C the spears slowly lignify and lose flavour, although deterioration is only just noticeable during the first week. At higher temperatures deterioration is more rapid and above 3°C the spears will continue to grow and bend upwards if kept for more than a few hours.

Initial cooling and extraction of field heat will be facilitated if the boxes of spears are stacked so that air can circulate freely around and through each individual stack. After initial cooling, the boxes or stacks are covered with polythene to prevent dehydration during the remaining period of storage.

Asparagus spears can be injured by exposure to excessively low temperatures, precise temperature control is therefore essential.

TOMATOES:-

Optimum storage conditions : Temperature 7.5 - 8.0°C
Relative humidity 85 per cent.

At 7.5 to 8°C tomatoes may be held in store successfully storage upto ten days. A relative humidity higher than 85 per cent may increase the likelihood of grey mould (Botrytis), especially on the calyx.

Tomatoes, being of tropical or sub-tropical origin, Its require storage temperatures considerably higher than most indigenous fruit and vegetables. At temperature below 7°C symptoms of injury from chilling will develop, either in store or during subsequent ripening at ambient temperatures. The extent of the injury will depend on the temperature and duration of storage. Slight chilling is characterised by changes in pigmentation of the skin which develops a somewhat orange hue, in contrast to the normal, deep red colour. Several injury will occur at 2°C where the symptoms are rogues or even pitted skins, blotchy, uneven coloration with a translucent appearance : ultimately a large proportion develop bladery. Water soaked area. In general, the riper, the fruit, the less succepitable it becomes to injury.

The following procedure is recommended for the successive starve of tomatoes. The fruit must be selected at the stage of one-quarter ripe since some colouring up will occur during storage. After picking, over-ripe, damaged or diseased fruit must than be called and fruit that is free of blemish transferred to shallow stacking boxes or baskets arranged on pallet bases. The containers can be moved to the storage room and the temperature set at 7.5 to 8.0°C. The time interval between picking the fruit and reaching the store must be kept to the minimum.

When required for market, the fruit should be transferred to a war,, dry well ventilated room or passage where condensation will disperse within two-three hours. When dry, the fruit is ready for grading and packing into retail or wholesale containers.

POTATOES: (For marketing as new)

Optimum storage conditions : Temperature 4-5°C
Relative humidity 95 per cent.

Only very limited quantities of immature potatoes for canning as new are held in refrigerated stores, is usually required for short periods of about three months but can be particularly valuable in allowing the canning of potatoes on processing lines used for other crops and for helping to level out irregular supplies.

Potatoes for canning must be kept at a low temperature to maintain their new condition and so, after a curing period, they should be held at 4-5°C, since new potatoes are characteristically sweet, the sweetening associated with low temperature storage is not a disadvantage. Humidities in the region of 95 per 9cent are required.

7

PRINCIPLES OF FRESH FOOD STORAGE

All foods have a useful storage life and this period can be prolonged or shortened depending on the conditions of storage and the physical abuse the food products receive prior to, during and following storage. In overall analysis the cool storage of nearly all foods, fresh or preserved, is beneficial to the retention of quality. In this chapter we will explore the technology of storage of fresh foods.

NATURE OF HARVESTED CROPS :

The quality of harvested fruits and vegetables is dependent on the conditions of growth and on postharvest treatments. The climatic factors and cultural practices are complex. Fruits as well as vegetables, which are botanically fruits, form a special class of foods which can maintain an independent existence when detached from the tree or vine. The length of storage is a function of composition, resistance to attack by microorganisms, the external conditions of temperature, and the gases in the environment.

A mature harvested fruit contains a variety of oxidizable substrates and the molecular machinery required to perform oxidative reactions. Respiration is the major process of concern and its mechanism is essentially the same in fruits as in other plant and animal life. In fruits, as in other materials, biological oxidants involve a number of metabolic pathways in which synthetic and degradative reactions are interdependent.

Ripening in fruit is a critical period of transition from the stages of cell disorganization and death. Ripening means those changes in sensory factors of color, texture and taste which render the fruit acceptable to eat. It is reported that these changes may be detected by analyzing transformations in pigments, pectins, carbohydrates, acids, tannins, etc. Fruits of different species differ in the nature of and rate of these changes, but most of them share a respiratory pattern known as the climacteric.

The significance of the upsurge in respiration at the end of the maturation phase and preceding breakdown. After harvest the decline in the rate of oxygen uptake and CO_2 evolution to a low value *(preclimacteric minimum)* is followed by a sharp rise to a peak, terminating in a post-climacteric minimum stage. The peak to minimum ratio tends to increase with temperature. This ratio varies among fruits. For example, it is much higher for a banana than for an apple. Fruit reaches the eating stage at the climacteric peak or sometime after the peak, depending upon the species and to some extend upon the conditions of storage. Unique changes take place during the sharp rise in respiration from the preclimacteric peak. The slope of the rise varies with species, maturity, temperature, and the oxygen and carbon dioxide content of the storage chamber.

A multitude of physioligical processes is present in edible plant tissues at the time of harvest. For example, on removal of vegetative parts *(such as fruits, roots, stems etc.)* from the parent plant, the tissues are deprived of their normal supply of water, minerals and, in some intances, of simple organic molecules(e.g., sugars, hormones) which previously would have been translocated to them from other parts of the plant. Although photosynthetic activity is then negligible, most tissues retain capabilities of a diversity of metabolic reactions which are specific to a given commodity and variety. These are seen in events such as rotting, ripening, sprouting, toughening, yellowing etc. The kind and intensity of activity in detached plant parts determines to a large extent their storage life.

Seeds, fleshy roots, tubers and bulbs are morphologically and physiologically designed in nature to maintain the tissues in a dormant condition until favorable envoirmental situations are available for germination or growth. Metabolic activity is low but not completely halted in such tissues.

Fruits, leaves and stems, on the other hand, are physologically conditioned for senescence rather than dormancy. Fleshy fruits are unusual in that the ripening process is followed by the development of optimal eating qualities.

PLant Product Storage :

Fresh fruits and vegetables maintain life processes during storage. So long as they are alive, they are able to resist the growth of spoilage organisms to some degree.

Treatments to Control Postharvest Decay of fresh Produce

Crop	Treatment
Apple	Sodium o-pehnylphenate
Pear	thiabendazole benomyl
Banana	thiabendazole bcnomyl
Citrus fruits	Sodium carbonate borax Sodium o-phenylphenate thia bendazole benomyl 2-aminobutane (sec-butylamine) biphenyl 2,4-dicholorophenoxyacetic acid nitrogen trichloride fumigation
Grape	Sulfur dioxide fumigation
Peach	hot water
Nectarine	2,6-dichloro-4-nitroaniline
Cherry	benomyl
Pineapple	sodium o-phenylphenate salicylanilide
Papaya	hot water
Mango	hot water, benomyl
Potato	hypochlorite
Vegetables	chloramines

DECAY CONTROL :

Antimicrobial agents and senescence inhibitors can be used to delay the onset of spoilage in storage. Two methods of applying these agents are used :

(1) A spray or dip in a solution or suspension in water/wax formulations.

(2) Fumigations.

Heat Evolved by Living Tissues :

Freshly harvested fruits, vegetables, grains and beans are alive. These living tissues respire and energy is released in the form of heat. The amount of heat released varies with the commodity and increases as the temperature of the storage chamber increases.

HEAT EVOLVED IN THE RESPIRATION OF FRUITS AND VEGETABLES

Commodity	Btu[1] per Ton per 24 Hr (0°C)	(4°C)	(15°C)
Apples Jonathan or Winesap	300 to 800	590 to 840	2,270 to 3,470
Beans, green	5,500 to 6, 160	9,160 to 11,390	32, 090 to 44, 130
Broccoli	7,450	11,000 to 17,600	33, 870 to 50,000
Cabbage	1,200	1,670	4,080
Carrots, topped	2,130	3,470	8,080
Celery	1,620	2,420	8,220
Corn, sweet	560	9,390	38, 410
Onions	600 to 1,100	1,760 to 1,980[2]	----
Oranges	420 to 1,030	1,300 to 1,560	3,650 to 5,170
Peaches	850 to 1,370	1,440 to 2,030	7,260 to 9, 310
Pears, green	8,160	13,220	39,250
Potatoes	440 to 880	1,100 to 1,760	2,200 to 3,520
Spinach	4,240 to 4,860	7,850 to 11, 210	36,920 to 38,000
Strawberries	2,730 to 3,800	3,660 to 6,750	15,460 to 20,280
Sweet Potatoes	1,190 to 2,440	1,710 to 3,350	4,280 to 6,300
Tomatoes			
Mature green	580	1,070	6,230
Ripe	1,020	1,250	5,640

It is also becoming clear that the storage life of living matter, within limits,varies inversely with the rate of respiration. It was postulated and then found that reducing the rate of respiration could prolong storage life.

Temperature of Cold Storage Rooms :

Temperature control in storage rooms is most important. Variations from desired conditions may be most damaging. These variations can be prevented if the storage rooms are sufficiently insulated, have adequate refrigeration equipment, and the spread between the temperature of the refrigerating coils and the temperature of the storage room is minimum. In a room with a desired temperature of 10°C, cooled by coils operating at -3°C, the air temperature may vary by a number of degrees. A room kept at 0°C with sufficient coils at a temperature -3°C should vary in temperature by less than one degree. The difference between the temperature of the refrigerant and the temperature of the storage room is important in maintaining desired humidities.

Metabolism a Function of Temperature :

The metabolism of living tissue is a function of the temperature of the envoironment. Living organisms have a temperature which is optimum for growth. Higher temperatures are injurious. Lower temperatures greatly retard metabolism. Low temperatures, near the freezing point of water, are effective in reducing the rate at which respiration occurs. Such temperatures have been found to be valuable in short term preservation of foods. For every 10°C the temperature is lowdered, it may be estimated that the rate of reaction will be halved. Storage of food at temperatures near 0°C to 5°C may be anticipated to prolong the period in which foods may be stored. Not only is the respiration rate of such foods as fruits decreased, but the growth of many spoilage microorganisms as well is retarded.

There are generally considered to be three types of microorganisms: those with optimum temperature for growth at 55°C, called thermophiles; those with an optimum at 37°C, called mesophiles, which include most organisms pathogenic for man; and those with an optimum growth below 10°C, called psychrophiles. Temperature control then is a positive means of influencing the growth of microorganisms associated with foods.

RECOMMENDED STORAGE TEMPERATURES, RELATIVE HUMIDITIES, APPROXIMATE STORAGE LIFE AND AVERAGE FREEZING POINTS OF FRUITS AND NUTS

Commodity	Storage Temperature (0°C)	RH (%)	Approx. Storage Life	Average Freezing Point (%)
Apples	-2- to -1	85 to 90	[1]	-2
Apricots	-1 to 0	85 to 90	1 to 2 weeks	-2
Avocados	2 to 8	85 to 90	[1]	-2
Bananas	11 to 15	85 to 90	1 to 3 weeks	2
Berries				
Blackberries	-1 to 0	85 to 90	7 to 10 days	-1
Dewberries	-1 to 0	85 to 90	7 to 10 days	-1
Gooseberries	-1 to 0	85 to 90	3 to 4 weeks	-1
Loganberries	-1 to 0	85 to 90	7 to 10 days	-1
Raspberries				
Black	-1 to 0	85 to 90	7 to 10 days	-1
Red	-1 to 0	85 to 90	7 to 10 days	-0
Strawberries	-1 to 0	85 to 90	7 to 10 days	-1
Cherries	-1 to 0	85 to 90	10 to 14 days	[4]
Coconuts	1 to 2	80 to 85	1 to 2 weeks	-3
Cranberries	2 to 4	85 to 90	1 to 3 months	-2
Figs	-1 to 0	85 to 90	10 days	
Grapefruit	see text	85 to 90	[1]	-2
Grapes				
Vinifera	-2 to -1	88 to 92	3 to 6 months	-3
American	-1 to 0	80 to 85	3 to 8 weeks	-2
Lemons	12 to 14	85 to 90	1 to 4 months	-2
Limes	7 to 8	85 to 90	6 to 8 weeks	-1
Mangoes	10	85 to 90	15 to 20 days	-1
Nuts	0 to 2	65 to 70	8 to 12 months	[4]
Olives	7 to 10	85 to 90	4 to 6 weeks	-1
Oranges	see text	85 to 90	8 to 10 weeks	[5]
Papayas	7	85 to 90	15 to 20 days	-1
Peaches	-1 to 1	85 to 90	2 to 4 weeks	-1
Pears	-1 to 1	88 to 92	2 to 7 months	[6]
Persimmons	-1	85 to 90	2 months	-2
Pineapples				
Mature green	10 to 15	85 to 90	3 to 4 weeks	-1
Ripe	4 to 7	85 to 90	2 to 4 weeks	-1
Plums, Prune	-1 to 0	85 to 90	3 to 8 weeks	-2
Pomegranates	-1 to 0	85 to 90	2 to 4 months	-2
Quinces	-1 to 0	85 to 90	2 to 3 months	-2

RATE OF RESPIRATION OF APPLES RELATED TO TEMPERATURE OF ENVIRONMENT

Variety	Temperature (°C)	MgCO_2 Evolved, Per kg per hr.
Grimes Olden	0	4.76
	4	8.34
	16	29.25
	34	67.82
Winesap	0	2.75
	4	5.30
	16	20.45
	34	33.95

Creating Energy Deficits :

Ice has been employed since early times to prolong the storage life of foods. It is the energy deficit of ice which has great utility. However, when all the energy deficit of ice is supplied, water remains; the temperature of the water-food substrate begins to come into equilibrium with the envoironment. Protective mechanisms (insulation) prolong this process. When the temperature of the waterfood substrate reaches that where microorganisms can multiply, the food will deteriorate very rapidly. Ice is therefore used presently where its characteristics are of value. One feature of ice in cooling foods is that ice does not desiccate the food.

Creating Energy Deficits Mechanically :

One of the important inventions of man is mechanical refrigeration. A simple diagram of an ammonia system is shown in fig. Both the first and second laws of thermodynamics are operative. Ammonia gas takes up energy as it is expanded. This heat is taken from the atmosphere, or chamber, or environment. The expanded ammonia gas is then compressed. This requires energy to be exerted on the system. The compressed gas is now hot. Heat is removed from the compressed gas by means of running water or. circulating air over the tubes containing the hot gas. The gas is liquefied. The cycle is then repeated. The gas is allowed to evaporate under controlled conditions, the gas takes up heat, the hot gas is compressed, the heat is removed, and the gas returns to the liquid state. With such a system accurate temperature control is possible. The refrigeration developed may be made to work directly on the food, or the refrigeration system may be employed to cool a brine which in turn is employed to cool. Many alternatives in refrigerants and systems are possible.

USEFUL TEMPERATURES

Temperature (^{0}C)	Effect
100	Boiling point of water at standard pressure ; short exposure kills most vegetative cells.
93	Steam-cabinet sterilization of utensils for 5 min. at this temperature.
76	Hot water sterilization of utensils in 5 min.
73	Cooking starts.
71	High temperature, short -time pasteurization of milk (15 sec) upper range of growth of thermophiles, ropy bacteria killed.
62	Holding pasteurization of milk (30 min)
58	Brucella (anthrax), typhoid-dysentery bacteria, and pathogenic streptococci killed (30 min)
56	Temperature for caustic solution in soaking-type washer for bottles
46	Temperature for water and cleaner for hand washing utensils
38	Temperature of cow's body
37	Temperature of man's body
26	In 12-24 hr. bacteria may multiply 3000 times.
21	In 12-24 hr. bacteria may multiply 700 times.
15	In 12-24 hr. bacteria may multiply 15 times.
12	Average well water temperature in northern belt for U.S.
10	In 12-24 hr. bacteria may multiply 5 times.
4	In 12-24 hr. bacteria may double numbers.
-1 to 1	Common cold storage temperature.
0	Freezing point of water; very slow growth of most microorganisms.
-17 to -23	Common frozen food storage.
-28 to -34	Common food freezing temperature.
-62	All water probably as crystals in frozen foods.

Once mechanical devices capable of imparting motion were invented, machines to power apparatus evolved. The ability to transform electrical energy to mechanicalenergy yielded such devices. With motors, pumps and compressors, the elements of a refrigeration device were available. Applying cumulative knowledge of gases and vapors, with these mechanical devices, mechanical ice-making machines evolved. The process of invention took 300 years.

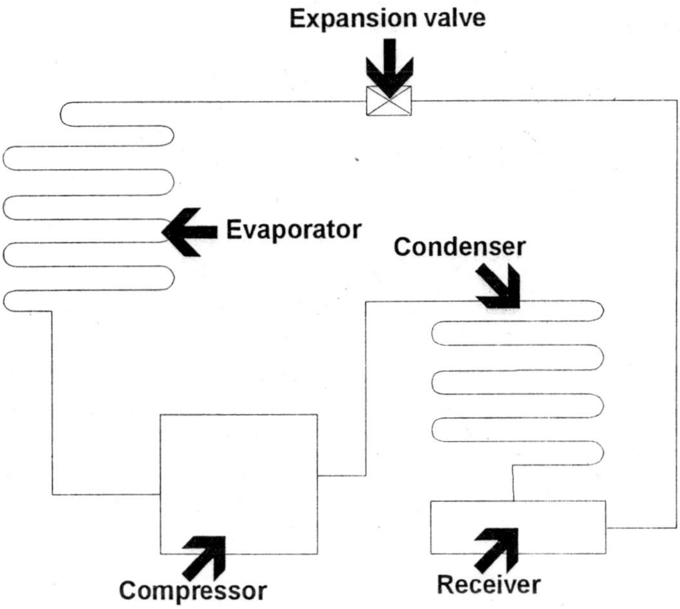

SCHEMATIC DIAGRAM OF A SIMPLE AMMONIA REFRIGERATION SYSTEM

Determining Refrigeration Load Needed :

In order to establish the refrigeration requirement for a chamber of fruit or vegetable, certain information must be known. We must know the initial temperature of the food, the final storage temperature, the rate of respiration and heat evolved, the specific heat of the food, and the amount of food to be placed in the room.

If we could instantaneously lower the temperature of a food to the storage temperature, the heat load would be obtained by multiplying the specific heat for the food by the number of degrees the temperature will be lowdered, by the weight of food.This value is generally reported

in terms of the British Thermal Unit (Btu). One Btu is equal to the amount of heat required to raise one pound of water one degree Fahrenheit at or near the water's point of maximum density.
(1 Btu = 0.252 Kg Calories per ^{0}C)

The Btu value obtained from this calcution is called the sensible heat. In practice, the cooling period is extended and is not instantaneous. Therefore, while the cooling process is occurring , the fruits or vegetables live on and evolve heat. While foods cool the rate at which they evolve heat decreases, but this calculation must be included, as it may be of great magnitude if the cooling period extends for a week or more. It is necessary, therefore, to establish the heat that will be evolved by the fruit or vegetable while the cooling process occurs, and also, to add the heat that will be evolved while the food is being stored. As a rule of thumb, for every 10^{0}C that the temperature is lowered, it may be expected that the rate of respiration will be halved, as noted earlier.

The Heat evolved in the respiration of fruits and vegetables stored at several tamperatures in given in table. in terms of Btu per ton per 24 hr. In this table it is assumed that the foods will be cooled to 0^{0}C. These figures are based on experimental evidence by many researchers. The data given have been obtained by assuming that the heat of respiration is produced solely by the oxidation of glucose to carbon dioxide and water. Because of little other evidence, and the fact that this system is workable, these values are useful in establishing the refrigeration load for storage of commodities.

Specific Heat of Foods :

The specific heat of food is required in calculating the refrigeration load. The specific heat for a food can be estimated from the equation:

$$\text{Specific heat} = 0.008\ (\text{percent } H_2O \text{ in food}) + 0.20$$

For example, apples have 85% moisture. The specific heat of apples can be estimated to be 0.008 X 85 + 0.20, or 0.88 (Actual values are given in table.)

Cold Injury to Fruits and Vegetables :

Fruits and vegetables are susceptible to cold injury at above freezing temperatures. Some foods are injured with a slight exposure to freezing temperatures; other foods can be frozen and thawed several times without permanent injury. The freezing point of foods are not enough in itself to explain this problem. Tomatoes and parsnips, as examples,

COMMODITIES SUSCEPTIBLE TO COLD INJURY WHEN STORED AT ONLY MODERATELY LOW TEMPERATURES

Commodity	Lowest Safe Temperature (°C)	Character of injury when stored between 0°C & safe Temperature
Apples Certain varieties	1-2	Internal browning, soggy breakdown
Avocados	7	Internal browning
Bananas Green or ripe	13	Dull color when ripened
Beans (snap)	7-10	Pitting increasing on removal, russeting on removal
Cranberries	1	Low-temperature breakdown
Cucumbers	7	Pitting, water-soaked spots, decay
Eggplants	7	Pitting or bronzing, increasing on removal
Grapefruit	7	Scald, pitting, waterby breakdown, internal browning
Lemons	12-14	Internal discoloration, pitting
Limes	7	Pitting
Mangoes	10	Internal discoloration
Melons Cantaloups Honey Dew Casaba Crenshaw & Persian Watermelons	 7 4-10 4-10 4-10 2	 Pitting, surface decay Pitting, surface decay Pitting, surface decay Pitting, surface decay Pitting, objectionable flavor
Okra	4	Doscoloration, water-soaked areas, pitting, decay
Olives, fresh	7	Internal browning
Oranges, California	1-2	Rind disorders
Papayas	7	Breakdown
Peppers, sweet	7	Pitting, discoloration near calyx
Pineapples Mature-green	7	Dull green when ripened
Potatoes Chippewa & Sebago	4	Mahogany browning
Squash, winter	10-12	Decay
Sweet Potatoes	12	Decay, pitting, internal discoloration
Tomatoes Mature-green Ripe	 12 10	 Poor color when ripe, tendency to decay rapidly breakdown

freeze at - 1°C. Parsnips can be left in the soil over winter with no apparent damage. The first frost ruins tomatoes. Green tomatoes held at 2°C for three days do not ripen properly if warmed. Some varieties of potatoes may turn brown internally if held at less than 4°C. Their sugar content also increases. In any event living tissues must be kept living if their food values and eating qualities are to be maintained by cold storage practices.

Animal Product Storage :

Microorganisms causing spoilage of fresh meat, poultry, eggs and most dairy products have optimum temperatures for growth at 20°C to 35°C. To obtain the maximum refrigerated shelf-life of these foods, microorganisms which grow best at room temperature as well as those that can also grow at refrigeration temperatures must be controlled. This general observation also conveys insight into potential sources of contamination and what to expect from sanitation practices and refrigeration of the environment and processing equipment. While pseudomonads are the major cause of spoilage for most fresh meats, poultry, eggs and bulk tank raw milk, other bacteria may be the dominant spoilage organism.

Meat : The two most critical factors influencing spoilage rate are temperature and initial level of contamination. Research on beef, poultry and pork show that small changes in temperature in the range of 0° TO 7°C have an effect on refrigerated shelf-life and on the types of bacteria growing on fresh meat. Coli-aerogenes and micrococci are found at very low levels in spoiled beef held at 4°C. These groups increase to moderate levels at 9°C and become a significant portion of the spoilage population at 15°C. Pseudomonads dominate the spoilage flora at all temperatures studied. With chicken meat, Pseudomonads dominate at 1°C and bocome of less significance as holding temperature increased. Acinetobacter and members of the family Enterobacteriaceae are of little consequence at 1°C but increased significantly with the higher temperatures of 10°C and 15°C.

Milk : The importance of temperature as well as time in holding milk cannot bo overstated. Manufacturing-grade milk received into a plant with bacterial counts in the low millions requires little time to spoil further. This is especially true for milk received at 7°C or more, where the generation time may be only 8 hr or less compared to 12 hr at at 5°C and 16 hr at 2°C. This is due to the psychrotrophic nature of the majority of bacteria in the milk.

In general, coliforms do not rapidly multiply in adequately refrigerated milk. Psychrotrophic coli-aerogenes bacteria may constitute 5 to 20% of the psychrotrophic microflora of farm bulktank milk at time of retailing. They may increase only 100 or 1000 fold in 3 days at

REPORTED GENERATION TIMES FOR SOME PSYCHROTROPHS AT 0°C TO 32°C

Generations Time (hr.)

	0°	2°-2.5°	4°-5°	10°	14°-15°	20°	30°-32°
Clostridiumr hastiforme	—	—	73	25.5	14.5	—	—
Clostridium 61	17	—	—	9	5	3.5	—
Bacillus W25	23	—	8.5	6	3	2.5	—
Bacillus W16B	24	—	11.5	7	2.8	2.5	—
Bacillus coagulans	—	24-30	—	—	—	—	—
Bacillus (Group A)	30	13-19	7.5-14	4-4.5	—	—	—
Pseudomonas 92	26.6	—	11.7	5.4	2.3	1.7	0.90
Pseudomonas 69	29.1	—	14.7	6.5	2.7	1.9	0.75
Pseudomonas fluoroescens	—	—	8.2	3.5	2	1.5	1.2
Pseudomonas fluroscens (P-200)	35	13.7	—	4	2	1.5	0.85
Pseudomonas fluroscens	30.2	—	6.7	—	—	1.4	—
Pseudomonas fragi	11.3	7.7	5	2.6	—	1.1	—
Pseudomonas (21-3c)	20	9.2	7.3	3.2	2	1.3	0.77
Pseudomonas (1-3b)	10.3	8	7	2.7	2.3	1.6	0.93
'Aerobacter aerogenes (Ps 43)	37.7	—	12.2	4.1	2.2	1.3	0.8
Gram negative rod							
Aerobic	21.2	—	4.3	—	—	1.4	—
Anaerobic	23.4	—	9.8	—	—	0.6	—
Gram negative rod	20	—	7.6 (6°C)	1.9 (12°C)	—	—	0.78
Achromobacter # 7	—	7.1	5.3	2.5	1.8	1.4	1.6
Achromobacter # 438	—	7.8	6	2.5	1.8	1.3	1.5
Achromobacter # 5	—	—	7.4	3.1	1.8	1.4	—
Pseudomonas # 451	—	13.8	9.7	4.0	2.0	1.2	0.8

DISTRIBUTION OF 3880 SAMPLES OF MANUFACTURING GRADE MILK ACCORDING TO BACTERIAL LEVELS

Standard Plate Comt/ml	Canned Milk (%)	Bulk Milk (%)
100,000	22.3	41.5
100,000-1,000,000	30.9	30.1
1,000,000-3,000,000	11.1	10.3
3,000,000	35.7	18.1

RELATIONSHIP BETWEEN TEMPERATURE AND LEVELS OF COLI-AEROGENES AND MICROCOCCI IN SPOILED BEEF

	No./g at Time of spoilage		
	4^0C	9^0C	15^0C
Coli-aerogenes	$2x10^4$	$1.5x10^5$	$1.6x10^7$
Micrococci	$3x10^3$	$6.3x10^4$	$1.9x10^6$

RELATIONSHIP BETWEEN TEMPERATURE AND TYPES OF BACTERIA CAUSING SPOILAGE OF CHICKEN MEAT

	Percentage		
	1^0C	10^0C	15^0C
Pseudomonas sp.	90	37	15
Acinetobacter	7	26	34
Enterobacteriaceae	3	15	27
Streptococci	—	6	8
Aeromonas	—	4	6
Others	—	12	10

3^0C to 5^0C, yet rarely attain dominance in milk at temperatures of less than 8^0C to 10^0C.

Eggs : The spoilage pattern of eggs is also dependent upon the degree of refrigeration. Tests on raw albumen for 3 weeks at 5^0, 10^0, 15^0 and 20^0C reveal that pseudomonas sp. dominate at 5^0C and decrease in significance as the holding temperature approaches 20^0C. Conversely, Enterobacter liquifaciens was not detected at 5^0C and increased in significance as the holding temperature was raised to 20°C. In whole eggs held at 10°, 20° and 30°C, Pseudomonads dominate at 10°C and are of lesser importance as the temperature increases to 30°C. It is clear that temperature markedly influences the rate of spoilage of animal products and the types of bacteria. It is logical to assume that there may be a seasonal effect relative to the types of bacteria in the environment. Probably less than 1% of the microorganisms contaminating meat carcasses as they leave the killing floor and enter the cooler are of the psychrophilic type. Refrigerated processing areas may act as a selective breeding ground for the psychrotrophic bacteria most likely to cause spoilage of the refrigerated packaged product. One must also consider that environmental temperature can influence the types and numbers of bacteria present in a processing area.

The limiting factor for refrigerated shelf-life has been recontamination after pasteurization with psychrotrophs. It is found that during recent years it has been profitable to use aseptic packaging conditions to exclude these psychrtrophs from speciality dairy products (e.g., whipping cream, half-and-half, nondairy creamer, chocolate milk). Aseptic packaging has extended refrigerated shelf-life of 6 weeks to 6 months.

The spoilage pattern for fresh meats, poultry, eggs and raw milk is very similar. The degree of refrigeration not only markedly influences refrigerated shelf-life but also the types of bacteria causing spoilage. Advantage may be gained bu minimizing contamination with the bacteria which occur in refrigerated processing areas which can cause spoilage of perishable refrigerated foods.

General :

Meats must be refrigerated at all stages from butchering to eating.

RELATIONSHIP BETWEEN TEMPERATURE AND TYPES OF BACTERIA CAUSING SPOILAGE OF ALBUMEN

	Percentage			
	5°C	10°C	15°C	20°C
Pseudomonas sp.	89	71	79	23
Enterobacteria[1]	—	10	14	77
Not identified	—	19	7	—

If we desire to hold meat for a week we must rapidly get its temperature down below 4⁰C, otherwise the meat will begin to spoil. Most commercial meat we eat fresh is consumed within a week or ten days from the time it is slaughtered. Beef is sometimes "aged" for 4 or even 6 weeks. If we want to keep meat longer, we must use the more drastic methods of preserving (freezing, canning, irradiating, drying, curing).

The heat present in the freshly killed animal must be removed rapidly to avoid decomposition and retard losses in body weight. The period required to remove this heat is less than 24 hr. The temperature of the carcasses entering the cooler will be about 37⁰C. The thickest section of the carcass should reach a temperature of 0⁰C to -1⁰C. Beef at this temperature can be stored for 8 days, lamb for 6, and veal for 6, before entering retail channels.

Calculation of Refrigeration load :

Meat.-The animal carcass body heat to be removed is sensible heat. Dead tissues do not respire. Calculation of refrigeration needs for meat chilling is then a multiplication of the specific heat of the flesh by the weight of meat to be cooled. Multiplied by the temperature drop and divided by the conversion factor. This will yield the tons of refrigeration needed to chill the carcasses. It is assumed that this cooling will be accomplished in 24 hr. Heat losses must be considered for the storage room, lights, etc., in establishing the total refrigerated needs for the storage chambers.

For quick marketing of fresh meat, temperatures near 0⁰C are used in storage rooms. For delayed marketing, meat is frozen and held at -17⁰C or lower.

BACON FLAVOR SCORES AS INFLUENCED BY TEMPERATURE AND TIME OF STORAGE

Storage Time (Weeks)	Temperature (-2⁰C)	(2⁰C)	(7⁰C)
0	2.0[1]	2.0	2.0
2	2.0	2.0	1.6
4	2.0	1.6	1.2
6	1.6	1.2	1.0

The humidity of the storage room is a factor requiring attention.

The carcass will lose nearly 2% of its weight in the chilling process, due to loss of moisture. If the relative humidity of the storage room is above 90% the meat will mold. If the relative humidity is less than 90% the carcass will lose excessive weight.

Mold and slime formation on chilled carcasses can be retarded by using ultraviolet lights in the storage chamber. Ultraviolet light at a wavelength of 2700A has germicidal power. If the carcass is exposed thoroughly to the germicidal rays, the meat will not mold. However, the exterior fat may turn rancid sooner than would be the case if it is not exposed to ultraviolet light.

Fish.- Fresh fish is more perishable than meat. Storage of fish in ice slows the process, but the flesh becomes soft and flabby. The bright color of the skin dulls. The sweet fresh fish flavor is lost. Unpleasant, strong odors develop. When caught at sea, fish is packed quickly into crushed ice, and iced again along the line from the sea to our tables. Soft fish like the whiting will not keep long under any circumstances. If cod is kept at 0°C it can be held for three weeks. For inland markets much of our fish is frozen and distributed in that condition.

Selfish may be kept for a week if cooled to ice temperatures. Shrimp, lobster and crab are very perishable,keeping in storage for a few days at the most. Lobsters are often held alive in sea water. Immersion in fresh water causes their quick death.

Egg Storage :- Eggs should be stored at the lowest temperature possible yet not permit the interior of the egg to solidify. If the interior solidifies the resulting expansion may cause shells to crack. This results in difficulties as eggs with firm, thick albumen solidify at a higher temperature than thin-albumen type eggs. Shell characteristics also affect the storage quality of eggs, as thick shells withstand the solidification better than thin-shelled eggs. It is considered that-1°C is the ideal storage temperature for eggs. The room must be maintained at constant temperature for best results. A relative humidity between 82 and 85% is generally considered optimum for eggs. Lower humidities result in desiccation, and therefore an enlargement of the air cell, which is undesirable. Eggs may pick up odors during storage and therefore should not be stored in the same room with other commodities.

Recommendations for cold storage of selected foods are present in tables.

QUALITY LOSSES IN SHELL EGGS ON STORAGE AT DIFFERENT TEMPERATURES LOSSES IN MOISTURE AND THINNING OF WHITES DECREASES EGG QUALITY

Storage (Months)	Grade A Eggs remaining (%)		
	-1°C	7°C	15°C
0	100	100	100
3	80	50	0
6	70	0	0

RECOMMENDED COLD STORAGE TEMPERATURES FOR SELECTED FOODS

Food	Temperature (0°C)
Dairy Products	
Butter[1]	1
Cheese (cream)	-1 to 2
Cheese (soft)	0 to 2
Condensed milk (bulk)	1 to 4
Cream (fresh)	0 to 1
Margarine	0 to 1
Milk (fresh)	0 to 1
Milk (evaporated)	2 to 4
Storage of Fish & Fish Products	
Fresh fish	0
Fish (dried)	1 to 4
Oysters	0 to 1
Storage of Miscllaneous Products	
Beer	0 to 4
Chocolate	3 to 5
Cider	0 to 2
Honey	4 to 7
Maple syrup	4 to 7
Molasses	4 to 7
Olive oil	1 to 4
Sauerkraut	1 to 3
Wine	4 to 7

[1] If Butter is to be stored for a longer than 2 or 3 weeks, it should be held at -17°C to -23°C

RECOMMENDED STORAGE TEMPERATURES, RELATIVE HUMIDITIES, APPROXIMATE STORAGE LIFE AND FREEZING POINTS OF VEGETABLES

Commodity	Storage Temperature (°C)	RH (%)	Approx. Storage Life	Average Freezing Point (%)
Artichokes,Jerusalem	0	90 to 95	2 to 5 months	-2
Asparagus	0	90 to 95	3 to 4 weeks	-1
Beans				
Green	7	85 to 90	8 to 10 days	-1
LIma-unshelled	0	90 to 95	2 to 4 weeks	-1
Shelled	0	90 to 95	15 days	-1
Beets				
Topped	0	90 to 95	1 to 3 months	-2
Not topped	0	90 to 95	10 to 14 days	-2
Broccoli, Italian	0	90 to 95	7 to 10 days	-1
Brussels sprouts	0	90 to 95	3 to 4 weeks	1
Cabbage	0	90 to 95	3 to 4 months	-1
Carrots				
Topped	0	90 to 95	4 to 5 months	-1
Not topped	0	90 to 95	10 to 14 days	-1
Cauliflower	0	90 to 95	2 to 3 weeks	-1
Celery	-1 to 0	90 to 95	2 to 4 months	-1
Corn, green	-1 to 0	90 to 95	4 to 8 days	-1
Cucumbers	7 to 10	90 to 95	10 to 14 days	-1
Egg plants	7 to 10	90 to 95	10 days	-1
Endive	0	90 to 95	2 to 3 weeks	-1
Garlic	0	70 to 75	6 to 8 months	-3
Horseradish	0	90 to 95	10 to 12 months	-3
Leeks, green	0	85 to 90	1 to 3 months	-1
Lettuce	0	90 to 95	2 to 3 weeks	-1
Melons (ripe)				
Watermelon	2 to 4	80 to 85	1 to 2 weeks	[1]
Muskmelon	4 to 10	80 to 85	10 to 14 days	[2]
Honeydew	4 to 10	80 to 85	2 to 4 weeks	[3]
Casaba, Persian	4 to 10	80 to 85	4 to 6 weeks	
Mushrooms	0	85 to 90	5 days	-1
Okra	10	85 to 95	2 weeks	-1
Olives	7 to 10	85 to 90	4 to 6 weeks	-1
Onions	0	70 to 75	6 to 8 months	-1
Peas, green	0	85 to 90	1 to 2 weeks	-1
Peppers, green	7	85 to 90	8 to 10 days	-1
Potatoes	3 to 7	85 to 90	6 to 9 months	-1
Pumpkins	10 to 12	70 to 75	2 to 6 months	-1
Rhubarb	0	90 to 95	2 to 3 weeks	-3
Rutabagas	0	90 to 95	2 to 4 months	-1
Spinach	0	90 to 95	10 to 14 days	-1
Squashes				
Summer	4 to 10	85 to 95	2 to 3 weeks	1
Winter	10 to 12	70 to 75	4 to 6 months	-1
Sweet potatoes	12 to 15	80 to 85	4 to 6 months	-1
Tomatoes				
Ripe	4 to 10	85 to 90	7 to 10 days	-1
Mature green	12 to 21	80 to 85	3 to 5 weeks	-1

[1] Rind (-1°C) flesh (-1°C)

[2] Rind (-2°C) flesh (-1°C)

[3] Rind (-1°C) flesh (-1°C)

Effect of Cold Storage on Quality

An unrefrigerated fruit or vegetable usually spoils rapidly and soon has little food value for man. If similar fruits and vegetables are held temporarily in cool storage, life processes are retarded, but the net result is a longer period in which the food is acceptable for man to eat.

Some of the life activity is used by storing the tissues. It is not to be expected that a fruit after seven months storage will be identical to a freshly harvested fruit. If the temperature and humidity conditions optimum for the storage of a fruit or vegetable are adhered to, there will be ample time for cold-stored commodities to be marketed through usual channels. Very perishable fruits and vegetables, those having a short period during which they keep cold storage, must be consumed shortly after being removed from storage rooms. It cannot be expected that cold storage will make extremely perishable foods nonperishable.

Occasionally it is necessary to refrigerate fruits and vegetables in common storage chambers. There can be substantial cross-transfer of odors. Apples should not be stored with celery, cabbage, potatoes or onions. Celery and onions damage each food's quality. Citrus fruits take up most strong odors. Apple and citrus odors are readily transferred to dairy products.Eggs stored with fish or certain vegetables lead off-flavored eggs.

Preserving Foods in a Microenvironment :

It is possible to preserve out foodstuffs if we alter the environment. As an example, the cold storage chamber is a modified environment in

LOSSES IN VITAMIN C IN SELECTED VEGETABLES ON COLD STORAGE

Produce	Storage conditions		Losses (%)
	Days	Temperature (^{0}C)	
Asparagus	1 7	1 0	5 50
Broccoli	1 4	7 7	20 35
Green beans	1 4	7 7	10 20
Spinach	2 3	0 1	5 5

CHANGES IN CAROTENE OF SWEET POTATOES STORED AT 10°C FOR FOUR MONTHS

Variety	At Harvest mg per 100g Wet Basis	After Storage
Maryland Golden	4.7	5.9
Nance Gold	5.4	5.7
Heartgold	6.7	7.4

which we place foods. The storage chamber is therefore a large package. The concept of microenvironment is the realm of individual packages for foods. Prepackaging perishable foods is an application of controlled environment.

The ability to control moisture losses inexpensively in fresh meats made major improvements in the economies of distribution and marketing of meats. This development had far-reaching implications, even to the relocation of livestock yards and meat processing plants further away from points of consumption.

Food packaging is an area of specialization in itself. A package has many functions. Four of the most important considerations of a package are the protection of the food, the economy of the package, the convienence of the package, and its appearance.

There are a number of factors to be considered for a package.

(1) Product properties : Tendency of the food to gain or lose moisture; free oil or fat content of the food; tendency of food to lose volatile flavors or pick up foreign odors; caking tendencies at different temperatures and different moisture contents; susceptibility of food to spoilage by light, susceptibility of food to spoilage by atmospheric oxygen; susceptibility of food to infestation by insects; particle size of food and sifting considerations.

(2) The conditions of environment which alter the package and contents must receive attention. These include: relative humidity of storage chamber, temperature, ventilation, pressure, warehousing and transportation problems.

(3) The packaging material must lend itself to being used with processing

equipment. The packing material must have specifications regarding tensile strength, tearing resistance, softness, ability to make dead folds, moisture content, thickness, heat sealing abilities, gluing requirements, vapor transmission factors, and a host of other considerations.

RELATION OF TEMPERATURE TO FIRMNESS OF BARLETT PEARS IN COLD STORAGE (MEASURED BY PRESSSURE TEST)

Temperature (^{0}C)	0	2	4	8
1	25[1]	19	12	9
4	25	7	4	2

THIAMIN, RIBOFLAVIN, AND NIACIN CHANGES IN COLD STORED PORK AND PORK PRODUCTS

Product	Days Storage (3^{0}C)	Retention		
		Thiamin (%)	Robiflavin (%)	Niacin (%)
Pork Loin	11	97	100	72
Ground Pork	14	94	104	97
Cured Pork	14	95	105	90

LOSS OF SWEETNESS IN SWEET CORN DURING STORAGE

Storage (hr.)	Loss in Total Sugars (%)	
	0^{0}C	20^{0}C
24	8.1	25.6
48	14.5	45.7
72	18.0	55.5
96	22.0	62.1

Packaging Materials Tests Which May be Performed :

Weight per unit of area, weight per 100 units, caliper or thickness, specific gravity or density, bursting strength, tearing resistance, tensile strength, folding endurance, stiffness, moldability, elonganation, porosity, transmission of air and gases, transmission of water vapor, transmission of organic vapors, oil and grease resistance, water absorption (penetration), moisture content, wax content, surface wax, melting and softening range, pressure and heat blocking, sealing strength, stability (heat and light), resistance to chemicals, printability, gloss, smoothness, opacity, transparency, and color are criteria of quality for packaging materials.

Formed Container Tests.-Compression tests, standard method or offset method, drop test, impact and vibration test may be used to determine the quality of the formed containers.

Knowing the specifications for a food package, the check list for three types of packaging materials provides a guide to make a descision as to which material to select.

PARTIAL CHECKLIST FOR FLEXIBLE PACKAGING FILMS

Qualities	Film I	Film II	Film III
Water-vapor transmission rate	Fair	Excellent	Good
Grease resistance	Poor	Excellent	Excellent
Resistance to passage of O_2 and CO_2	Good	Excellent	Excellent
Resistance to passage of organic vapors	Fair	Excellent	Excellent
Strength	Good	Fair	Excellent
Dimensional stability	Good	Good	Good
Stiffness	Poor	Good	Poor
Tear fold	Poor	Excellent	Poor
Type of seals	Heat	Good	Heat
Strength of seals	Excellent	Fair	Excellent
Appearance of film	Good	Good	Good
Printability	Fair	Good	Fair
Price	Satisfactory	Satisfactory	Too high
Decision	Reject	Accept	Reject

Disorders of Stored Foods :

Our fruits, vegetables, eggs, meats and dairy products may be harvested, gathered or slaughtered some time prior to going into refrigerated storage. Food deterioration may have already begun. A food will not improve in quality if harvested, gathered or slaughtered in a decayed condition. Only sound foods should be given the attention required for successful cold storage. Even under optimum conditions, storage in a cool chamber only retards food deterioration.

8

REFRIGERATION

Refrigeration is the use of mechanical or heat-activated machinery for cooling purposes. The production of extremely low temperatures, <-15^{0}C (1), is usually thought of as cryogenics (qv), and the use of refrigeration equipment to provide human comfort is known as air conditioning (qv). This article deals only with refrigeration which, in its broadest sense, covers such diverse uses as food processing and storage, supermarket display cases, skating rinks, ice manufacture, and biomedical applications such as blood and tissue storage or hypothermia used in surgery. The first commercial machine used for refrigerations was built in 1844 (2). In this article, chemical industry applications are emphasized, although the basic principles are valid for other uses of refrigeration.

The chemical industry uses refrigeration in installations covering a broad range of cooling capacities and temperature levels. The variety of applications results in a diversity of mechanical specifications and equipment requirements. Nevertheless, the methods for producing refrigeration are well-standardized.

Principles in Basic :

Thermodynamic principles govern all refrigeration processes. For a review of the basic laws of thermodynamics and the nature of the reverse Carnot cycle, ie, the refrigeration cycle. Refrigeration is accomplished in this cycle by using a fluid that evaporates and condenses at suitable pressures for practical equipment designs. The vapor cycle is illustrated by a pressure-enthalpy diagram.

The compressor raises the pressure of the refrigerant vapor so that its saturation temperature is slightly above the temperature of an available cooling medium, eg, air or water. This difference in temperature allows transfer of heat from the vapor to the cooling medium so that the vapor can condense. The liquid next expands to a pressure such that its saturation temperature is slightly below the temperature of the product to be cooled. This difference in temperature allows transfer of heat from the product to the refrigerant, causing the refrigerant to evaporate. The vapor formed must be removed by the compressor at a sufficient rate to maintain the low pressure in the evaporator and keep the cycle operating.

Many of today's chemical plants use pumped recirculation of refrigerant rather than direct evaporation of refrigerant to service remotely located or specially designed heat exchangers. This technique provides the users with wide flexibility in applying refrigeration to complex processes and greatly simplifies operation. Secondry refrigerants or brines are also commonly used today for simple control and operation. Direct application of ice and brine storage tanks may be used to level-off batch cooling loads and reduce equipment size. This approach provides stored refrigeration where temperature control is vital as a safety consideration to prevent runaway reactions or pressure buildup.

All mechanical cooling results in the simultaneous production, somewhere else, of a greater amount of heat. It is not always realized that this heat can be put to good use by applying the heat-pump principle. This requires provision to recover the heat normally rejected to cooling water or air in the refrigeration condensor. Recovery of this waste heat at temperature up to 65°C is frequently employed in modern plants to achieve improved heat balance and operating economy.

If a steady supply of waste heat is available, an absorbtion machine can be chosen for continuous-cooling duty. Heat at elevated temperatures, ie, steam or hot water, is required in the generator to drive off the high pressure refrigerant. The heat rejected to the cooling-tower water from both the absorber and the condenser is the sum of the waste heat supplied plus the cooling produced. This requires a larger cooling tower and greater cooling-water flow than for the vapor-compression cycle.

For water-chilling service, absorbtion (qv) systems generally use water as the refrigerant and lithium bromide as the absorbent solution. For process applications that require chilled fluid $<7^0$C, the ammonia -

water pair is used, with ammonia serving as the refrigerant. Single-

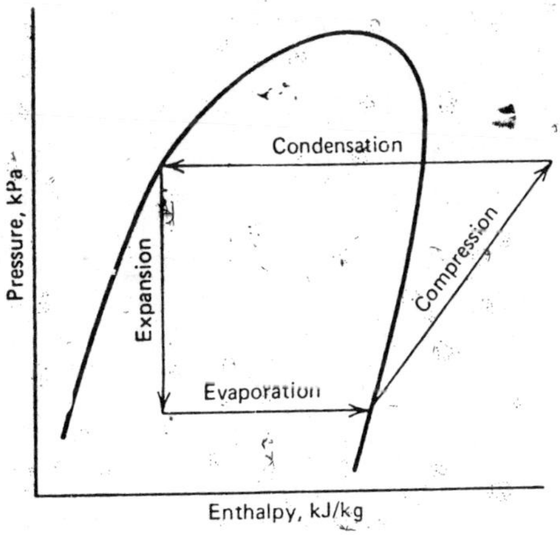

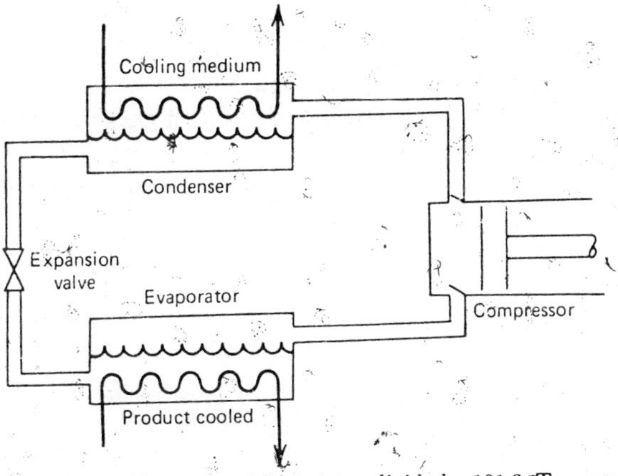

Basic vapor cycle. To convert kPa to atm, divide by 101.3. To convert kJ/kg to Btu/lb multiply by 0.4302.

stage systems are most common with generator heat input <95⁰C. The coefficient of performance (COP) of a system is the cooling achieved in the evaporator divided by the heat input to the generator. The COP of a lithium bromide machine is generally 0.65-0.70 for water-chilling duty.

Absorption machines can be built with a two-stage generator for heat input temperatures $\gtrsim$ 150⁰C. Such machines are called dual-effect machines. Coefficients of performance above 1.0 can be obtained, but at the expense of increased design and operating complexity.

Historically, capacities of mechanical refrigeration systems have been stated in tons of refrigeration, a unit of measure related to the ability of an ice plant to freeze one short ton (907 kg) of ice in 24 h. Its value is 3.51 kW_t (12,000 Btu/h). Often a kilowatt of refrigeration capacity is identified as KW_t to distinguish it from the amount of electricity (KW_e) required to produce the refrigeration.

Refrigeration Cycles and System Overview :

Refrigeration can be accomplished in either closed-cycle or open-cycle systems. In a closed cycle, the refrigerant fluid is confined within the system and recirculates through the processes in the cycle. In an open cycle, the fluid used as the refrigerant passes through the system once on its way to be used as a product or feedstock outside the refrigeration process. An example is the cooling of natural gas to separate and condense heavier components.

In addition to the distinction between open- and closed-cycle systems, refrigeration processes are also described as simple cycles, compound cycles or cascade cycles. Simple cycles employ one set of components and a single refrigeration cycle as in Figure. Compound and cascade cycles employ multiple sets of components and two or more refrigeration cycles. The cycles interact to accomplish cooling at several temperatures or to allow a greater span between the lowest and highest temperatures in the system than can be achieved with the simple cycle.

Closed-Cycle Operation.

For a simple cycle, the lowest evaporator temperature that is practical in a closed-cycle system is set by the pressure-ratio capability of the compressor and by the properties of the refrigerant. Most high speed reciprocating compressors are limited to a pressure ratio of 9:1, so that the simple cycle is used for evaporator temperatures of 2 to - 50°C. Below these temperatures, the application limits of a single reciprocating compressor are reached. Beyond that there is a risk of excessive heat which may break down lubricants, high bearing loads, excessive oil foaming at startup, and inefficient operation because of reduced volumetric efficiency.

Centrifugal compressors with multiple stages can generate a pressure ratio up to 18:1, but their high discharge temperatures limit the efficiency of the simple cycle at these high pressure ratios. As a result, they have practical evaporator temperatures in the same range as reciprocating compressors.

The compound cycle achieves temperatures of ca-100°C by using two or three compressors in series and a common refrigerant. This keeps the individual machines within their application limits. A refrigerant gas cooler is normally used between compressors to keep the final discharge temperature at a satisfactory level.

Below - 100°C, most refrigerants with suitable exaporator pressures have excessively high condensing pressures. For some refrigerants, the specific volume of refrigerant at low temperature may be so great as to

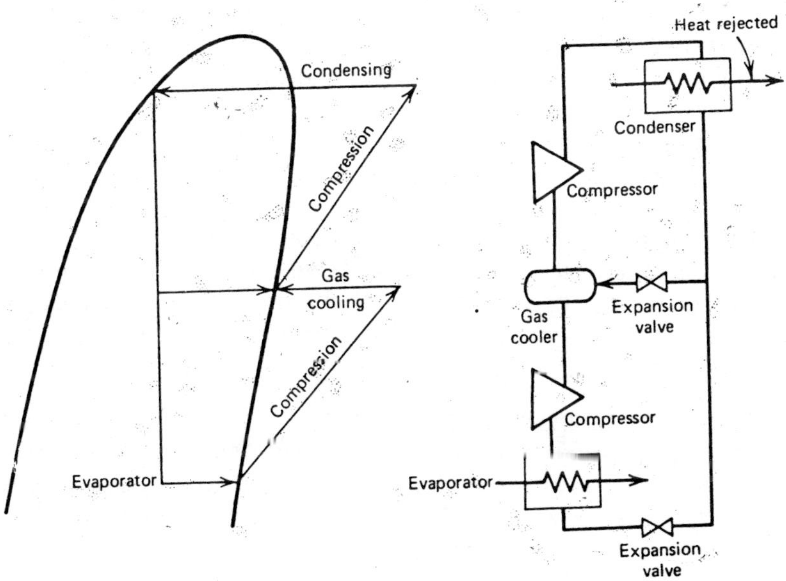

Compound cycle.

require compressors and other equipment of uneconomical size, in other refrigerants, even though the specific volume of refrigerant is satisfactory at low temperature, the specific volume may become too small at the condensing condition. In some circumstances, although none of the above limitations is encountered and a single refrigerant is practical, the compound cycle is not used because of oil-return problems or difficulties of operation.

To satisfy these conditions, the cascade cycle is utilized. This consists of two or more separate refrigerant cycles. The cascade condensor-evaporator rejects heat to the evaporator of the high temperature cycle, which condences the refrigerant of the low temperature cycle. This makes possible the use of refrigerant such as R-13 in the low stage, with pressure-temperature-volume characteristics well suited to the low temperature. Refrigerants with pressure-temperature-volume characteristics more favorable at higher temperatures, eg, R-12 or R-22, are used in one or more higher stages. For extremely low temperatures, more than two refrigerants may be cascaded as, for example, methane-ethylene-propane to produce - 160^{0}C evaporator temperatures. Expansion tanks, sized to handle the low temperature refrigerant as a gas at ambient temperatures, are used during stand by to hold pressure at levels suitable for economical equipment design.

Compound cycles using reciprocating compressors or any cycle using a multistage centrifugal compressor allow the use of economizers or intercoolers between compression stages. Economizers reduce the discharge gas temperature from the preceding stage by mixing relatively cool gas with discharge gas before entering the subsequent stage. Either flash-type economizers, which cool refrigerant by reducing its pressure to the intermediate level, or surface-type economizers, which subcool refrigerant at condensing pressure, may be used to provide the cooler gas for mixing. This keeps the final discharge gas temperature low enough to avoid overheating of the compressor and improves compression efficiency.

Compound compression with economizers also affords the opportunity to provide refrigeration at an intermediate temperature. This provides a further thermodynamic efficiency gain because some of the refrigeration is accomplished at a higher temperature, and less refrigerant must be handled by the lower temperature stages. This reduces the power consumption and the size of the lower stages of compression.

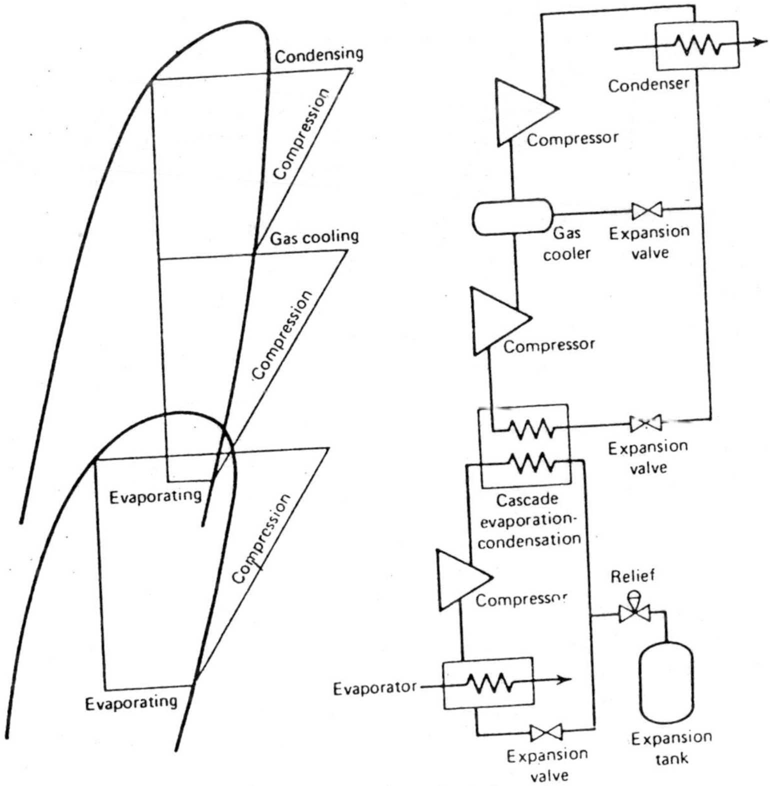

Cascade cycle.

Figure shows a typical system schematic with flash-type economizers. Process loads at several different temperature levels can be handled by taking suction to an intermediate compression stage as shown. The corresponding pressure-enthalpy (P-H) diagram illustrates the thermodynamic cycle.

• Flooded refrigeration systems are a version of the closed cycle which may reduce design problems in some applications. In flooded systems, the refrigerant is circulated to heat exchangers or evaporators by a pump. Figure shows the flooded cycle, which can employ any of the simple or compound closed-refrigeration cycles.

The refrigerant-recirculating pump pressurizes the refrigerant liquid and moves it to one or more evaporators or heat exchangers which may be remote from the receiver. The low pressure refrigerant may be used as single-phase heat-transfer fluid as in (a) of figure, which eliminates the extra heat exchange step and increased temperature difference encountered in a conventional system that uses a secondry refrigerantor brine. This approach may simplify the design of process heat exchangers where the large specific volumes of evaporating refrigerant vapor would

REFRIGERANT NUMBERING SYSTEM (ASHRAE 34-78)[a]

Refrigerant number designation	Chemical name	Chemical formula	Molecular weight	Normal boiling point, °C	Group classification[b]
10	carbon tetrachloride	CCl_4	153.8	77	2
11	tetrachlorofluoromethane	CCl_3F	137.4	24	1
12	dichlorodifluoromethane	CCl_2F_2	120.9	-30	1
13	chlorotrifluoromethane	$CClF_3$	104.5	-81	1
22	chlorodifluoromethane	$CHClF_2$	86.5	-41	1
23	trifluoromethane	CHF_3	70.0	-82	
113	1,1,2-trichlorotrifluoroethane	CCl_2FCClF_2	187.4	48	1
114	1,2-dichlorotetrafluoroethane	$CClF_2CClF_2$	170.9	48	1
Hydrocarbons					
50	methane	CH_4	16.0	-161	3
170	ethane	CH_3CH_3	30	-89	3
290	propane	$CH_3CH_2CH_3$	44	-42	3
600	butane	$CH_3CH_2CH_2CH_3$	58.1	0	3
600a	isobutane	$Ch(CH_3)_3$	58.1	-12	
Inorganic compounds					
717	ammonia	NH_3	17.0	-33	2
732	oxygen	O_2	32.0	-183	
744	carbon dioxide	CO_2	44.0	-78	1
764	sulfur dioxide	SO_2	64.1	-10	2
Unsaturated organic compounds					
1140	vinyl chloride	$CH_2 = CHCl$	62.5	-14	
1141	vinyl fluoride	$CH_2 = CHF$	46	-72	
1150	ethylene	$CH_2=CH_2$	28.1	-104	3
1270	propylene	$CH_3CH = CH_2$	42.1	-48	3
Azeotropes[d]	Composition	Azeotropic Temp. °C			
500	R-12/152a(73.8/26.2 wt%)	0	99.31	-33	1
502	R-22/115(48.8/51.2 wt%)	19	112	-45	1

be troublesome. Alternatively, the pumped refrigerant in the flooded system may be routed through conventional evaporators as in (b) and (c), or special heat exchangers as in (d).

The flooded refrigeration system is helpful when special heat exchangers are necessary for process reasons, or where multiple or remote exchangers are required.

Refregerant Selection for the Closed Cycle.

In any closed cycle, the choice of the operating fluid is unrestricted and is based on the one whose properties are best suited to the operating

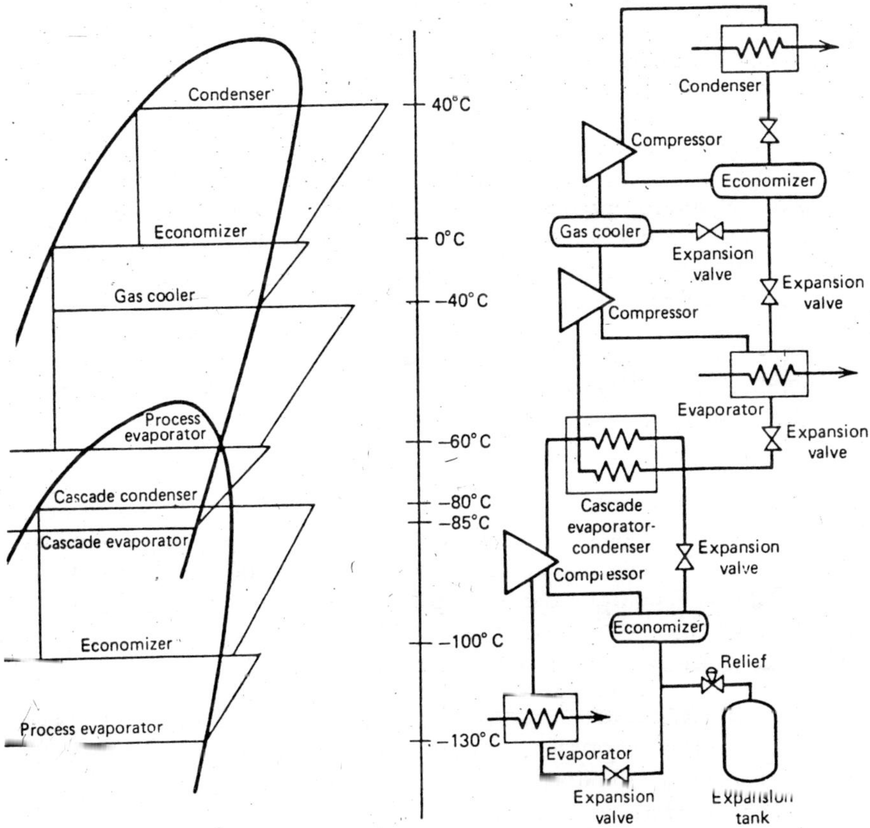

System with flash economizers.

conditions. The choice depends on a variety of factors, some of which may not be directly related to the refrigerant's ability to remove heat. For example, flammability, toxicity, density, viscosity, availibility, and similar characteristics are often deciding factors. The suitability of refrigerant also depends on factors such as the kind of compressor to be used (ie, centrifugal, rotary or reciprocating), safety in application, heat-exchanger design, application of codes, size of the job, and temperature ranges. The factors below should be taken into account when selecting a refrigerant.

Discharge (condensing) pressure should be low enough to suit the design pressure of commercially available pressure vessels, compressor casings, etc. However, discharge pressure, ie, condensor liquid pressure, should be high enough to feed liquid refrigerant to all the parts of the system that require it.

Suction (evaporating)pressure should be above ca 3.45 kPa (0.5 psi)for a practical compressor selection. When possible, it is preferable to have the suction pressure above atmospheric to prevent leakage of air and moisture in to the system. Positive pressure normally is considered a necessity when dealing with hydrocarbons because of the explosion hazard presented by any air leakage into the system.

Standby pressure (saturation at ambient temperature) should be low enough to suit equipment design pressure unless there are other provisions in the system for handling the refrigerant during shutdown, eg, inclusion of expansion tanks.

Critical temperature and pressure should be well above the operating level. As the critical pressure is approached, less heat is rejected as latent heat compared to the sensible heat from desuperheating the comp[ressor discharge gas, and cycle efficiency is reduced. Methane (R-50) and chlorotrifluoromethane (R-13) usually are cascaded with other refrigerants because of their low critical points.

Suction volume sets the size of the compressor. High suction volumes require centrifugal compressors and low suction volumes dictate the use of reciprocating compressors. Suction volumes also may influence evaporator design, particularly at low temperatures, since they must include adequate space for gas-liquid separation.

Freezing point should be lower than minimum operating temperature. This generally is no problem unless the refrigerant is used as a brine.

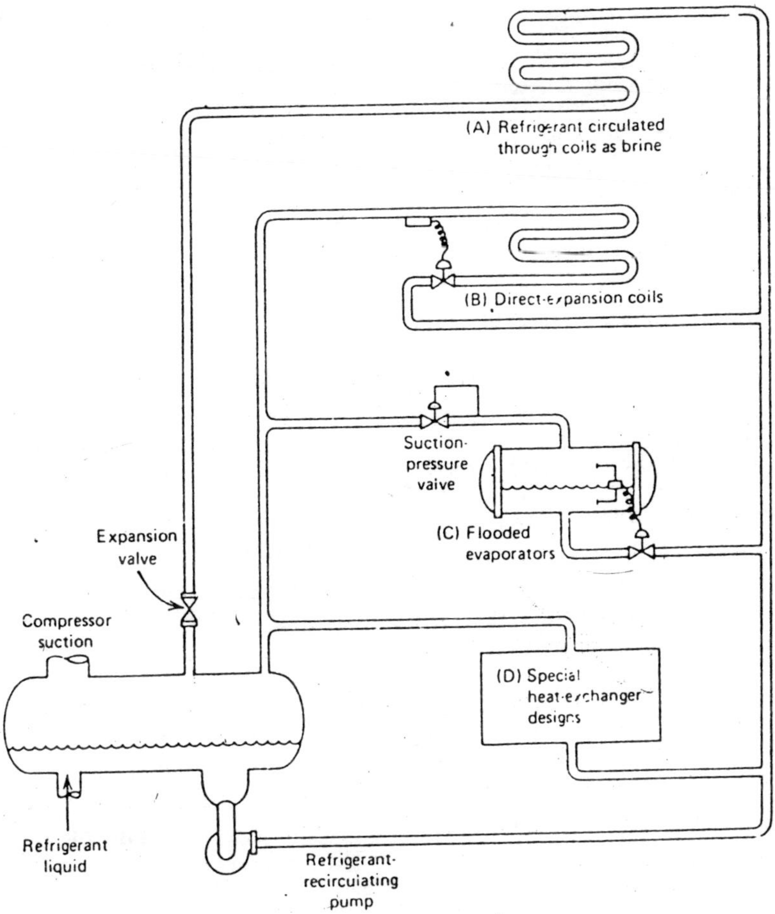

Liquid recirculation.

Theoretical power required for adiabatic compression of the gas is slightly less with some refrigerants than others. However, this is usually a secondry consideration offset by the effects of particular equipment selections, eg, line-pressure drops, etc, on system power consumption.

Vapor density (or molecular weight) is an important characteristic when the compressor is centrifugal because the lighter gases require more impellers for a given pressure rise, ie, head, or temperature lift. On the other hand, centrifugal compressors have a limitation connected with the acoustic velocity in the gas, and this velocity decreases with the increasing molecular weight.

Low vapor densities are desirable to minimize pressure drop in long suction and discharge lines.

Liquid density should be taken into account. Liquid velocities are comparatively low so that pressure drop is usually no problem. However, static head may effect evaporator temperatures, and should be considered when liquid must be fed to elevated parts of the system.

Latent heat should be high because it reduces the quantity of refrigerant that needs to be circulated. However, large flow quantities are more easily controlled because they allow use of larger, less sensitive throttling devices and apertures.

Refrigerant cost depends on the size of the installation and must be considered both from the standpoint of the initial charge and of composition owing to losses during service. Although a domestic refrigerator contains only a few dollars worth of refrigerant, the charge for a typical chemical plant may cost thousands of dollars.

Other desirable properties. Refrigerants should be stable and noncorrosive. For heat-transfer considerations, a refrigerant should have low viscosity, high thermal conductivity, and high specific heat. For safety to life or property, a refrigerant should be non toxic and nonflammable, should not contaminate products in case of a leak, and should have a low leakage tendency through normal materials of construction.

Refrigerants.

No one refrigerant meets all these requirements for the wide range of temperature and the multitude of applications required by modern chemical processing. However, the tendency in the chemical industry is towards the use of, even insistence upon, low cost fluids such as propane and butane whenever they are available in the process. These rediscovered hydrocarbon refrigerants, often thought of as too hazardous because of flammability, are entirely suitable for use in modern compressors and frequently add no more hazard than already exists in the oil refinery or petrochemical field. These low refrigerants are used in simple, compound, and cascade systems, depending on operating temperatures.

With a flammable refrigerant, extra precautions may have to be taken in the engineering design if it is required to meet the explosion-proof classification. It may be more economical to use a higher cost, but nonflammable, refrigerant.

Most of the nontoxic, nonflammable refrigerants are halogenated hydrocarbons containing one or more of the halogens: fluorine, chlorine, and occasionally bromine.

A standard numbering system, shown in table has been devised to identify the refrigerants without the use of cumbersome chemical name. Numbers assigned to the hydrocarbons and halohydrocarbons of the methane, ethane, propane and cyclobutane series are such that the number uniquely specifies the refrigerant compound.

The American National Standards Institute (ANSI) groups refrigerants in three classes, depending on toxicity and flammibility. Group 1 refrigerants are nontoxic and nonflammable; Group 2 are slightly toxic or flammable; Group 3 are highly toxic or flammable. The most commonly used refrigerants are shown in Table.

The group 1 refrigerants generally fulfill the basic requirements for an ideal refrigerant with considerable flexibility as to refreigeration capacity. They are ideal for comfort air conditioning since they are nontoxic and nonflammable. These refrigerants are used selectively in terms of compressor displacement and operating temperature levels desired.

Refrigerant 12, dichlorodifluoromethane, is at present the most widely known and used refrigerant. It is ideal for close-coupled or remote systems ranging from small reciprocating to large centrifugal units. It has been used for temperatures as low as -90°C although -85°C is more practical lower limit because of the high gas volumes necessary for attaining these temperatures. It is suited for single-stage or compound cycles using reciprocating and centrifugal compressors.

Refrigerant 22, chlorodifluoromethane, is used in many of the same applications as R-12, but its lower boiling point and higher latent heat permit the use of smaller compressors and refrigerant lines than R-12. The higher pressure characteristics also extend its use to lower temperatures in the range of -100°C.

Refrigerant 11, trichlorofluoromethane, has a low pressure-high volume characteristic suitable for use in close-coupled centrifugal compressor systems for water or brine cooling. Its temperatutre range extends no lower than ca-7^{0}C.

Refrigerant 114, Dicholorotetrafluoroethane, is similar to R-11 but its slightly higher pressure and lower volume characteristic than R-11 extend its use to ca-17^{0}C and higher capacities.

Refrigerant 13, cholorotrifluoromethane, is used in low temperature applications to ca-126^{0}C. Because of its low volume, high condensing pressure, or both, and because of its low critical pressure and temperature, R-13 is usually cascaded with other refrigerants at a discharge pressure corresponding to a condensing temperature in the range of -56^{0}C to -23^{0}C.

Of the group 2 refrigerants, only ammonia is still used to any extent. Although toxic and flammable within specific limits, ammonia is one of the best and most widely used refrigerants. Ammonia liquid has a high specific heat, an acceptable density and viscosity, and high conductivity. This makes it an ideal heat-transfer fluid with reasonable pumping costs, pressure drop, and flow rates. As a refrigerant, ammonia provides high heat transfer except when affected by oil at temperatures below ca -29^{0}C where oil films become viscous. To limit the ammonia-discharge-gas temperature to safe values, its normal maximum condensing temperature is 38^{0}C. Generally, ammonia is used with reciprocating compressors, although relatively large centrifugal compressors ($\geq$ .3.5 MW_t or 1.2 X 10^6 Btu/h) with 8-12 impeller stages required by its low molecular weight are in use today. Materials that are to contain ammonia should contain no copper (with the exception of Monel metal).

. Refrigerants in Group 3 are generally applicable where a flammibility or explosion hazard is already present and their use does not add to the hazard. These refrigerants have the advantage of low cost and, although they have fairly low molecular weight, they are suitable for centrifugal compressors of larger sizes. Because of the high acoustic velocity in Group 3 refrigerants, centrifugal compressors may be operated at high impeller tip speeds, which partly compensates for the higher head requirements than Group 1 refrigerants.

These refrigerants should be used at pressures greater than atmospheric to avoid increasing the explosion hazard by the admission of air in case

PROPERTIES OF COMMON REFRIGERANTS

Refrigerant number[a]	Chemical formula	Normal temp. range, ^0C	System capacity	Cycle type	Compressor type	Recommended equipment: Relative cost	Recommended equipment: Design pressure, kPa[b] High side	Recommended equipment: Design pressure, kPa[b] Low side
Group 1, Nontoxic and nonflammable								
R-11	CCl_3F	-5 to 60	low	simple	centrifugal	medium	210	210
R-114	$CClF_2CClF_2$ CCl_2FCF_3	-20 to 65	low	simple	centrifugal	medium	450	450
R-12	CCl_2F_2	-90 to 60	medium	simple and compound	centrifugal and reciprocating	medium	1650	1140
R-22	$CHClF_2$	-100 to 60	high	simple and compound	centrifugal and reciprocating	medium	2170	1140
R-13	$CClF_3$	-125 to -20	high	cascade	centrifugal and reciprocating	high	2170[c]	2170[c]
Group 2, slightly toxic and flammable								
R-717	NH_3	-30 to 40	high		reciprocating	medium	2170	1140
Group 3, Highly toxic or flammable								
R-600	$CH_3CH_2CH_2CH_3$	2 to 60	low	simple	centrifugai	low	760	450
R-290	$Ch_3Ch_2CH_3$	-40 to 60	medium	simple	centrifugal and reciprocating	low	2170	1140
R-1270	$CH_3CH{=}CH_2$	-45 to 60	high	simple	centrifuagl and reciprocating	low	2170	1140
R-170	CH_3CH_3	-90 to -5	medium	cascade	centrifugal and reciprocating	low	217^0C	217^0C
R-1150	$CH_2{=}CH_2$	-105 to -30	high	cascade	centrifugal and reciprocating	low	217^0C	217^0C
R-50	CH_2	-160 to -110	high	cascade	centrifugal and reciprocating	low	217^0C	217^0C

of leaks. In designing the system, it also must be recognized that these

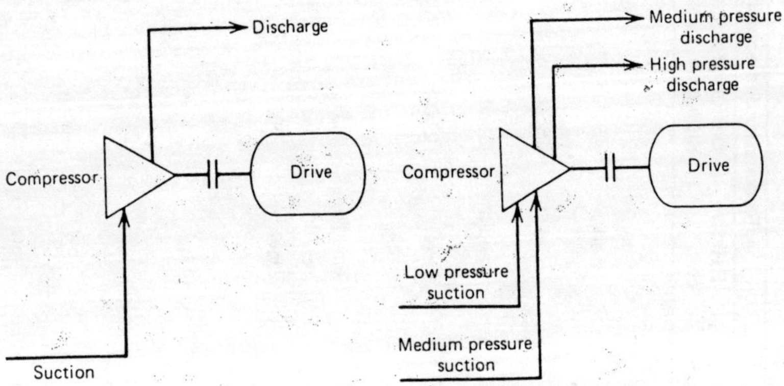

Open-cycle compressors.

refrigerants are likely to be impure in refrigerant applications. For example, commercial propane liquid may contain about 2 wt% ethane, which in the vapor phase, might represent as much as 16-20 vol%. Thus, ethane may appear as a noncondensable. Either this gas must be purged or the compressor displacement must be increased ca-20% if it is recycled from the condensor, otherwise, the condensing pressure will be higher than required for pure propane and the power requirement will be increased.

Propane is the most commonly used Group 3 refrigerant. It is well suited for use with reciprocating and centrifugal compressors in close-coupled or remote systems. Its temperature range extends to ca-40^{0}C.

Propylene is similar to propane but has slightly higher pressure characteristics.

Butane occasionally is used for close-coupled systems in the medium temperature range of 2^{0}C. It has a low pressure and high volume characteristic suitable for centrifugal compressors where the capacity is too small for propane and the temperature is within range.

Ethane normally is used for close-coupled or remote systems at -87 to -7^{0}C. It must be used in cascade cycle because of the high pressure characteristics.

Ethylene is similar to ethane but has a slightly higher pressure, lower volume characteristic which extends its use to -104 to -29^{0}C. Like ethane it must be used in the cascade cycle.

Methane is used in an ultralow range of -160 to -110^{0}C. It is limited to cascade cycles. Methane condensed by ethylene, which is in turn condensed by propane, is a cascade cycle commonly employed to liquefy natural gas.

Open-Cycle Operation.

In many chemical processes, the product to be cooled can itself be used as the refrigerating liquid. An important example of this is in the gathering plants for natural gas. Gas from the wells is cooled, usually after compression and after some of the heavier components are removed as liquid. This liquid may be expanded in a refreigeration cycle to further cool the compressed gas, which causes more of the heavier components to condense. Excess liquid not used for refrigeration is drawn off as product. Another example is in ammonia synthesis. The product is cooled, condensed, and held in spheres or other tanks at low temperatures (-33^{0}C) and atmospheric pressure. In the transportation of liquefied petroleum gas and of ammonia (qv) in ships and barges, the open refrigeration system can be used. The LPG or ammonia is compressed, cooled, and expanded. The liquid portion after expansion is passed on as product until the ship is loaded.

Open-cycle is similar to closed cycle operation, except that one or more parts of the closed cycle may be omitted. For example, the compressor suction may be taken directly from gas wells, rather than from an evaporator. A condensor may be used, and the liquefied gas may be drained to storage tanks.

Compressors may be installed in series or parallel for operating flexibility on for partial standby protection. While multiple reciprocating compressors, or with a centrifugal compressor, gas streams may be picked up or discharged at several pressures if there is refrigerating duty to be performed at intermediate temperatures. It is always more economical to refrigerate at the highest temperature possible.

Principal concerns in the open cycle involve dirt and contaminants, wet gas, compatibility of materials and lubrication circuits, and piping to and from the compressor. The possibility of gas condensing under various ambient temperatures either during operation or during standby must be considered. Beyond these considerations, the open-cycle design and its operation are govered primarily by the process requirements. The open system can use standard refrigeration hardware. It is not necessary to go to the expensive speciality field for the equipment.

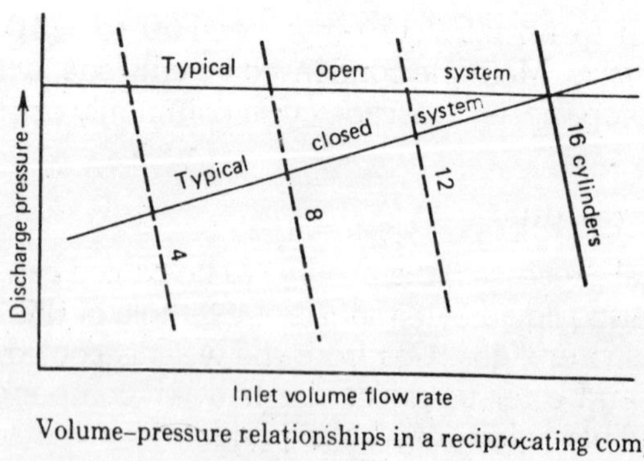

Volume–pressure relationships in a reciprocating compressor.

Open-Cycle Refrigerant Selection.

Process gases used in the open cycle include chlorine, ammonia, and mixed hydrocarbons. These create a wide variety of operating conditions and corrosion problems. Gas charateristics affect both heat exchangers and compressors, but their impact is far more critical on compressor operation. All gas properties and conditions should be clearly specified to obtain the most economical and reliable compressor design. Many installations are greatly overspecified, resulting in design features that not only add significant cost but also complicate the operation of the system and are difficult to maintain. Specifications should consider the following:

Composition. Molecular weight, enthalpy-entrophy relationship, compressibility factor, and operating pressures and temperatures influence the selection and performance of compressors. If process streams are subject to periodic or gradual changes in composition, the range of variations must be indicated.

Corrosion. Special materials of construction and types of shaft seals may be necessary for some gases. Gases that are not compatible with lubricating oils or that must remain oil-free may necessitate reciprocating compressors designed with carbon rings or otherwisen made oilless, or the use of centrifugal compressors designed with isolation seals. However, these features are unnecessary on most installations. Standard designs usually can be used to provide savings in first cost, simpler operation, and reduced maintenance.

Dirt and Liquid carryover. Generally, the carryover of dirt and liquids can be controlled more effectively by suction scrubbers than by costly compressors design features. Where this is not possible, all anticipated operating conditions should be stated clearly so that suitable materials and shaft seals can be provided.

Polymerization. Gases that tend to polymerize may require cooling to keep the gas temperature low throughout compression. This can be handled by liquid injection or by providing external cooling between stages of compression. Provision may be necessary for internal cleaning with steam.

These factors are typical of those encountered in open-cycle gas compression. Each job should be thoroughly reviewed to avoid unnecessary cost and obtain the simplest possible compressor design for ease of operation and maintenance. Direct coordination between the design engineer anf manufacturer during final stages of system design is strongly recommended.

Use of Ice.

Where water is not harmful to a product or process, ice may be used to provide refrigeration. Direct application of ice or of ice and water is a rapid way to control a chemical reaction or remove heat from a process. The rapid melting of ice furnishes large amounts of refrigeration in a short time and allows leveling-out of the refrigeration capacity required for batch processes. This stored refrigeration also is desirable in some processes where cooling is critical from the standpoint of safety or serious product spoilage.

However, ice still is used extensively, and equipment to make flake or cube ice at the point of use is commonly employed. This method avoids the loss of crushing and minimizes transportation costs.

Compressors.

Reciprocating or centrifugal compressors can be used singly or parallel and series combinations for process compresion and refrigeration applications.

Modern high speed reciprocating compressors with displacements up to 0.283-0.472m ^{3}/s (600-1000 cfm) generally are limited to a pressure ratio of about 9. The reciprocating compressor is basically a constant-volume variable-head machine. It handles various discharge pressures with relatively small changes in inlet-volume flow rate as shown by the heavy line in Figure.

Open systems and many processes require nearly fixed compressor suction and discharge pressure levels. This load characteristic is represented by the horizontal typical open-system line of Figure. In contrast, condenser operation in many closed systems is related to ambient conditions, eg, through cooling towers, so that on cooler days the condenser pressure can be reduced. When the refrigeration load is lower, less refrigerant circulation is required. The resulting load characteristic is represented by the typical closed-system line on Figure.

The compressor must be capable of matching the pressure and flow requirements imposed upon it by the system in which it operates. The reciprocating compressor matches the imposed discharge pressure at any level up to its limiting pressure ratio. Varying flow requirements can be met by providing devices that unload individual or multiple

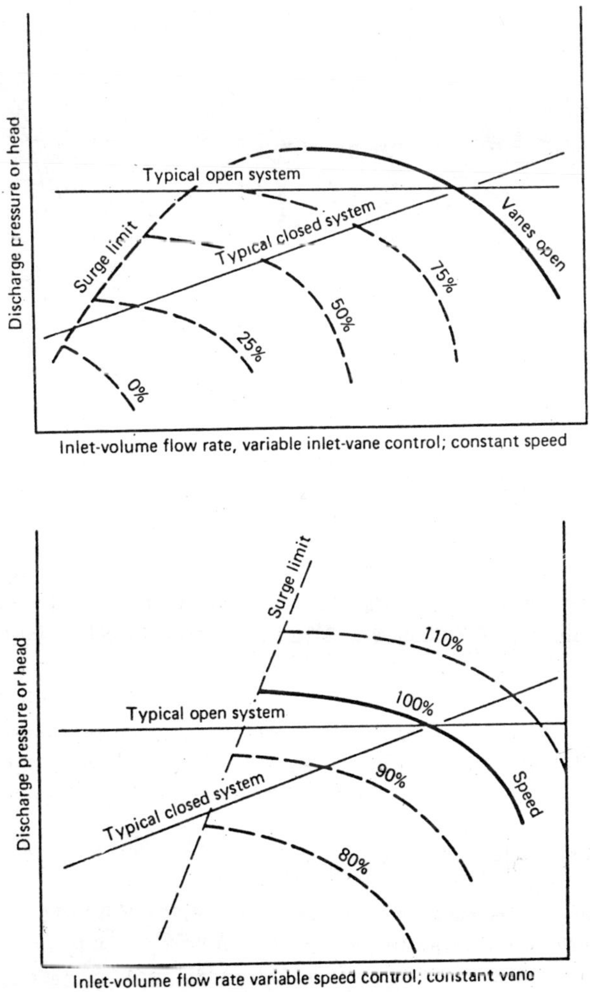

Volume–pressure relationships in a centrifugal compress

cylinders. This unloading is accomplished by blocking the suction or discharge values that open either manually or automatically. Speed control also can be used to effect changes in capacity.

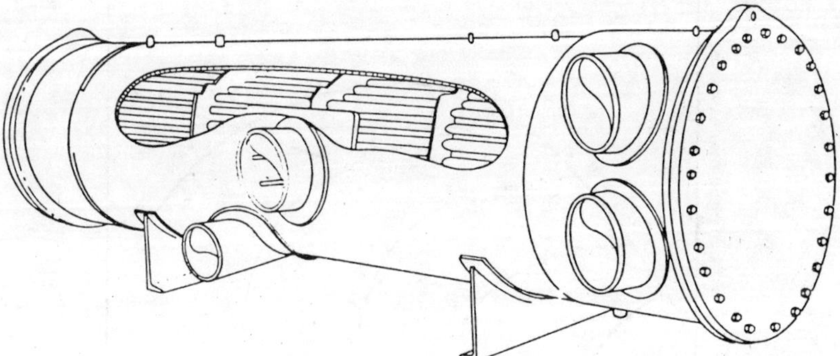

Typical refrigerant condenser.

Most reciprocating compressors have a lubricated design. Oil is pumped into the process gas stream or refrigeration system during operation. Thus, systems must be designed carefully to return oil from various parts of the system to the compressor crankcase to provide for continuous lubrication and also to avoid contaminating heat-exchangers surfaces. At very low temperatures (ca -50^{0}C or lower, depending on refrigerants used) oil becomes too viscous to return, and provision must be made for periodic plant shutdown and warmup to allow manual transfer of the oil.

Compressors usually are arranged to start unloaded so that normal torque motors are adequate for starting. When gas engines are used for reciprocating compressor drives, careful torsional analysis is essential.

The centrifugal compressor is preferred whenever the gas volume is high enough to allow its use, because it offers better control, simpler hookup, minimal lubrication problems and lower maintenance. Single-impeller designs are directly connected to high speed drives or driven through an internal speed increaser. These machines are ideally suited for clean, noncorrosive gases in moderate-pressure process or refrigeration cycles in the range of 0.236-1.89 m^3/s (500-400 cfm).

Multistage centrifugal compressors are built for direct connection to high speed drives or for use with an external speed increaser. Designs available from suppliers generally provide for two to eight impellers per casing covering the renge of 0.236-11.8 m^3/s (500-25,000 cfm) depending on the operating speed. A wide choice of materials and shaft seals to suit any gas composition, including dirty or corrosive process streams, as available.

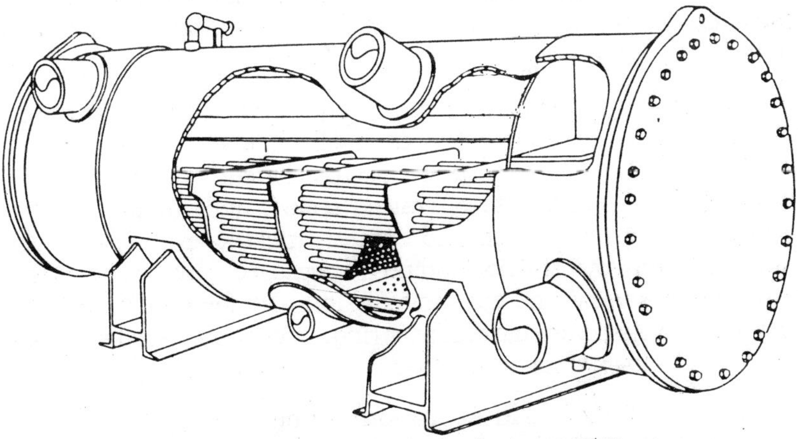

Typical fixed-tube-sheet evaporator.

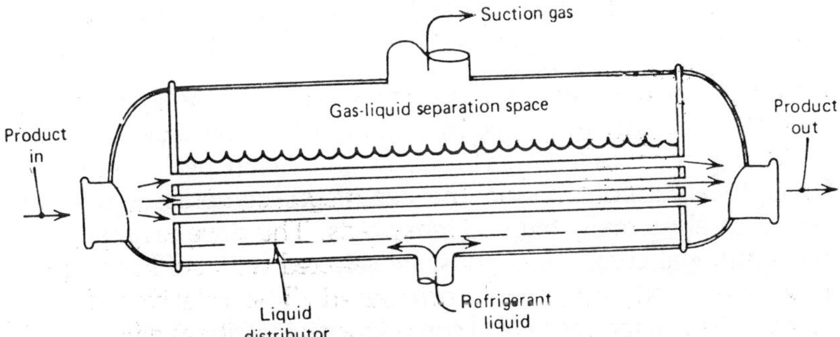

Typical flooded shell-and-tube evaporator.

The centrifugal compressor has a more complex head-volume characteristic than reciprocating machines. Changing discharge pressure may cause relatively large changes in inlet volume, as shown by the heavy line in Figure. Adjustment of variable inlet vanes or of a diffuser allows the compressor to operate anywhere below the heavy line to match conditions imposed by the system. A variable-speed driver offers an alternative way to match the compressor's characteristics to the system load, as shown in the lower half of Figure. The maximum head capability is fixed by the operating speed of the compressor. Both methods have advantages; generally, variable speed usually is more efficient. Maximum efficiency and control can be obtained by considering both methods of control.

The centrifugal compressor has a surge point, ie, a minimum-volume flow below which stable operation cannot be maintained. The percentage of load at which the surge point occurs depends on the number of impellers, design-pressure, operating speed, and variable inlet-vane setting. The system design and controls must keep the inlet volume above this point by artificial loading if necessary. This is accomplished with a bypass valve and gas recirculation. Combined with a variable inlet-vane setting, variable diffeuser ring, or variable speed control, the gas bypass allows stable operation down to zero load.

Provision for no-load operation strongly recommended for all chemical plant installations, regardless of expected fluctuations in plant load. This permits the refrigeration system to be started up and thoroughly checked uot independently of the chemical process.

The contrast between the operating characteristics of the reciprocating compressor and the centrifugal compressor are important considerations in plant design to achieve satisfactory performance. Unlike a reciprocating compressor, the centrifugal compressor will not be rebalance abnormally high system heads. The drive arrangement for the centrifugal compressor must be selected with sufficient speed to meet the maximum head anticipated. The relatively flat head characteristic of the centrifugal compressor necessitates different control approaches than for reciprocating machines, particularly when parallel compressors are utilized. These differences, which account for most of the troubles experienced in centrifugal-compressor systems, cannot be overlooked in the design of a plant.

A system that uses centrifugal compressors to start with high suction density existing during standby poses a special problem of starting torque. This situation can be handled by the driver if it has sufficient starting torque. If not, the system must have provisions to reduce the suction pressure at startup. This problem is particularly important when using single-shaft gas-turbine engines, or reduced-voltage starters on electric drives. Split-shaft gas turbines are preffered for this reason.

Drive ratinge that are affected by ambient temperatures, altitudes, etc, must be evaluated at the actual operating conditions. Refrigeration installations normally require maximum output at high ambient temperatures, a factor that must be considered when using drives such as gas turbines and gas engines.

Condensers.

The refrigerant condenser is used to reject the heat of compression and the process heat load picked up in the evaporator. This heat can be rejected to cooling water or air; both of which are commonly used.

The heat of compression depends upon the compressor horsepower and becomes a sifnificant part of the load on low temperature systems affecting the size of condensers. The condenser heat-rejection rate can be expressed as follows:

$$\text{rejection rate} = \text{evaporator load} + \text{motor power}$$

Where both rejection rate and evaporator load are in kilowatts (kJ/s). Approximate condenser heat-rejection rates are summarized in Table for various evaporator temperatures.

APPROXIMATE CONDENSER HEAT-REJECTION RATES

Evaporator temperature, 0°C	Approximate kJ rejection per kJ evaporator load
10	1.2
-20	1.5
-50	1.8
-80	2.2
-110	2.5
-140	2.8
-160	3.1

Water-cooled shell-and-tube condensers designed with finned tubes and fixed tube sheets generally provide the most economical exchanger design for refrigerant use. Figure shows a typical refrigerant condenser. Commercially available condensers confirming to ASME Boiler and Pressure Vessel Code (6) construction adequately meet both construction and safety requirements for this duty. Design practices essential to many special process exchangers used in refineries and chemical industries add unnecessary expense and, in most cases, result in exchangers less suited for this application than standard condensers specifically developed for refrigerant condensing.

It is common practice in chemical plants to tie in refrigeration equipment with a water-cooling system serving the entire plant needs. The temperature and water flow rate variation must be carefully surveyed. Separate controls on the cooling water for the refrigeration condenser may be needed. For example, water temperatures, which control condensing pressure, may have to be maintained above a minimum value to ensure proper refrigerant liquid feeding to all parts of the system. Separate valving may be necessary to shut off the condenser water supply when the refrigeration unit is shut down.

Cooling towers and spray ponds are frequently used for water-cooling systems. These generally are sized to provide 29°C supply water at design load conditions. Circulation rates typically are specified so that design cooling loads are handled with a 5.6°C cooling-water temperature rise. Pump power, tower fans, makeup water (ca 3% of the flow rate) and water treatment should be taken into account in operating cost studies.

River or well water, when available, provides an economical cooling medium. Quantities circulated will depend on initial supply temperatures and pumping cost but are generally selected to handle the cooling load with 8.3-16.6°C water temperature range. Water treatment and special exchanger materials frequently are necessary because of the corrosive and scale-forming characteristics of the water. Well water, in particular, must be analyzed for corrosive properties, with special attention given to the presence of dissolved gases, eg, H_2S and CO_2. These are extremely corrosive to many exchanger materials, yet difficult to detect in sampling. Pump power, water treatment, and special condenser material should be evaluated when considering costs.

Allowances must be made in heat-transfer calculations for fouling or scaling of exchanger surfaces during operation. This ensures sufficient surface to maintain rated performance over a reasonable interval of time between cleanings. Scale-factor allowances are expressed in $(m^2.k)/kW$ as additional thermal resistance.

Commercial practice normally includes a scale-factor allowance of 0.088. However, the long hours of operation usually associated with chemical-plant service and the type of cooling water frequently encountered generally justify a greater allowance to minimize the frequency of downtime for cleaning. Depending on these conditions, an allowance of 0.18 or 0.35 is recommended for chemical-plant service. Scale allowance can be reflected in systen designs in two ways-as more heat-exchanger surface or as higher design condensing temperatures with attendant increase in compressor power. This is illustrated in Figure. Generally, a compromise between these two approaches is most economical. For extremely bad water, parallel condensers, each with 60-100% capacity, may provide a more economical selection and permit cleaning one exchanger while the system is operating.

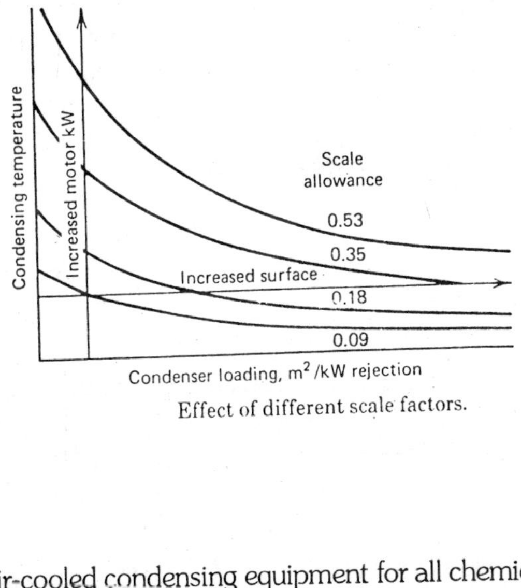

Effect of different scale factors.

Use of air-cooled condensing equipment for all chemical-plant service in on the increase. With tighter restrictions on the use of water, air cooled equipment is used even on larger centrifugal-type refrigeration plants, although it requires more physical space than cooling towers. The service required of an air-cooled condenser in a chemical-plant atmosphere frequently dictates the use of the more expensive alloys in tube construction or of conventional materials with higher wall thickness to give acceptable service life. A battery of air-cooled condensers, with propeller fans located at the top, pull air over the condensing coil. Circulating fans and exchanger surface are usually selected to provide design condensing temperatures of 49-60°C with 35-38°C ambient dry-bulb temperature.

The design dry-bulb temperature should be carefully considered since most weather data reflect an average or mean maximum temperature. If full load operation must be maintained at all times, care should be taken to provide sufficient condenser capacity for the maximum recorded temperature. This is particularly important when the compressor is centrifugal because of its flat-head characteristics and the need for adequate speed. Multiple-circuit or parallel air-cooled condensers must be provided with traps to prevent liquid backup into the idle circuit at light load. Pressure drop through the condenser coil must also be considered in establishing the compressor discharge pressure.

In comparing water-cooled and air cooled condensers, the compression horsepower at design conditions is invariably higher with air-cooled condensing. However, ambient air temperatures are considerably below the design temperature most of the time, and operating costs frequently compare favourably over a full year. In addition, air-cooled condensers usually require less maintenance, although dirty or dusty atmospheres may affect this.

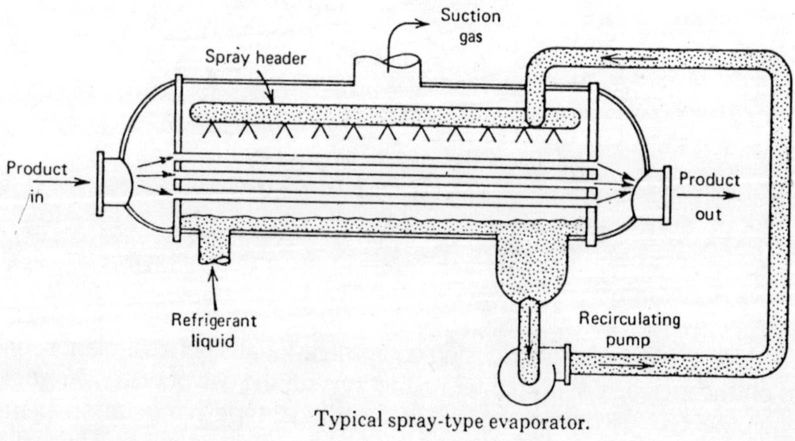

Typical spray-type evaporator.

Evaporators.

The broad range of chemical-plant cooling requirements has led to an extremely wide variety of refrigerant evaporator designs. The chemical-plant design engineer is concerned with heat-exchanger design for nearly every process. Familiarity with heat-exchanger requirements may tempt the chemical engineer to treat the design of the evaporator for a refrigeration system in a fashion identical to evaporators for nonrefrigeration service. Although the general laws of heat transfer apply in both cases, there are special requirements for evaporators in refrigeration service that are not always present in other types of heat-exchanger design. These include problems of oil return, flash-gas distribution, gas-liquid separation, and submergence effects.

Oil Return.

When the evaporator is used with reciprocating-compression equipment, it is necessary to assure adequate oil return from the evaporator. If oil will not return in the refrigerant flow, it is necessary to provide an oil reservoir for the compression equipment and to remove oil mechanically from the low side of the system on a regular basis. Evaporators used with centrifugal compressors do not normally require oil return from the evaporator since centrifugal compressors pump very little oil into the system. However, even with centrifugal equipment, low temperature evaporators eventually may become contaminated with oil which must be reclaimed.

Flash-Gas Distribution.

As a general rule, refrigerants are introduced into the evaporator by expanding liquid from a higher pressure. In the expansion process, a significant amount of refrigerant flashes off into gas. This flash gas must be introduced properly into the evaporator for satisfactory performance. Improper distribution of this gas can result in liquid carryover to the compressor and in damage to the exchanger tubes from erosion or from vibrations.

Gas-Liquid Separation.

The suction gas leaving the evaporator must be dry to avoid compressor damage. The design should provide adequate separation space or include mist eliminators. Liquid carryover is one of the most common sources of trouble with refrigeration systems.

Submergence Effect.

In flooded evaporators the evaporating pressure and temperature at the bottom of the exchanger surface is higher than at the top of the exchanger surface owing to the liquid head. This static head or submergence effect significantly affects the performance of refrigeration evaporators operating at extremely low temperatures and low suction pressures.

Beyond these basic refrigeration-design requirements, the chemical industry imposes many special conditions. Exchangers frequently are applied to cool highly corrosive process streams; consequently, special materials for evaporator tubes and channels of particularly heavy wall thicknesses are dictated. Corrosion allowances, ie, added material thicknesses, in evaporator design may be necessary in chemical service.

High pressure and high temperature design, particularly on the process side of refrigerant evaporators, is frequently encountered in chemical-plant service. Process-side construction may have to be suitable for pressures seldom encountered in commercial service, and differences between process inlet and leaving temperatures $\geq 55^0$C are not uncommon. In such cases, special consideration must be given to thermal stresses within the refrigerant evaporator. U-tube construction or floating -tube-sheet construction may be necessary. Minor process-side modifications may permit use of less expensive standard commercial fixed-tube-sheet designs. However, coordination between the equipment supplier and chemical-plant designer is necessary to tailor the evaporator to the intended duty. Relief devices and safety precautions common to the refrigeration field normally meet chemical-plant needs but should be reviewed against individual plant standards. Here again, it must be the mutual responsibility of the refrigeration equipment supplier and the chemical-plant designer to evaluate what special features, if any, must be applied to modify commercial equipment for chemical-plant service.

Process requirements in the chemical plant may call for very sudden or unexpected load changes on the refrigeration evaporator. Possible thermal shocks, with attendant stresses, must be evaluated in the design phase and the evaporator suitability designed to meet all conditions of its particular service.

Evaporators in chemical-plant duty normally require inspection and cleaning on an annual basis. For this reason, it is sometimes necessary to modify commercial designs for increased accessibility and ease of tube replacement.

Possible contamination of the process stream by leakage from the refrigerant side, or contamination of the refrigerant side by process fluid leakage, should be evaluated in the design of chemical-plant evaporators. Special means of leak detection may be dictated.

Low temperature refrigeration in the chemical-plant industry frequently results in extremely high viscosities on the process side of the equipment. When this is the case, special evaporator designs may be necessary to minimize process-side pressure drops and maintain optimum heat transfer. In general, the process stream is on the tube side of the evaporator to simplify cleaning. Although commercial practice in evaporator design calls for tubes of small inside diameter to achieve optimum heat-transfer performance, the small tube diameters may be incompatible with the process stream. Extra large tube sizes may be required in some chemical-plant evaporators. In extremely low temperatures and extremely viscous chemical-plant cooling duties, evaporators may be provided with rotating internal scrapers within the tubes to provide for continual scraping of the heat-transfer wall and to assure flow of high viscosity fluid through the evaporators.

Refrigeration evaporators are usually designed to meet the Boiler and Pressure Vessel Code (6), which provides for a safe reliable exchanger at economical cost. In refrigeration systems, these exchangers generally operate with relatively small temperature differentials for which fixed-tube-sheet construction is preferred. Refrigerant evaporators also operate with simultaneous reduction in pressure as temperatures are reduced. This relationship results in extremely high factors of safety on pressure stresses, eliminating the need for expensive nickel steels from -29 to -59^{0}C. Most designs are readily modified to provide suitable materials for corrosion problems on the process side.

The basic shell-and-tube exchanger with fixed tube sheets is most widely used for refrigeration evaporators. Most designs are suitable for process fluids up to ca 2170 kPa (300 psig) and for operation with up to 38^{0}C temperature differences. Above these limits, specilized heat exchangers generally are used to suit individual requirements.

With the process fluid on the tube side, the shell side is flooded with refrigerant for efficient wetting of the tubes. Designs must provide for distribution of flash gas and liquid refrigerant entering the shell and for separation of liquid from the gas leaving the shell before it reaches the compressor.

In low temperature applications and large evaporators, the exchanger surface may be sprayed rather than flooded. This eliminates the submergence effect or static-head penalty, which can be significant in large exchangers, particularly at low temperatures. The spray cooler is recommended for some large coolers to offset the cost of refrigerant inventory or charge which would be necessary for flooding.

Where the Reynolds number in the process fluid is low, as for a viscous or heavy brine, it may be desirable to handle the fluid on the shell side to obtain better heat transfer. In these cases, the refrigerant must be evaporated in the tubes. On small exchangers, commonly referred to as direct-expansion coolers, refrigerant feeding is generally handled with a thermal-expansion valve.

On large exchangers, this can best be handled by a small circulating pump to ensure adequate wetting of all tubes. An oversize channel box on one end provides space for a liquid reservoir and for effective liquid-gas separation.

System Design Considerations :

Chemical processes may be continuous or batch. Continuous processing is characterized by temperatures, pressures, flow levels, compositions, and other parameters that do not change with time. Associated with continuous operation are refrigeration start-up and shutdown conditions that invariably differ, sometimes widely, from those of the process itself. These conditions, although they occupy very little time in the life of the installation, must be properly accomodated in the design of the refrigeration system. Consideration must be given to the amount of time required to achieve design operating conditions, the need for standby equipment, etc.

In batch processing, operating conditions are expected to change with time, usually in a repetitive pattern. The refrigeration system must be designed for all extremes. Use of brine storage or ice banks can reduce equipment sizes for batch processes.

Cooling loads can generally be classified in three types in refrigeration systems : sensible cooling, condensing, and partial condensing.

Many chemical cooling loads extend over a wide temperature range.

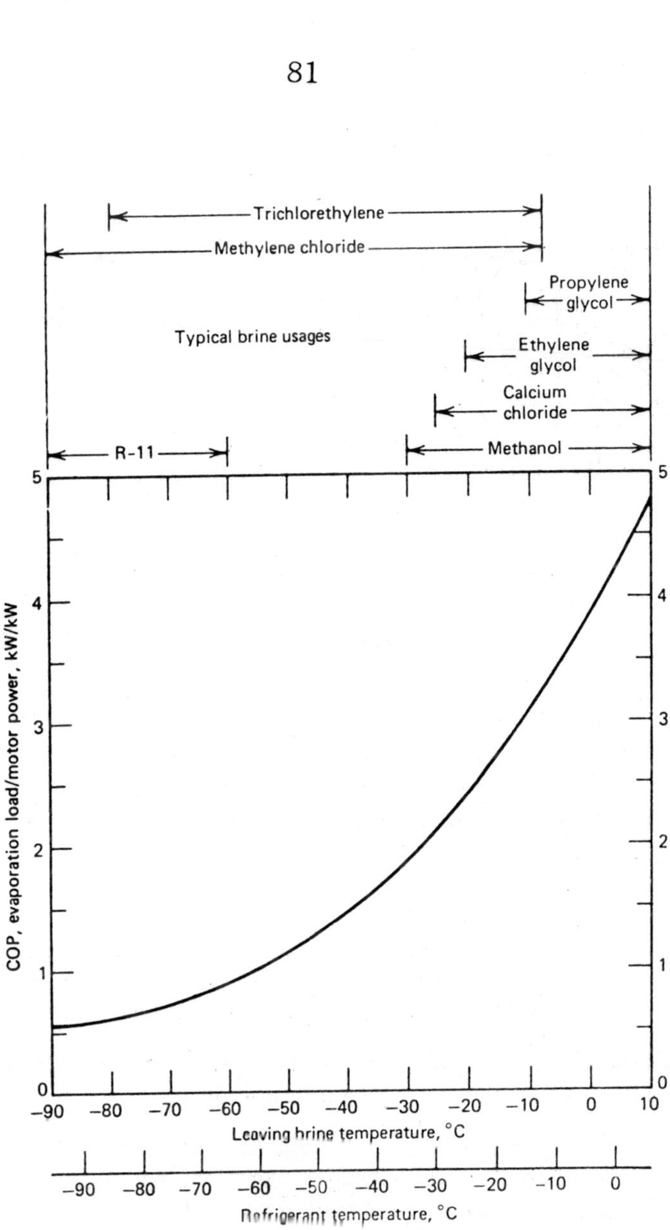

Power requirements at various temperature levels. Centrifugal brine chilling

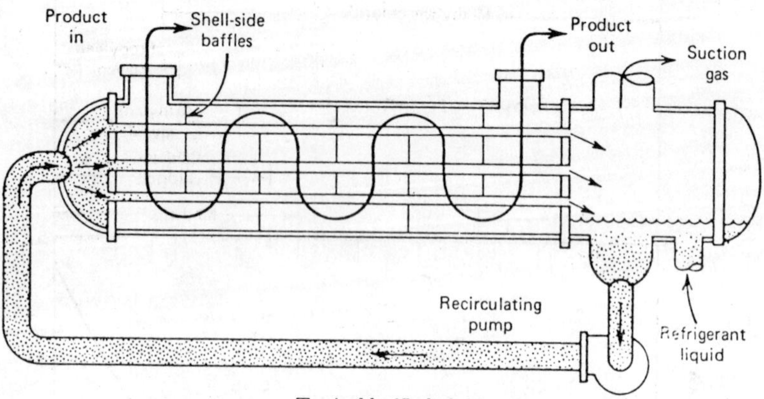

Typical baffled-shell evaporator.

With sensible cooling, the load is almost directly proportional to temperature reduction. Particularly in larger plants, applying refrigeration in several stages improves operating economy. If all of the cooling is done at the final lowest temperature, the compression power required is a maximum. Because compression power increases substantially as temperatures are lowered, the power can be reduced by breaking the load into several stages and cooling part of it at higher temperatures. The number of stages must be balanced against the first cost of equipment, which increases as the number of stages is increased.

Condensing loads are essentially isothermal. Refrigeration must be applied at the required condensing temperature.

Partial condensing, which is frequently encountered in chemical processes because of impurities such as air or high pressure constituents, justifies staged cooling. In most situations, the process stream requires a small amount of sensible cooling. Condensing then generates a significant cooling load as temperature is reduced through the next few degrees. From this point, the load diminishes. Significant temperature reduction is required to accomplish the final stages of condensing, however, because of the increasing percentage of noncondensables which rapidly reduce the partial pressure and required condensing temperature of the condensing constituent.

Closed-cycle operation involves both liquid and gas phases. System designs must take into account liquid-flow problems in addition to gas-flow requirements and must provide for effective separation of the liquid and gas phases in different parts of the system. These factors require careful design of all components and influence the arrangement or elevation of certain components in the cycle.

Liquid pressures must be high enough to feed liquid to the evaporators at all times, especially when evaporators are elevated or remotely located. In some cases, a pump must be used to suit the process requirements. The possibility of operation with reduced pressures caused by colder condensing temperatures than the specified design conditions must also be considered. Depending on the types of liquid valves and relative elevation of various parts of system, it may be necessary to maintain condensing pressures above some minimum level, even if doing so increases the compression power.

Provision must be made to handle any refrigerant liquid that can drain to low spots in the system upon loss of operating pressure during shutdown. It must not be allowed to return as liquid to the compressor upon startup.

The operating charge in various system components fluctuates depending on the load. For example, the operating charge in an air-cooled condensor is quite high at full load but is low, ie, essentially dry, at light load. A storage volume such as a liquid receiver must be provided at some point in the system to accomodate this variation. If the liquid controls permit the evaporator to act as the variable storage, the level may become too high, resulting in liquid carry over to the compressor.

Abnormally high process temperatures may occur either during startup or process upsets. Provision must be made for this possibility, for it can cause damaging thermal stresses on refrigeration components and excessive boiling rates in evaporators, forcing liquid to carry over and damage the compressor.

Factory-designed and built packages, which provide cooling as a service or utility, can require several thousand kilowatts of power to operate, but in most cases, they require no more installation than connection of power, utilities, and process lines. As a result, there is a single source of responsibility for all aspects of the refrigeration cycle involving the transfer and handling of both saturated liquids and saturated vapors throughout the cycle, oil return, and other design requirements. These packages are custom engineered, including selection of components, piping, controls, base designs, torsional and critical speed analysis, and individual chemical process requirements. Large packages are designed in sections for shipment but are readily interconnected in the field.

As a general rule, field-erected refrigeration systems should be close-coupled to minimize problems of oil return and refrigerant condensation in suction lines. Where process loads are remotely located, pumped recirculation or brine systems are recommended. Piping and controls should be reviewed with suppliers to assure satisfactory operation under all conditions.

Refrigeration System Specifications :

To minimize costly and time-consuming alternations owing to unexpected requirements, the refrigeratión specialist who is to do the final design must have as mush information as possible before the design is started. Usually, it is best to provide more information than thought necessary, and it is always wise to note where information may be sketchy, missing, or uncertain. Carefully spelling out the allowable margins in the most critical process variables and pointing out portions of the refrigeration cycle that are of least concern is always helpful to the designer.

A checklist of minimum information needed by a refrigeration specialist to design a cooling system for a particular application may be helpful.

Process Flow Sheets.

Seeing the process flow sheets is the best overall means for the refrigeration engineer to become familiar with the chemical process for which the refrigeration equipment is to be designed. In addition to providing all of the information shown in table, they give the engineer a feeling for how the chemical plant will operate as a system and how the refrigeration equipment fits into the process. This will allow the engineer to be on the lookout for any areas where savings or more reliable operation in the refrigeration equipment can be achieved or where problem areas may occur. Inability to see the complete process flow sheets, eg, for reasons of process secrecy, will limit the refrigeration engineer's effectiveness in providing the proper refrigeration system for the job. In this case, it is extremely important that the refrigeration

85

engineer to be given all of the information specified in the checklist.

Basic Specifications.

This portion of table fills in the detailed mechanical information that is not found on the flow sheets. The information requested tells the refrigeration engineer how the equipment should be built, where it will be located, and specific safety requirements. This determines which standard equipment can be used and what special modifications need to be made.

Instrumentation and Control Requirements.

These tell the refrigeration engineer how the system will be controlled by the plant operators and how it will connect to the rest of the chemical-process controls. Particular controller types as well as control sequencing and operation must be spelled out to avoid misunderstandings and costly redesign. The refrigeration engineer needs to be aware of the degree of control required for the refrigeration system; for example, the process may require remote starting and stopping of the refrigeration system from the central room. This could influence the way in which the refrigeration safeties and interlocks are designed.

Off-Designed Operation.

It is likely that the most severe operation of the refrigeration system will occur during startup or shutdown of the chemical process. The rapidly changing pressures, temperatures, and loads experienced by the refrigeration equipment can cause motor overloads, compressor surging, orloss of control if they are not anticipated during design.

48

Disorders of Stored Foods :

Our fruits, vegetables, eggs, meats and dairy products may be harvested, gathered or slaughtered some time prior to going into refrigerated storage. Food deterioration may have already begun. A food will not improve in quality if harvested, gathered or slaughtered in a decayed condition. Only sound foods should be given the attention required for successful cold storage. Even under optimum conditions, storage in a cool chamber only retards food deterioration.

9

TECHNICAL & DESIGN SECTION

Cooling Coils

The selection of the correct cooling coil for any storage application is one of the main factors that will influence the relative humidity of the storage environment produced. Where high humidities are required it is important to size the cooling coil for the smallest practical TD. * (Selection should be based on a TD of between 3 and 5°C.) Such a selection inevitably leads to a coil with a large surface area. Where copper tubes and aluminium fins are used the primary to secondary surface area ration should be around 1-18. If galvanise steel fins and tubes are used are used the ration should be around 1-11.

The number of rows of tubes in the direction of air flow also effects the coils performance. For high humidity applications a deepcoil having six or more rows of tubes is generally satisfactory. The face velocity of the air passing through the cooling coil also affects the coils performance. Typical design figures are 2-3 m per second. Such a velocity will give rise to a pressure drop in the the air flowing across the coil of 60-80 pa.

Fin spacing affects the resistance to airflow offered by the cooler. Restricted airflow results in a reduced efficiency of the cooling system. In stores that will run at temperatures above 4°C a fin spacing of 4 mm between fins is acceptable. For store temperatures below 4°C fins should spaced at 6 mm apat to allow for a certain amount of frosting to occur before the airflow is severely restricted. It is important to avoid obstructions before and after the cooling coil as these may give rise to poor air distribution. The effect of poor distribution is to reduce the effective surface area of the coil resulting in lower humidities than were originally intended in the design.

*TD is the difference between the temperature of the air entering the cooler and the temperature.

Some storage applications require low humidities in the store atmosphere rather than high ones. If suitably selected and controlled, the cooling coil can act as a dehumidifier to provide the required conditions. The dehumidification process requires a low coil temperature. Low cooler temperatures will result when the produce is subjected to a suitable vaccum, some of this water is evaporated taking its heat of vaporisation from the produce and there by cooling it. In fact, to cool produce by 10° requires on average the evaporation of water equivalent to 1.8 per cent of the weight of the produce.

The mechanism of vaccum cooling is such that the cooling effect is generated within the produce. This has the important advantage of enablingh even and rapid cooling of tightly stacked produce. It is even possible to cool produce that has been pre-packed ready for market, providing some ventilation holes are left in the packing materials. Vacuum cooling is most successful with flowers, mushrooms and with thin leafy produce, for example lettuce. it is perfectly possible to cool solid products like apples and strawberries but the larger the individual items are the longer it will be before their centre temperatures have been reduced to the required level.

By comparison with other cooling systems, vaccum cooling requires a higher capital investment.

Provided that the cooler is fully used for a long season the cost of cooling by this method are comparable to refrigerated cooling techniques. The vaccum cooler has the advantage of rapid uniform cooling regardless of method of stacking; an attribute which cannot be ascribed to forced air cooling systems.

Hydro Cooling:

Hydro cooling is an effective method of quickly removing field heat. Cooling times are comparable with those achieved by vaccum cooling. The method suffers from several disadvantages. The produce comes from the cooler in a very wet state which may make packing or handling difficult. The cooling water must be recirculated to retain the cooling effect and as a result it may become heavily containminated with soil, plant sap; plant debris and disease organisms. Such conditions are conducive to the spread of fungal and bacterial disease which may in turn considerably shorten the shelf life of the produce. In some circumstances the disposal of used cooling water may present a serious effluent problem.

Compressors and condensing Sets:-

Positive displacement single stage compressors are used almost exclusively in agricultural an horticultural storage work. Direct drive by electric motor is most common, though some machines may be driven via a belt.

The compressor is often mounted in a frame which also carries the liquid receiver, refrigerant filter/drier, slight glass and the condensing coil together with its cooling fan. Such a unit is called a condensing set. When specifying the cooing capacity of a condensing set, it is essential to state the condensing and evaporating temperatures to which the capacity applies. The cooling power of a condensing set varies considerably at different temperatures, and for this reason the size of the compressor motor can only be considered as a guide to plant capacity. Condensing sets function most effectively when they are mounted in the plant on the roof of the store, this is not recommend. Such a site is inaccessible for maintenance and cleaning. The air temperature is often well above ambient and vibration may damage gas barriers in the controlled atmosphere stores.

Remote Condensers:-

In some installations it may be necessary to locate the condenser away from the compressor. Two tipes of remote condeser are available. The air cooled condenser consists of a finned tube block similar to a vehicle radiator, and arrangement is generally used on medium and small sized plants. The alternative, a water cooled condenser is more expensive, but is often preferred on larger plants because of the increased efficiency of the refrigeration system which results from the lower condensing temperature that can be obtained during warm weather. Water cooled condensers provide for greater flexibility in positioning since they do not have to be located near a good supply of cooling air. It is generally necessary to economise in the use of water: for this reason it will be desirable to recirculate the cooling water through a cooling tower. Water cooled condensers are generally only considered economic for plants rated at more than 50 Kw refrigeration. With water cooled systems precuations must be taken to prevent possible frost damage.

Evaporator/Cooler:-

The principle of the bank cooler is not new but its use has largely been restricted to the cooling of milk. The technique can be easily adopted to the cooling of vegetables.

The principle of operation is that a refrigeration compressor with sufficient capacity to meet the average daily cooling requirement is run continuously to produce blocks of ice. When it is required to cool produce, the cooling effect is released by melting the ice. Under suitable conditions the ice can be melted much more rapidly than it was made: thus enabling the cooling to be completed in a time only limited by the rate at which the produce can give up its heat. A further advantage of the ice bank system is that if correctly designed it will produce very high humidities in the store, minimising the weight loss that inevitably occurs during the cooling process.

Direct Refrigeration :

In some cases, where the annual use of facilities is very short, the installation of a vapour compressing refrigeration system cannot be justified. In such situations it may be practicable to provide refrigeration by evaporating liquid nitrogen, or solid carbon dioxide. The high cost of the refrigerant and the fact that it is lost and cannot be recirculated, tends to exclude this method of refrigeration from applications which require the quick extraction of large quantities of field heat. It can, however, be successfully used for refrigerating transport vehicles to prevent cooled produce from warming up too quickly on its journey to market. it is important to remember that direct refrigeration systems of this type temt to influence the atmosphere composition. It care is not taken produce may be damaged, though in general terms the modificatons in atmpsphere may be slightly beneficial. Care must also be taken by personnel who enter the storage chamber. Adequate time should be allowed after the doors are opened to ensure that the atmosphere is normal.

Cooling with ambient air:-

For same crops the use of refrigerated storage facilities may not be justified. An improvement in stroage life can be obtained by selective ventilation, using outside air. The principle of operation is that only air that is colder than the stock of produce is used for ventilation. it will be obvious that such a system depends for its effectiveness on an adequate supply of air at a temperature below the required storage temperature.

As storage is extended into the spring, the number of hours available for ventilation decreases. In general, one may not with certainly maintain sufficiently low storage temperatures much beyond the beginning of April. For storage beyond this period it will be necessary to consider mechanical refrigeration, possibly as an adjunct to ambient air cooling.

QUICK COOLING METHODS

Perishable crops like soft fruit and select vegetables benefit greatly from rapid removal of field heat. Several techniques are available by which produce can be rapidly cooled. Whichever method as cooling is adopted it is important to potential benefits of cooling are to be fully ralissed. The high speed cooler must be backed up by cooled storage facilities.

Forced air cooling:

The rate at which heat can be transferred from produce to an air stream depends firstly on the temperature difference between the crop and the cooling air, and secondly on the speed at which the air passes over the crop. The more intimate the contact between the air stream and the crop, the less important in the speed. From the foregoing comments it will be seen that the size and shape of container and the method of stacking within the cooler will have a considerable effect on the cooling times achieved.

It may, if size of an installation warrants it, be worthwile considering a separate forced air cooling chamber where produce can be reduced to within a few degrees of storage temperature in a fairly short time, subsequently being removed to a separate building for storage. Admittedly such a system may involve double handling but with careful design this could reduced to a minimum.

Vaccum Cooling :

An alternative method for the rapid removal of field heat from produce is the vaccum cooler.

It is sometimes difficult to obtain details about the design of the powers and the method of fitting them together, but in all cases the principles of stability and suitability for performance must be followed and the proposals scrutinised accordingly.

Some proprietary systems use timber in the construction of panels in walls and ceilings and this timber must be pressure treated with preservative before fabrication. Ceiling and roof supports systems should be examined, also the methods of creation and fixing. Particular points to note are the panel junctions and the method of sealing: structural support for ceilings and general structural qualities. The methods used for supporting door hangings and hinges and the avoidance of unnecessary bolt and screw holes through the panels are other important items. The intending purchaser should always inspect examples of proprietary stores already in use before deciding to purchase stores of similar manufacture.

Insulation :

To limit the load on the refrigerating equipment, heat leakage into a store must be reduced to as low a level as is practicable. Insulating materials are incorporated in the store for this purpose, the method of application varying with the materials selected. The most important characteristics of such materials are : resistance to moisture transmission, ease of installation, absence of tain and, where exposed, low surface spread of flame.

Suitable materials can be found within the whole range of commercial, thermal insulants but in practice they tend to be selected from certain well known groups and include board or slab materials of a rigid or semi-rigid character, granular or loose fill materials, materials foamed in situ or sprayed on insulants. Some insulating materials, in particular plastics of various kinds, can constitute a fire hazard, both from the production of smoke and toxic fumes. Professional advice should be taken where there is any any doubt about the characterisitic and safe use of a material.

Examples of some types of insulating materials for refrigerated stores are given below, but this list is not complete. The Table in Appendix 2 lists some of the more usual material and indicates their effectiveness as shown by their K value (the K value is a measure of the heat transmission qualities of the material; the lower the K value the better the insulating value of the material) from the Kvalues of the various materials used in the structure of store, the overall insulating value of that structure can be derived.

Board or Slab Insulation :

These include plastics such as expanded polystyrenes and polyurethanes which, together with cork slab, are the most commonly used materials for lining the inside of store walls, ceilings and roofs. Plastics have tended to displace the more traditional cork due to the advantages of price, availability and weight. Methods of fixing include nailing, skewering with hard-wood pegs and adhesives. As with cork slab, plastic materials ca be used horizontally below the floor finish but high density quality must be selected to mechanically handed into and out of store. Slab insulations are also suitable for use in composite panel construction and for filling cavities.

Granuler and loose fill materials:-

These include regranulates cork, mineral wool and pelleted polystrene. It was formerly standard practice in some fruit store designs use regranulated cork, either between brick skins or within cevities in stud walls lined with timber or galvanised steel. Where a good wapour barrier was provided and where is the material was kept dry, the result was satisfactory but all granular materials are liable to settlement and it is almost impossible to check this settlement in vertical cavities once a store is completed and in use.

Framed 'in situ':-

Chemical foams and other insulating materials can be introduced into cavities in a similar way to granular materials. They can be effective and in certain circumstances the method is useful. It is important not to overall the fact that large quantities of water are produced in the process of foaming and this water must be allowed to dry out of the structure.

Sprayed-on Insulation:-

Urethane foams sprayed into walls, roofs and ceilings can be satisfactory but the application is a specialised one and particular care is needed in the choice of protective finishes.

Pre-Fored Panels :-

Factory produced panels utilising one or more of the above insulants are increasingly used and are of many types. Galvanised steel and Aluminium sheets, rigid plastics, plywood and flats asbestos are all available as the exterior components of the panels, Plastic insulating materials have several advantage in forming these panels, including relatively low cost, lightness and case of use and manufacture. Incorporating the materials within the panels protects against mechanical damage to which they are prone; in this situation they are also a reduced fire risk and are less likely to be damaged by vermin.

Insulation Thickness :

To determine the thickness of insulation required in any particular case, it is necessary to decide upon a theoretical U value for each element in the construction, that is, for the wall, ceiling and floor. (The U value is a measure of the hoat transmission characteristics of the structure, the lower the U value the better the insulation value. See Appendix - 2).

Calculations are necessary involving the store temperatures required, the periods of use, the type of equipment selected, the capita and running cost relationship, the degree of exposure of the store to prevailing winds, its construction, and the acceptable less of weight from the produce. For example, if low temperatures are required during the summer month, running costs can be high unless an appropriate thickness of insulation has been provided. Also, if defective construction loads to unnecessary air changes in the store from outside wind movement, then the theoretical value of the insulation will not be achieved. Thus each store has to be examined and calculated separately. There are, however, some broadly accepted figures for U values for particular for the stores illustrated are given in Appendix - 2, this particularly rolates to expanded plastics and it is essential that the manufacturer's advice be followed.

Structure :

Stores may be built as individual, freestanding structures (Store A. Fig - 4) or within a new or existing building (Store C. Fig.6). There is no single preferred method of construction to be used in all circumstances. Provided sound building practice is followed, any one of several recognised methods can be used.

Foundations:-

Foundation design is dependont upon the overall loading factors and the particular site conditions. Each cases has to be approached individually but it can be assumed that in most cases the usual types of strip foundation or reinforced concrete slab will be sufficient.

Floor :

Apart from small, sectional stores with their own timber framed floors, the usual specification is for a suitable concrete slab laid on polythene or other sheet type of water barrier over a layer of hard-core. Insulating material will in many cases be incorporated in the floor. Good quality concrete may sufficience as a wearing surface but, where fork lift trucks or other small wheel transporters are used, such a surface is liable to wear and deteriorate and a different finish will be required (see Internal Finishes, Doors and Hatches,

When under-floor ducts are necessary they can be built in bricks, concrete block or in situ concerete they must not admit water. They may need to be insulated in the same way as the floors, depending upon overall design. Dust covers may be in timber, steel or concrete; loose brick floors are not recommended for refrigerated storage chambers.

Exising concrete should be regarded with suspecion and be built on only when professional advice has been taken. In the case of small sectional stores incorporating their own insulated floors, existing concrete may well be acceptable to receive them but the resulting difference in levels between inside and outside floors may prove a handicapt to filling and emptying the store. Where such stores are built in situ (Store C. it may be necessary to provide perimeter insulation which consists of a vertical strip of insulating material placed in position around the edges of the floor of the chambers where heat leakage is usually maximum. This obviates the need to break up the existing concrete floor as would be necessary if a horizontal lear of insulation had to be incorporated.

Walls:-

A distinction must be made between stores where the produce is held in containers and these where it is in bulk with the produce likely to exert a lateral pressure on the walls.

In the first case traditional methods such as solid or mavity brick or block work are satisfactory. The interior of the store must be kept dry and a horizontal damp proof course (DPC) included. (Store A, Alternatively timber framing many be used to build the store (Store C., or the roof may be carried on stanchions within filling of various materials. These include composite panels of steel, asbestos, aluminium or timber combined with insulating materials.

In the second case when crops are stored in bulk the walling must be so as to accept the lateral loads and transfer them safely to the foundations. the magnitude of these loads will vary with the crop and the height of storage and for guidance on design methods to the followed reference should be made to BS 5500 (Code of practice for design of building and structures for agriculture) and its loading Addendum. Methods of construction include reinforced brickwork or concrete or, more usually, some form of prefabricated panel. Grain walling systems are adequate structurally but may need modifications to make them suitable fo vegetable storage

Roof:-

Sound construction and good workmanship are particularly important. In some cases a flat roof may be unavoidable but wherever possible it is preferable to construct stores with a pitched roof. Where a flat ceiling is required within the store, the space above this and below the pitched roof can be used for inspection and access to both stores and fans, and defects in the construction of the roof and ceiling can be seen and put right without delay.

Most pitched roof are built with steel, timber or concrete fames with purlins carrying sheet materials such as steel, asbestos or Aluminium. If constructed to good practice, there should be few problems but it is essential that laps and joints at ridges, verge and eaves be sealed and bedded closely to present fine show entering. Although ventilation should be provided, roof spaces should be kept as dark as possible inside to discourage entry of bricks. Other rood surfaces employing flexible sheet materials may be used, in accordance with sound, current building practice.

Ceilings:-

Where a flat ceiling is required, as in most CA stores
, it is usually formed from timber joists spanning between chamber walls, trusses or special steel and timber beams. In every case it is essential to design the framework so as to adequately accommodate the loads to be applied and to ensure a rigid with the minimum of deflection. Suitable materials for lining and insulation are discussed later .

In some cases supports for the walls and ceiling can be taken from the roof chambers over the store, using steel hangers and runners. In the case of sectional stores erected under existing roofs, the ceiling panels meat be designed as self supporting units or suspended form external frameworks or from the main roof in preference to relying on support from beams within the store itself

Sectional Stores:-

Recent developments in the design of sectional stores for board cell for special consideration (see Store B, Prefabrication boxes produce fabrication of the various part of a store, followed by assembly on size is now a recognised alternative in traditional methods of construction. In order to reduce the site work even further, complete designs of sectional stores are offered as package deals. Such stores may be supplied complete with refrigerating equipment and controls. The use of pre-formed, insulated, structural panels has made it.

TECHNICAL NOTE

Introduction :

Preservation of perishable foods, such as fruits, vegetables and dairy products etc. for long duration requires suitable cold storages operating at appropriate low temperature. A proper layout and design of a cold and both for reduction in power consumption and economy in overall cost of the cold storage. Based on the survey conducted by CBRI on cold storages in northern India, it has been found that there is a large variation in the specification of building, insulation and Plant and Machinery for the same capacity of cold storage for potatoes. There were large variations in the size and type of machinery used power consumption was found to be quite different for the same quantity of product stored, most important point was that none of the cold storage owners was familiar with the importance of vapour barrier in keeping the thermal efficiency of insulating materials intact.

This Technical Note aims to provide suggestions and guidelines on selection of site, layout, structural design, thermal insulation and choice of proper size of plant and machinery. it will enable selection of proper size of plant and machinery. It will enable selection of proper volume of the chamber for a given capacity, maintenance of correct temperature and relative humidity and also reduce initial and operating power consumption.

Selection of Site :

The selection of site is quite important. Following points should be considered while selecting the site of a cold storage.

1. The cold storage should be near the production and consuming centres.

2. The site should be near the main highway/Railway Station to facilitate transportation.

3. The site should not be in low lying areas and should be free from pits etc.

4. The location of cold storage should be such that the cost of local transport is minimum.

5. Adequate supply of electricity and power should be ensured.

6. Casual labour for loading and unloading of the product should be available.

Orientation and Building Form :

1. Since the major portion of the heat gain is through the surfaces exposed to solar radiation, efforts should be made to orient the longer walls facing N-S direction.

2. The western and eastern wall should have good plantation and covered verandah.

3. The surface area to volume ratio of the building should be minimum.

4. In big Cities where the land cost is quite high, the height of building may be increased while decreasing floor area to reduce land cost and operating power consumption.

Space Requirement :

Cold storage capacity is normally specified in terms of volume of the storage space. It does not include loading and drying platforms, machine and office rooms, precooling chamber depends upon the total quantity of the product to be stored methods of packing and handling of commodity, e.g. manual or mechanical, it is found that a storage space of 3.4 cubic meter/ton of potato (as against present variation from 2.8 to 3.6 M^3/ton) is most suitable for proper tacking and circulation of cold air assuming that loading of potato is being done generally. The height of the chamber varies from 3 to 10 m depending upon available available land area and prevailing land prices.

For case of loading and unloading operations the following steps are suggested.

1. The passage between the rows of the racks should not less than 75 cm.
2. The racks should be kept atleast 20 to 25 cm. away from thewalls.
3. A gap of atleast 30 cm should be provided between the ceiling and the product loaded in the topmost shelve of each rack.

For potato cold storage, the floor area for different heights of the room is given in Table . From the Table floor area for a particular height can be calculated.

Design of Building :

It is found that for heights exceeding 7.5 m. a R.C.C. skeleton with infilled walls is suitable. In places where land cost is extremely low, single storey construction is economical.

In such cases 35-45 cm. thick brick masonry walls (as against 46.70 cm. in the present practice) stiffened with brick pillasters can be safely used.

The most common type of roof employed in construction of cold storage is trangular steel trusses. Now a days R.C.C./R.B.C flat roofs are also inuse. But it has been found that use of open web parallel chord steel joists in such roofs results in at least 15-20% economy in total roofing cost including its insulation. Moreover, use of easily available M.S. angles and rods makes the system simple in fabrications.

Internal Racking System :

The space thus created by a system of walls and columns is divided into floors and then further subdivided into small cabins making use of timber or rolled steel sections in one direction and precast or insitu R.C.C. members in the cross direction. These cabins serve as the storage space. To minimise the spoilage, the appropriate size of a cabin may be selected by referring

Foundations :

Upto 3 storeyed construction, tradition all type of foundations can be followed. But beyond three stories, use of under reamed piles is suggested instead of usual reft foundations. It provides a substaintial saving in foundation cost.

Thermal Insulation :

The most important properties which in insulating material should satisfy are, insulating officiency, resistance to water vapour migration, durability at low temperature and resistance to fire.

The thickness of insulation required for wall, roof and floor of potato cold storage are given For roof it is larger than that for floors and for portion walls it should not be less than half the thickness used for exposed walls. Good insulation should be applied on each side.

Applications :

Insulation should be applied in two layers the second layer should be laid to break the joints in both directions on the first layer.

Vapour Barrier :

Success of the insulation system depends upon the correct application. The correct practice is to make outer skin as impervious as possible. The inner side should be of more permeable type so that no condensation takes place within the insulation. The method of application for saw dust and ricehusk are given in Building Digest No. 85 and for other materials, manufacturers specifications should be followed.

Cold Storage Doors :

Doors of a cold storage should be insulated to the same extent as walls. the doors are usually constructed with a core of insulation material covered on both sides with good and sheet metal and screwed to wooden frames, the joint being sealed with a sealing substance. Their actual dimension will depend upon the handling method employed, but the size most commonly used our country is 195 x 90 mm.

SELECTION OF THE REFRIGERATION PLANT CAPACITY & MACHINERY

1. Compressor :

The Compressor being the heart of refrigeration systems it must be selected very carefully. A slow speed compressor is better suited to our climatic conditions. The design specifications for cold storage of different capacities are total refrigeration load over two compressors, each with slightly more than half the capacity. This will not only ensure flexibility to cope with fluctuating load during the loading period, but also remove the necessity of providing a stand by compressor.

2. Refrigerant :

The refrigerent normally used are ammonia, freon 12 and freon 22. from the cost point of view there is not much difference in ammonia or freon plants. The consumption of electricity per ton of refrigeration is almost the same in both the plans. The price of ammonia is about one fourth lower in case of ammonia plants.

3. Condenser :

There are three types of condenser units. About 85 per cent of the cold storage plants in this country are using atmospheric type of condenser problem. Cell and tube condenser may be used when sufficient quantity of soft and filtered water is available whereas an evaporative condenser may be used when water is scare and there is no space to install cooling tower.

4. Air Circulation :

Forced air circulation is the best for a large cold storage cooled air should be distributed evenly with the help of G.T. ducts for maintaining uniform temperature and humidity throughout the cold chambers. Flooded systems are more economical compared to direct expension systems.

In states like West Bengal and U.P. there is a tendency to built a large chamber size 3000 to 5000 tons using bunker coil system where air circulation is done through the ceiling fans. such systems are reported to be economical in cost and consume less power as compared to force air circulation system.

5. Design Example :

The following example illustrates the design of a cold storage.

6. Example :

Design a cold storage to store 1000 T. of potato. Area of land available is 600 sq. m.

7. Solutions :

From Table , following combinations are possible :-

1. The capacity is close to requirement.
2. To cater for pre-cooling chambers/verandah, machine and

office room and space for movement of truck, an additional 40-50% of the chamber area is need which will not be available in case of alternative -1.

3. Third alternative shall result in wastage of available land area unless future expansion is also taken care of.

The area should be divided into suitable length and breath depending upon site restrictions and to satisfy the requirement of storages space as in Fig.

The roof is provided using open web steel joists and covering is made of A.C.C. or G.I.I., sheets. False ceiling, below the trusses is provided with 10 mm thick country wood plants.

The required thickness of insulation as per Table is provided on the false coiling, walls and floors. gives typical sections of roof, wall and floor to indicate the application of insulating material. The size of the compressor is selected

Concluding Remarks :

1. The thickness of insulation required should be calculated from Table For other storage be calculated from Table For other storage temperature and materials, the thickness of material as given in IS : 661-1974 should be selected.
2. Whenever saw husk or rice husk is used as an imulating material, the method of application for wall, roof and floor should be following as given in Building Digest No. 85.
3. These materials should not be allowed to remain not for a long time otherwise the efficiency of insulation will decrease and power consumption will increase.
4. The flat roof should be properly treated with water proofing material as per IS : 1366-1976 and IS : 4365-1967.
5. Plantlant capacity for a given size of cold storage should be calculated from Table
6. It is preferable to divide the total refrigeration load on two compressors. it will not ensure reduced power consumption and cost but also eliminate the need for a stand-by compressor.
7. Precooling chambers can be provided while using evaporativbe

coolers. The possibility of precooling chamber should be explored for reduction in plant capacity due to reduction in product load.

8. The longer walls of the cold storage should be oriented facing N-S direction the minimise solar heat gain.

9. For a given capacity of potatoes to be stored, the size of the chamber can be worked out based upon the storage density.

10. The thickness of wall should be decided based upon structural requirement and it should be designed as per IS : 1095 - 1969 for actual conditions of loading.

11. If good quality of bricks are not available (Having crushing strength more than 90 Km/cm^2) then a R.C.C. frame should be used. Adequate provision in the form of R.C.C. band should be provided in the walls as per IS : 4326 - 1975 to make the structure strong against earthquake hazards.

12. The precast R.C.C. members should be provided with a minimum bearing of 10 cm on beams/walls.

13. The wooden joists if used shall be of good quality timber and of size 7.5 x 10 cm section.

14. The buttons should be made of country woods, e.g. mango. The section of battons shall not be less than 3 x 5 cm. and spacking not more than cm in any case.

RECOMMENDED THICKNESS OF INSULATION FOR POTATO COLD STORAGE BUILDING SECTION

SL. No.	Name of Material	Density Kg./M	Insulation Thickness in Cms. Roof	Wall	Floor	Partition Wall	
1.	Resin bonded mineral wool	48.0	10.0	8.0	5.0	4.0	Applied on both sides
2.	Resin bonded fibre glass	24.0	10.0	8.0	5.0	4.0	" "
3.	Expanded polytyrene	16.0	10.0	8.0	5.0	4.0	" "
4.	Saw dust & rice husk	150.0	30.0	25.0	20.0	12.0	" "

CAPACITY OF THE COLD STORAGE FOR DIFFERENT HEIGHTS OF THE POTATO COLD STORAGE

	Quantity of Product to be stored (Tons) for heights of the room (Mts.)			
m^2	**4**	**6**	**8**	**10**
50	64	96	128	160
100	128	192	256	320
150	192	288	384	480
200	256	384	512	640
250	320	480	640	800
300	384	476	768	960
350	448	672	896	1120
400	512	768	1014	1280
450	576	864	1142	1440
500	640	960	1270	1600

DESIGN SPECIFICATION FOR COLD STORAGES OF DIFFERENT CAPACITIES

Sl.	Quantity		Height	Flour	Refrigeration Plant Capacity Area	Number
No.	(Ton)	(Meter)	(m^2)	of rooms	(Tons)	No. of compressors
1.	500	6 10	283 170	1 1	13.5 12.5	ONE
2.	1000	6 10	566 340	2 1	25.0 23.0	TWO
3.	2000	6 10	1132 680	4 2	48.0 45.0	TWO
4.	4000	10	1260	4	90.0	THREE

10

MAIN FEATURES OF AMMONIA COMPRESSORS

Ammonia Compressors must be manufactured from best quality material. The compressors should be assembled with utmost care and tested under the strict suprevision of highly experienced and qualified engineers.

Compressors sre double cylinders, vertical reciprocating type. These are designed for slow speed operation. The water jacket surrounds the cylinder heads which remove the sensible heat. Oil filter is fitted outside the crank case. Two valves are provided on both sides of the filter to make it easy to clean without removing the oil from the crank case. Safety valve is built in the valve box which by-pass the high pressure gas to the low pressure side in case the discharge pressure increases above 250 lbs per sq. in guage.

LUBRICATION :

The compressors are forced feed lubricated by the rotary gear pump fitted outside the crank case. This pump takes oil from the crank case through the oil filter and lubricates the main bearings, bigend bearings, gudgeon pin and bushes,. cylinders and shaft seal. Special lubricator manifold with sight glass is fitted with size $8^1/_2$" X $8^1/_2$" and $9^1/_2$" X $9^1/_2$" compressors for the extra lubrication of cylinders and valve. Pistons are fitted with oil scraper rings to remove the excess oil. The padestal bearing is lubricated by the chain turning with the crank shaft.

FORCE FEED LUBRICATING SYSTEMS :

In this system a rotary gear pump is fitted with the compressor. The gear rotates with the crank shaft . The pump takes oil from the crank case and force it to lubricate all the compressor parts. To charge oil in the compressor fitted with rotary gear pump and proceed as follows :

1. Close suction stop valve in the oil pipe line
2. Open the oil filling valve with which rubber pipe is fitted to charge oil from the container
3. Slightly open the vent valve and allow the oil to come from it, then close it.
4. See the oil level in the compressor gauge glass when the required quantity of oil have charged, close the oil filling valve.
5. Open the suction stop valve in the oil pipe line.

Note : Sometimes pump does not suck oil. In that case, close the suction stop valve of the valve box to pump out the crank case slightly.

INSTALLATION :

Installation work should be carried out under the supervision of qualified and experienced technician in refrigeration & air-conditioning field. The compressor should be installed in a clean, dry and well ventilated room.

COMPRESSOR FOUNDATION :

Make the foundation according to the Foundation Drawing supplied with the compressor. Use one part cement, two parts sharp sand and four parts crushed stone. Allow 48 hours to set the foundation. Mount the compressor on the Foundation and grout the foundation bolts with cement, sand and crushed stone. Level the compressor by placing spirit level on the cylinder top Fill the under-side of the compressor with one part cement and two parts sharp sand. Allow it to set for 36 hours.

The pipe line and pipe fittings should be thoroughly cleaned. There should be no rust or any foreign matter in the pipes. All the pipes should be properly supported to eliminate any vibration.

The compressor should be thoroughly cleaned before starting. Remove the head-covers, spring and head valves. Also remove the inspection-cover. Clean the oil pipe and fit with the compressor. Also clean the crank case and fill with new Refrigeration Oil to the proper level. Use any one quality of the oil given below :

1. Freezole 46 or 68 of Bharat Petroleum.
2. Servo Friz 57 or 68 of Indian Oil Company.
3. Sheetal N-68 of Hindustan Petroleum.

Note : Oil must be free from water and machine free from air.

INITIAL STARTING :

Remove the priming plugs on the oil pump and fill it with compressor oil. Replace the plugs. Check the alingment of the compressor fly-wheel and motor pulley. Also check the tension of the V-belt. Check the electrical system and run the compressor for 15 minutes. Check the oil pressure on the oil gauge which should be at least 25 psig. Stop the machine and refit the head valves, springs and head covers.

The compressors are fitted with manually operated full size by-pass valve assembly which equalizes the discharge and the suction pressure for easy starting.

Start the cooling water pump and check the water circulation. To start the compressor without load, open discharge stop valve and discharge by-pass valve. Start compressor. When the compressor attains full speed, close discharge by-pass valve. Open suction stop valve slowly until the suction pressure comes to 20 lbs. psig. Then open the suction stop valve full. During this operation, check the oil pressure and listen to any unusual noise. Open main liquid valve on the receiver. Check the solution and discharge pressure. Also check the cylinders and bearings for unusual over-heating.

Keep the discharge pressure as low and suction pressure as high as practicable. High suction pressure means saving in horse power per ton of refrigeration. Adjust the expansion valve to allow the frost to develop upto suction strainer.

Maintain the oil pressure 20 lbs. more than the suction pressure. Maintain the oil level in the crank case in the centre of oil gauge glass.

There should be no unusual noise in the compressor. Never allow the frost to develop beyond the suction strainer.

STOPPING THE COMPRESSOR :

1. Close main liquid valve on the receiver.
2. Close suction stop valve and pump out the crank case by opening vacuum valve.
3. Stop the compressor.
4. Close discharge stop valve.
5. Shut off cooling water pump.

PERIODICAL MAINTENANCE :

The periodical maintenance should be performed by a qualified mechanic in the field of refrigeration and air conditioning. For the trouble-free operation of the compressor, the maintenance is most important.

Some points are given below for periodical maintenance and checking :

Check oil level in the crank case, sight feed glasses and outer bearing, suction pressure, discharge pressure, cooling water circulation.

Check the condition of the crank case oil fortnightly. Clean the suction and oil strainer thrice in the first week, then after every month.

Check the compressor valves, water jacket, piston rings and play in the bearing annually.

TO CLEAN THE SUCTION STRAINER :

Close the suction stop valve and open the body vacuum valve run the compressor for a few minutes to pump out the gas from the crank case. Stop the compressor and close the discharge stop valve. Now remove the suction strainer from then valve box and clean it. Then replace it and start the compressor as mentioned before.

TO CLEAN THE OIL STRAINER :

To clean the oil strainer, stop the compressor as usual. Close the valves on both sides of the strainer. Remove strainer and clean the wire mesh and refit it. Now open the valves and start the compressor as usual.

SHAFT SEAL :

The compressor shaft seal is fitted at factory with great care. In case it leaks, remove the cover plate. Take out steel cones and rubber rings. Replace the rubber rings with new ones. Grind the bronze ring and steel cones with emery paste on a plain glass. Clean thoroughly with petrol and refit it.

PRINCIPLES OF REFRIGERATION :

Mechanical refrigeration is the process of absorbing undesirable heat from one substance and transferring this heat to the atmosphere through a cooling medium-water or air. In a mechanical refrigeration system, this transfer, of heat is possible and practicable because commercial refrigerants are capable of absorbing heat and boiling to gases at very low temperatures and of giving up this heat as temperatures. They condense to liquids at higher pressure and temperatures.

The amount of heat transferred by a system is expressed in tons of refrigeration. A ton of refrigeration is based upon the amount of heat required to melt one ton of ice in 24 hours. This equals to a cooling rate of 2,88,000 Btu per 24 hours. The amount of refrigeration a system can produce, depends upon the number of pounds of refrigerant circulated in a given time. Each compressor handles a definite volume of gas depending upon its size and speed. Since refrigerant gas is heavier at higher evaporator pressure and lighter at lower evaporator pressure, the tons of refrigeration in a system decreases rapidly as the evaporator pressure decreases.

SINGLE STAGE AMMONIA REFRIGERATION CYCLE :

The high pressure warm liquid refrigerant flows from the receiver to the evaporator coil through the expansion valve. In the evaporator the pressure drop due to the suction of the compressor and the liquid refrigerant boils to a gas, absorbing its latent heat of vaporization from the surrounding substance being cooled the compressor picks up this cold, low pressure gas from the evaporator and discharge it into the condenser at high pressure and temperature.

The condenser is air and water cooled. In the condenser the hot high pressure refrigerant gas gives up its latent heat of condensation to the cooling medium and returns to the liquid state. From the condenser the warm high pressure liquid again flows in to the receiver.

A simple refrigeration system consists of a compressor, condenser, receiver, liquid control valve and evaporator connected by suitable piping and stop valves. The function of each component is explained below :

RECEIVER :

The receiver stores a sufficient quantity of high pressure liquid refrigerant to assure a constant liquid supply to the liquid control device at all times during operation under varying load conditions.

LIQUID CONTROL :

The liquid control device is located in the liquid line immediately ahead of the evaporator. It may be either a thermostatic expansion valve, hand expansion valve or float valve. Its function is to meter the proper amount of liquid refrigerant to the evaporator and to maintain a seal between the high pressure and low pressure sides of the system.

EVAPORATOR :

The evaporator is the cooling component of the system. In the evaporator, the liquid refrigerant boils under controlled reduced pressure as it absorbs heat from the substance surrounding the coil in the conditioned space, liquid or air.

COMPRESSOR :

The compressor draws the cold heat laden refrigerant gas from the evaporator at low pressure and temperature and compresses this. gas, raising its pressure and temperature to the point at which the gas will condense to liquid at ordinary water & air temperature.

CONDENSER :

In the condenser, the heat absorbed by the refrigerant in the evaporator is transferred to the atmosphere through the condenser cooling medium, usually water or air.

POSSIBLE TROUBLE :

Their Causes and Remedies

TROUBLE	CAUSE	REMEDIES
Compressor does not start.	Fuse blown out.	Replace fuse
	Low voltage.	Check volt meter
	Defective motor.	Check motor
	Circuit open.	Check all controls.

Compressor stops.	Motor over load.	Check electric circuit
	High or low pressure cut-out	Check high & low pressure gauges.
Oil pressure too low.	Low oil level.	Charge oil
	Choke oil strainer.	Clean strainer.
	Defective oil pump.	Replace or repair oil pump.
	Oil suction stop Valve closed.	Open the valve.
Suction line temperature too low.	Evaporator over flooded.	Set expansion valve.
Suction temperatures too high	Lack of refrigerant. supply.	Set expansion valve.
Discharge temperature too low.	Wet suction gas.	Adjust refrigerant flow.
Discharge temperature too high	Over superheated Suction gas.	Adjust refrigerant control.
	Broken discharge plate	Replace with new
	Weak safety head spring.	Replace spring.
	Leaking bypass valve.	Repair valve seat.
	Leaking safety valve.	Repair valve seat

ABNORMAL SOUNDS :

Sudden pounding noise twice per revolution.	Liquid coming back to compressor.	Control by adjusting suction stop valve.
Chicking sound.	Drop in discharge gas temperature.	Control liquid feed valve.
	Broken valve.	Replace valve.
	Overheating of discharge line.	Adjust liquid feed valve.
Heavy bumping noise twice per revolution.	Loose flywheel.	Tighten flywheel
Lighter thumping Sound	Main bearing wornout.	
	Defective safety head spring.	Replace the defective parts.
	Loose connecting rod bearing/wrist pin.	

Frost on compressor.	Excess liquid in suction line.	Control liquid feed Valve.

LIST OF SPARE PARTS :

CYLINDER BLOCK ASSEMBLY

Sl. No.	Name of Parts
1.	Water Jacket
~~2.~~	~~Cylinder Head~~
3.	Safety Head Spring
4.	Head Valve Cage
5.	Safety Head
6.	Discharge Valve Spring
6a.	Discharge Valve Plate
6b.	Steel Ball
7.	Discharge Valve
8.	Discharge Valve Spring
9.	Set Screw with nut
10.	Piston
11.	Compression Rings
12.	Oil Rings
13.	Piston Pin
14.	Bush for Pin
15	Lock Bolts
16.	Suction Valve
17.	Connecting Rod

MAIN BODY ASSEMBLY :

Sl. No.	Name of Parts
18.	Bigend Bearing
19.	Bigend Bolts
20.	Bigend Nuts
21.	Oil Pump
22.	Oil Pump Gears (Set of Two)

24. Bronze Metal Ring
25. Steel Cone
26. Steel Plate
27. Seal Spring
28. Crank Shaft
29. Main Bearing

WHEEL ASSEMBLY :

30. Crank Shaft Key
31. Wheel Holding Plate
32. Wheel Holding Bolt
33. Safety Valve Spindle
34. Safety Valve Spring
35. Safety Valve Set Screw

PADESTAL BEARING ASSEMBLY

(For 8½" X 8½" and 9½" X 9½" two cylinders compressors.)

36. Bearing
37. Oiling Ring

FORCE FEED LUBRICATOR :

38. Plunger
39. Spring
40. Lubricator Glass

CONDENSED LIST OF COLD STORAGE TEMPERATURE :

PRODUCT	HOW PACKED	TEMPERATURE °F
Almonds	In Shells/bags	34-38
Apples	Boxes	34-36
Butter	Boxes or Crates	14-30
Cabbage	Bulk	32-34
Carrots	Bushel, Crates	32-34
Cherries	Fresh, In boxes/crates	32-34
Cheese	In Boxes	34-36
Condensed Milk	Bulk	32-36
Cream	Fresh, 40 kg. cans	32-36

Dates	Cured, boxes	34-36
Eggs	Crates, 30 dozen	28-30
Fish	Fresh, short period	25-30
Fish	Frozen, regular storing	0-10
Fruits	Crates	35-40
Grapes	Large Baskets	34-40
Meat	In Chill room	30-32
Milk	Fresh, 40 kg. Cans/Btls	32-35
Onions	Sacks	32-36
Oranges	Boxes	35-40
Peaches	Bushel, Baskets	32-34
Pineapples	Boxes	40-45
Potatoes	Sacks	34-38
Poultry	In Freezer	0-10
Vegetables	In barrels or crates	34-36
Watermelon	Short Period	34-36
Wines	Barrels	40-45

DAILY OPERATING LOG SHEET :

Date .... Comprerssor No. ....

Time	Suction Pressure	Discharge Pressure	Oil Pressure	Amps	Volts	Condensser Pump No.	Room 1 Dry	Room 1 Wet	Room 2 Dry	Room 2 Wet
0200										
0400										
0600										
0800										
1000										
1200										
1400										
1600										
1800										
2000										
2200										
2400										

AMMONIA COMPRESSORS : NOMINAL DIMENSIONS WITHOUT FLY-WHEEL

Compressor Size	3½"X3½"	4½"X4½"	5½"X5½"	6½"X6½"	7½"X7½"	8½"X8½"	9½"X9½"
Length	26½"	35"	40"	48"	56"	79"	82"
Breadth	17"	20"	25"	32"	34"	41"	43"
Height	27"	37"	44"	51"	55"	64"	72"
Flywheel Diameter	18"	24"	30"	36"	39"	42"	45"
Belt Groovve	3	4	4	5	7	9	8
Section of Groove	B	B	C	C	C	C	D
Size of V-belt with 1440 RPM Motor	94"	114"	134"	152"	170"	185"	200"
Size of Motor Pulley	5-5/8"	7-1/2"	9-3/8"	10"	10-7/8"	11-5/8"	12-1/2"

Soze of V-belt with 960 RPM Motor	98"	120"	142"	160"	178"	192"	210"
Size of Motor Pulley	8½"	11¼"	14¼"	15"	16¼"	17½"	18¾"
B.H.P. of Motor	10	15	30	50	70	100	150
No. of Cylinder	2	2	2	2	2	2	2
Bore of Cylinder	3½"	4½"	5½"	6½"	7½"	8½"	9½"
Stroke of each Cylinder	3½"	4½"	5½"	6½"	7½"	8½"	9½"
Size of Suction line	1"	1¼"	1½"	2"	2½"	3"	4"
Size of Discharge line	1"	1¼"	1½"	2"	2½"	3"	3"
R.P.M. (Maximum)	450	450	450	400	400	400	375
Maximum Discharge Pressure lbs. per Sq. inch	250	250	250	250	250	250	250
Full oil charge in litres	8	12	16	24	32	36	45

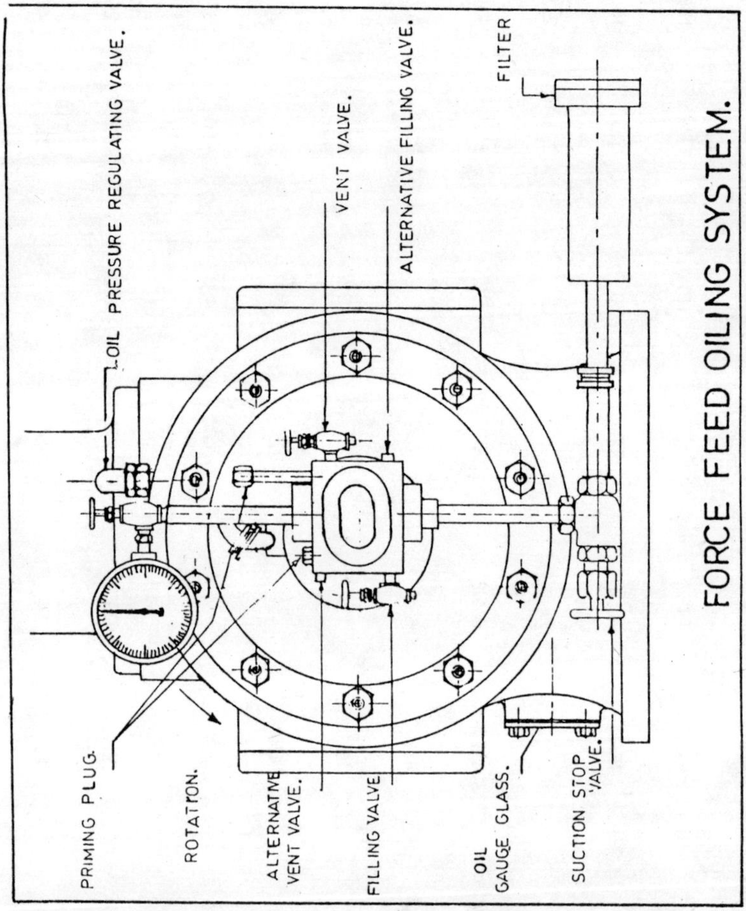

FORCE FEED OILING SYSTEM.

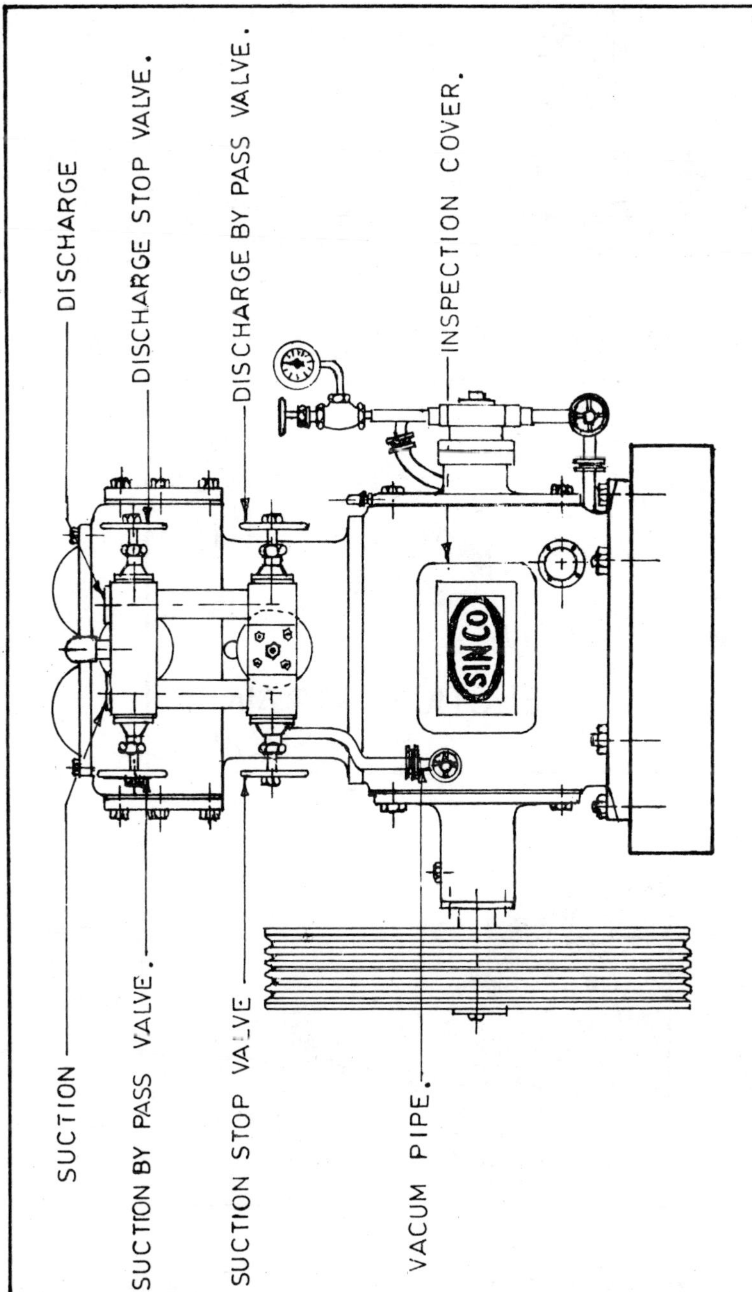

LOCATION OF COMP. OPERATING VALVE.

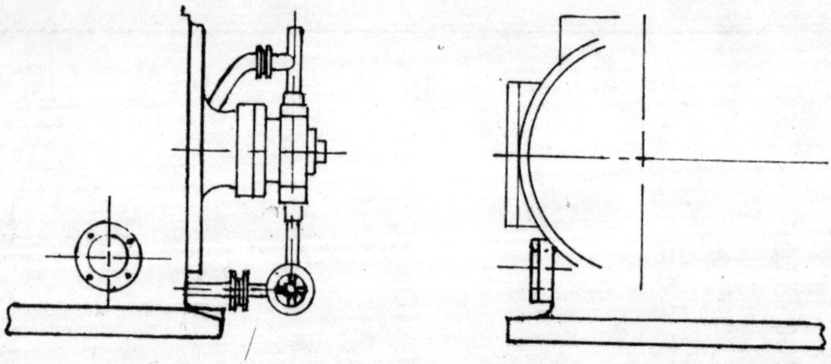

ARRANGEMENT OF OIL GAUGE GLASS.

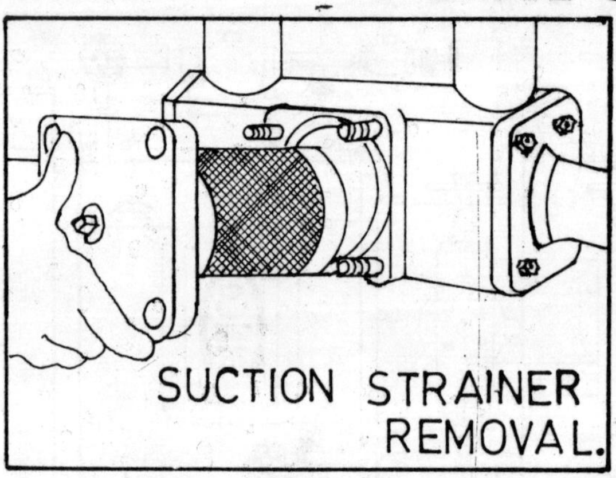

SUCTION STRAINER REMOVAL.

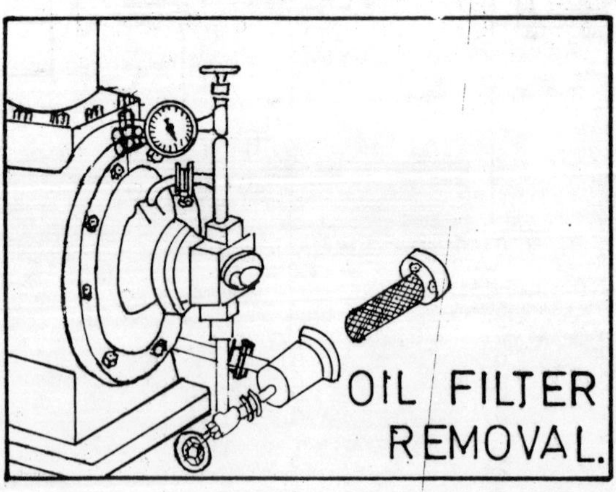

OIL FILTER REMOVAL.

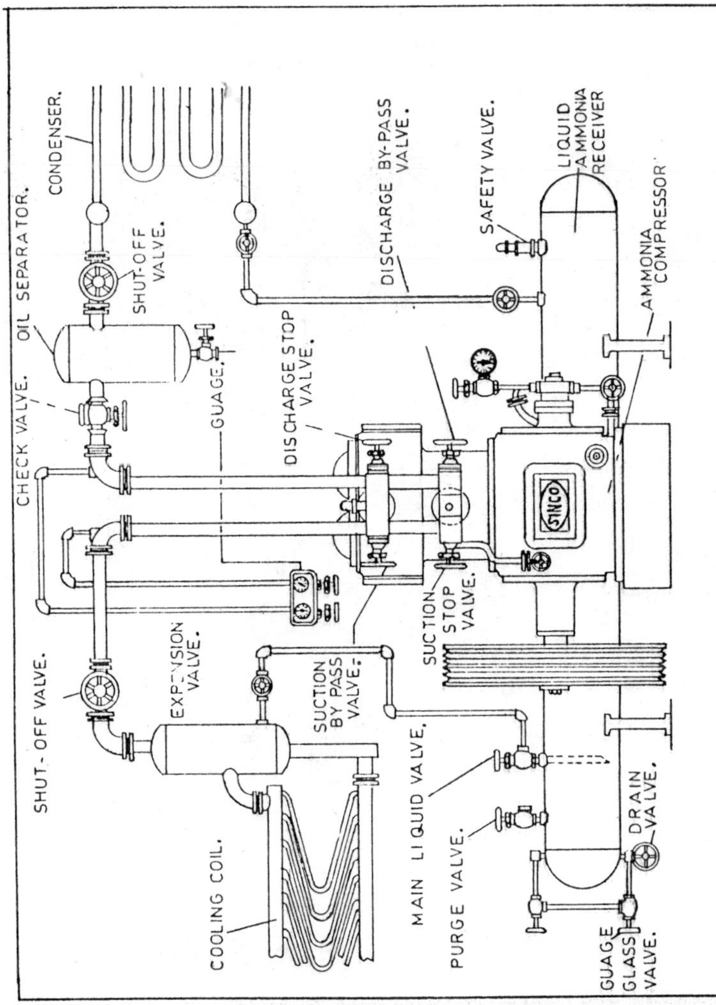

REFRIGERATION SYSTEM WITH SINCO COMPRESSOR

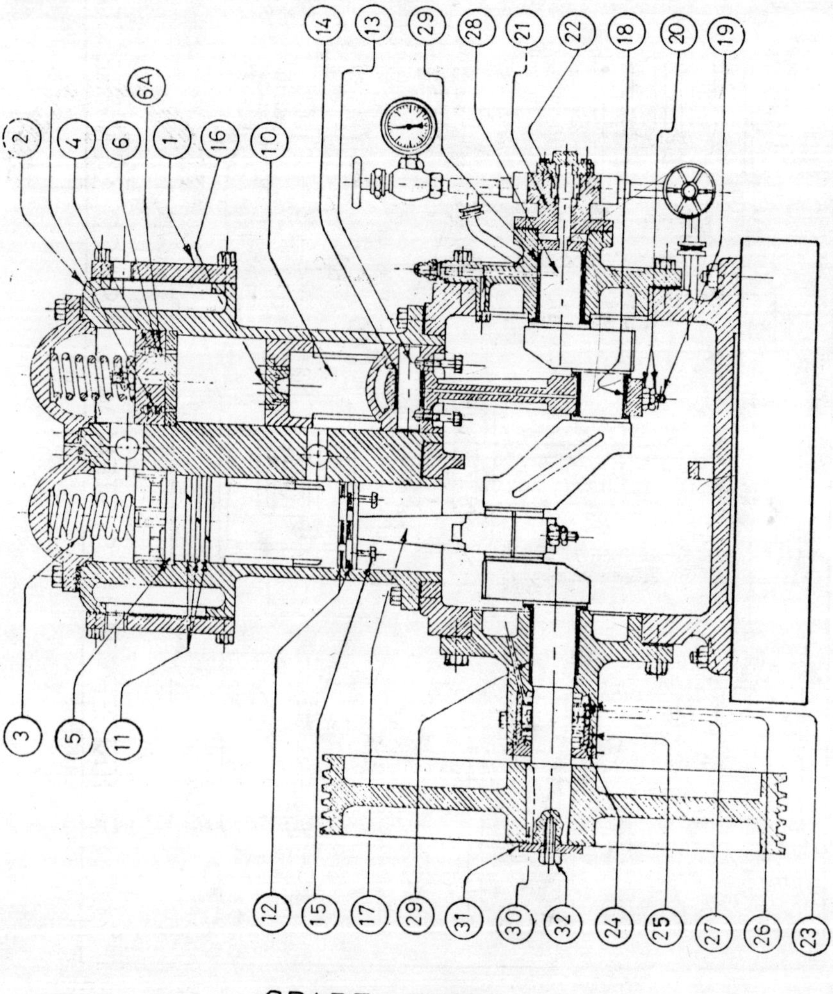
2
4
6
6A
1
16
10
14
13
29
28
21
22
18
20
19
3
5
11
12
15
17
29
31
30
32
24
25
27
26
23

SPARE PARTS.

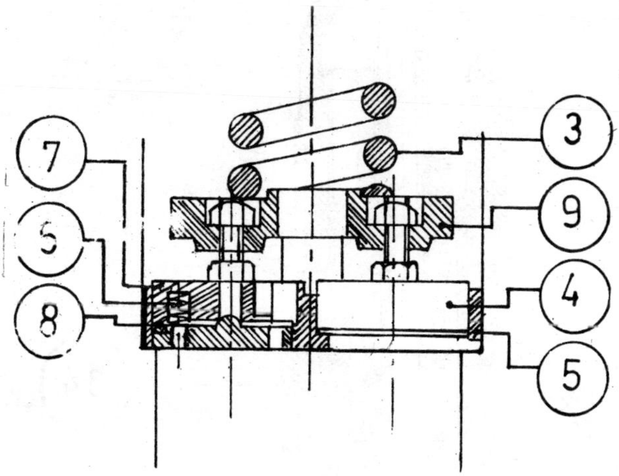

SPARE PARTS

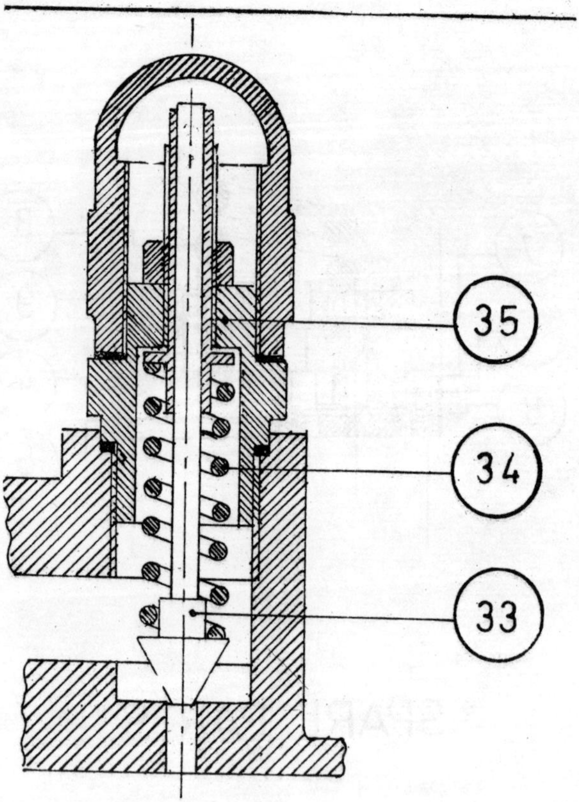
35
34
33

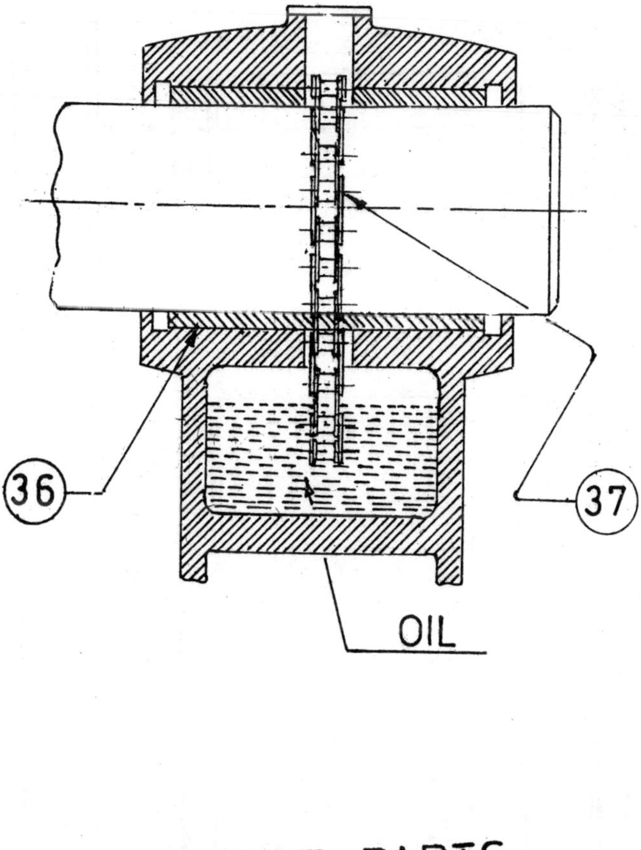

SPARE PARTS

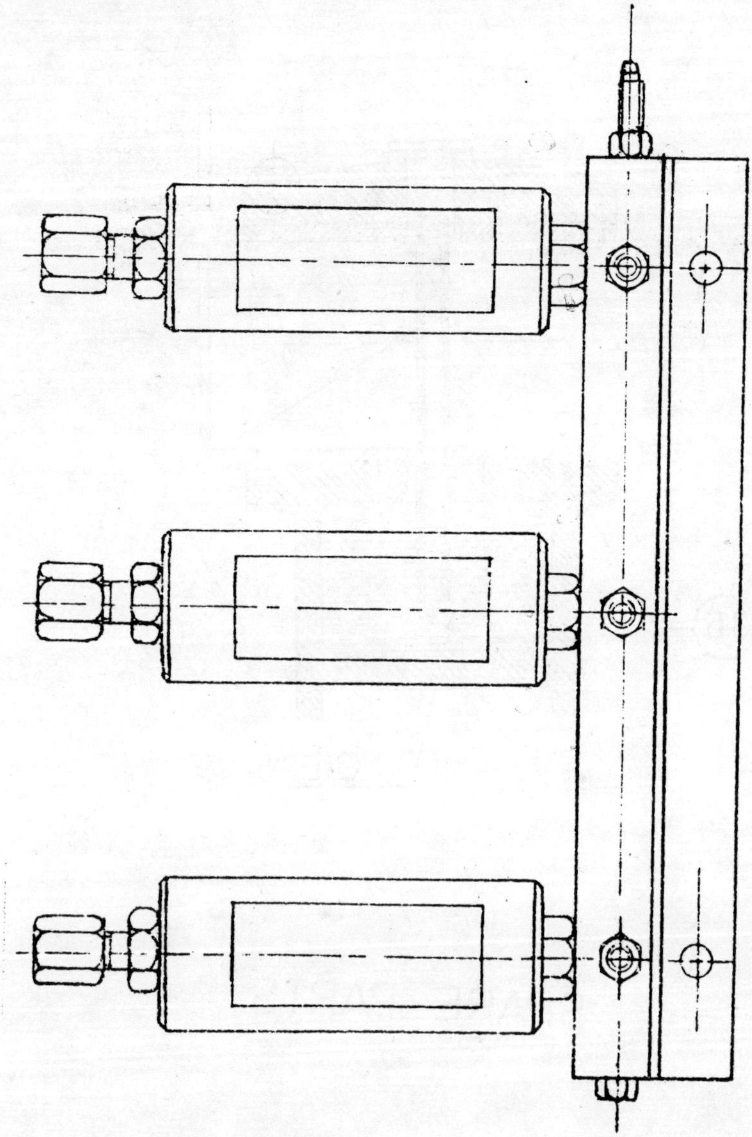

OIL LUBRICATION ARRANGEMENT.

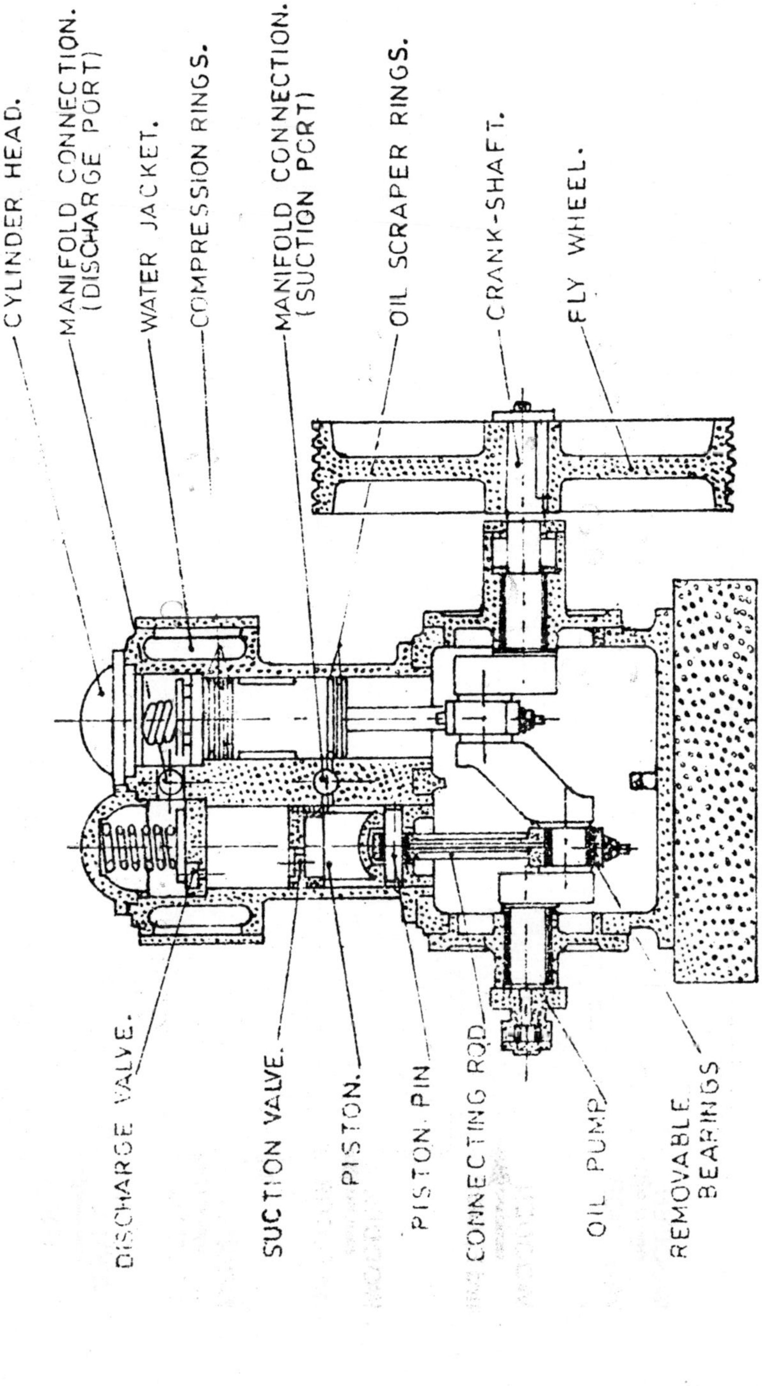
CYLINDER HEAD.
MANIFOLD CONNECTION. (DISCHARGE PORT)
WATER JACKET.
COMPRESSION RINGS.
MANIFOLD CONNECTION. (SUCTION PORT)
OIL SCRAPER RINGS.
CRANK-SHAFT.
FLY WHEEL.
DISCHARGE VALVE.
SUCTION VALVE.
PISTON.
PISTON PIN
CONNECTING ROD
OIL PUMP
REMOVABLE BEARINGS

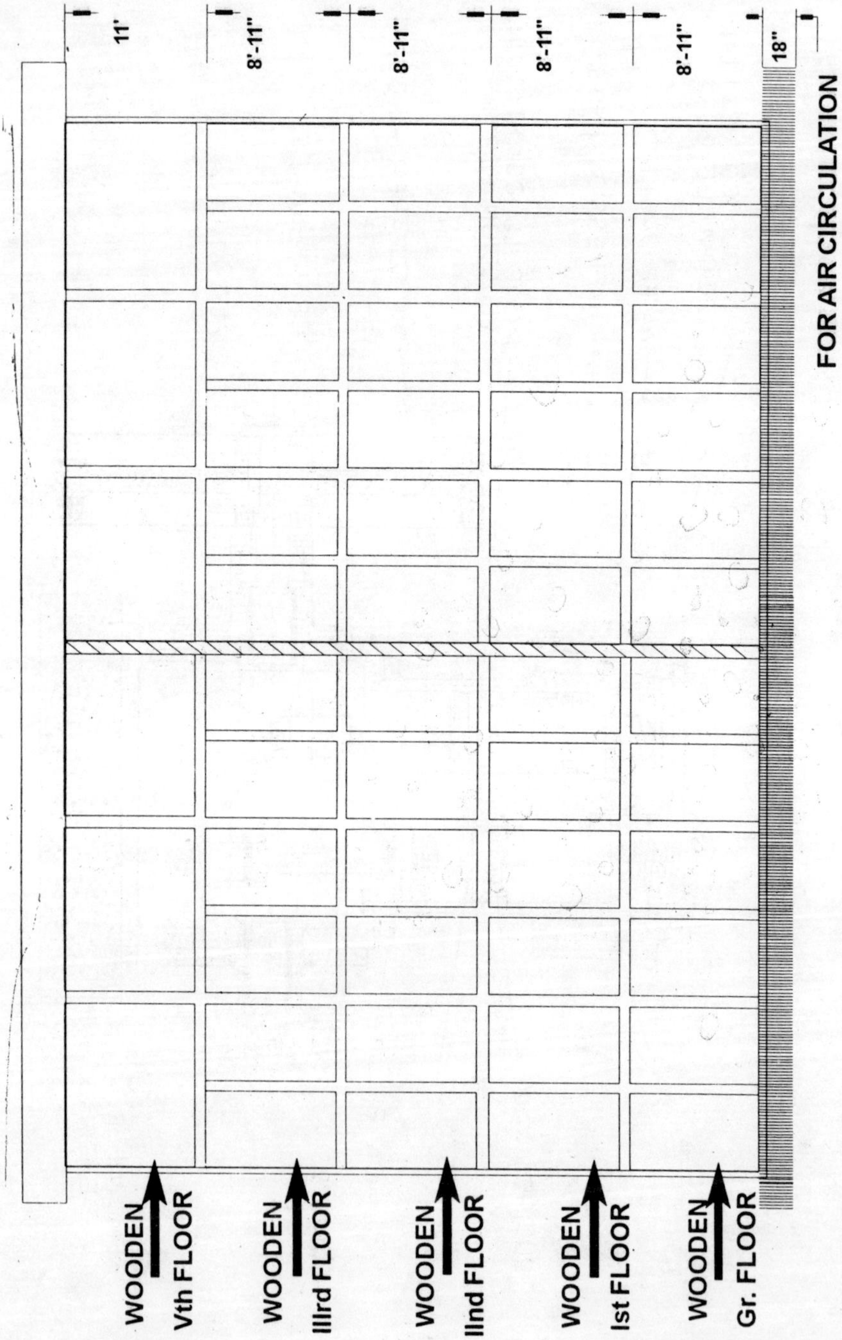
11'
8'-11"
8'-11"
8'-11"
8'-11"
18"
FOR AIR CIRCULATION
WOODEN
Vth FLOOR
WOODEN
IIIrd FLOOR
WOODEN
IInd FLOOR
WOODEN
Ist FLOOR
WOODEN
Gr. FLOOR

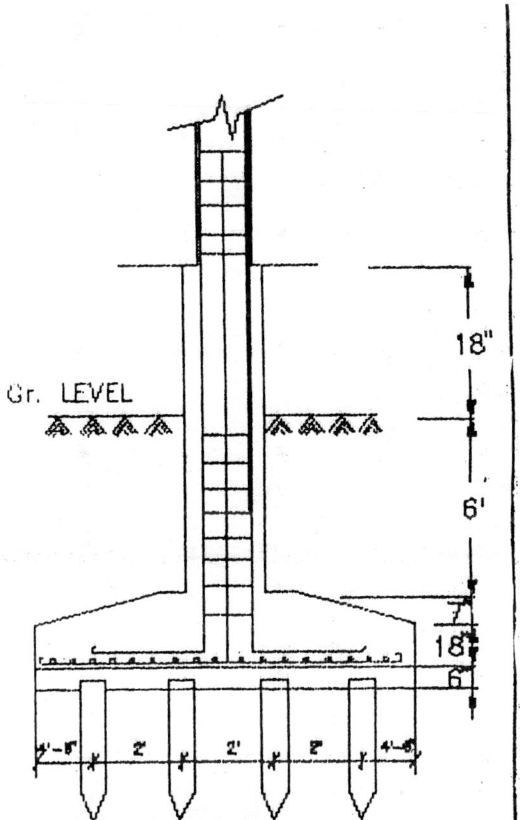

COLUMN

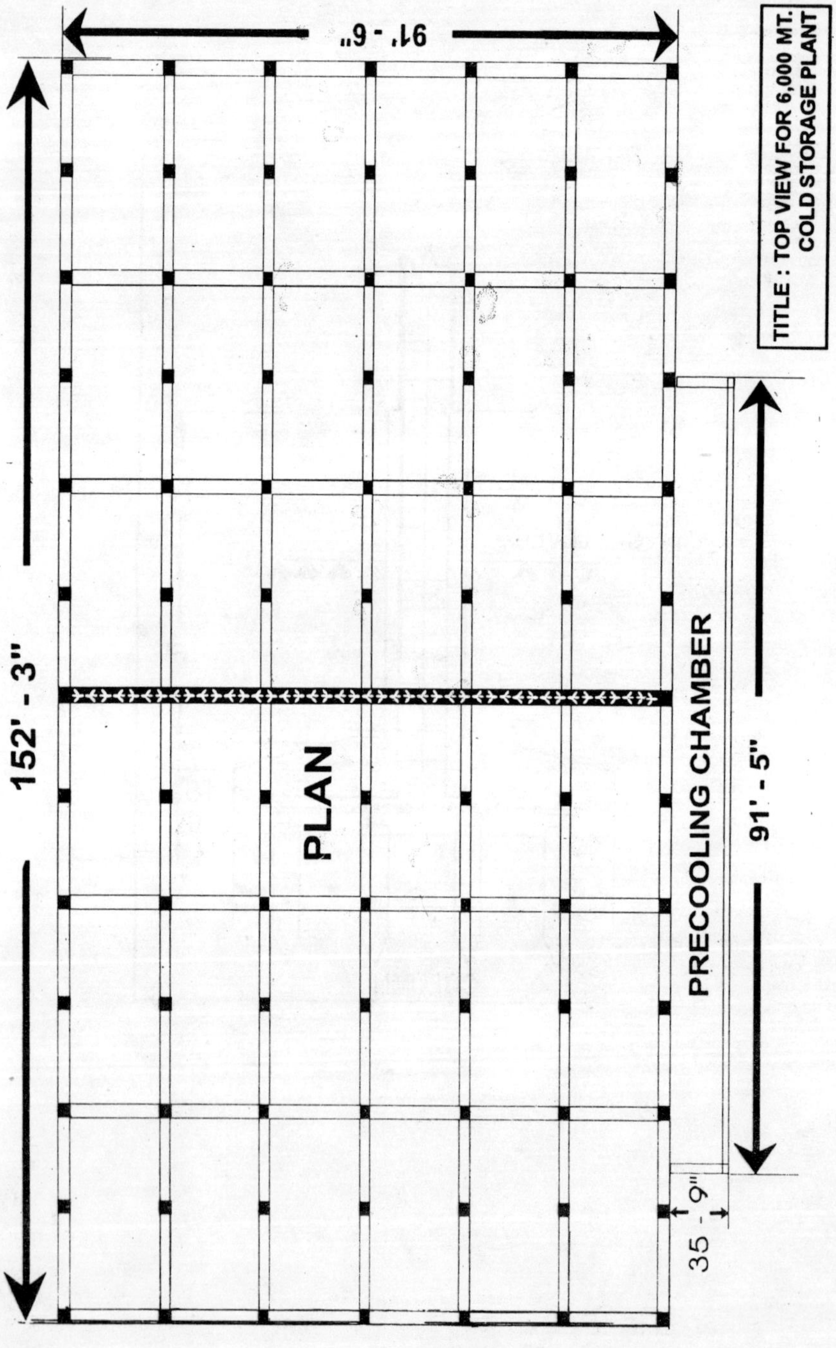

TITLE : TOP VIEW FOR 6,000 MT. COLD STORAGE PLANT

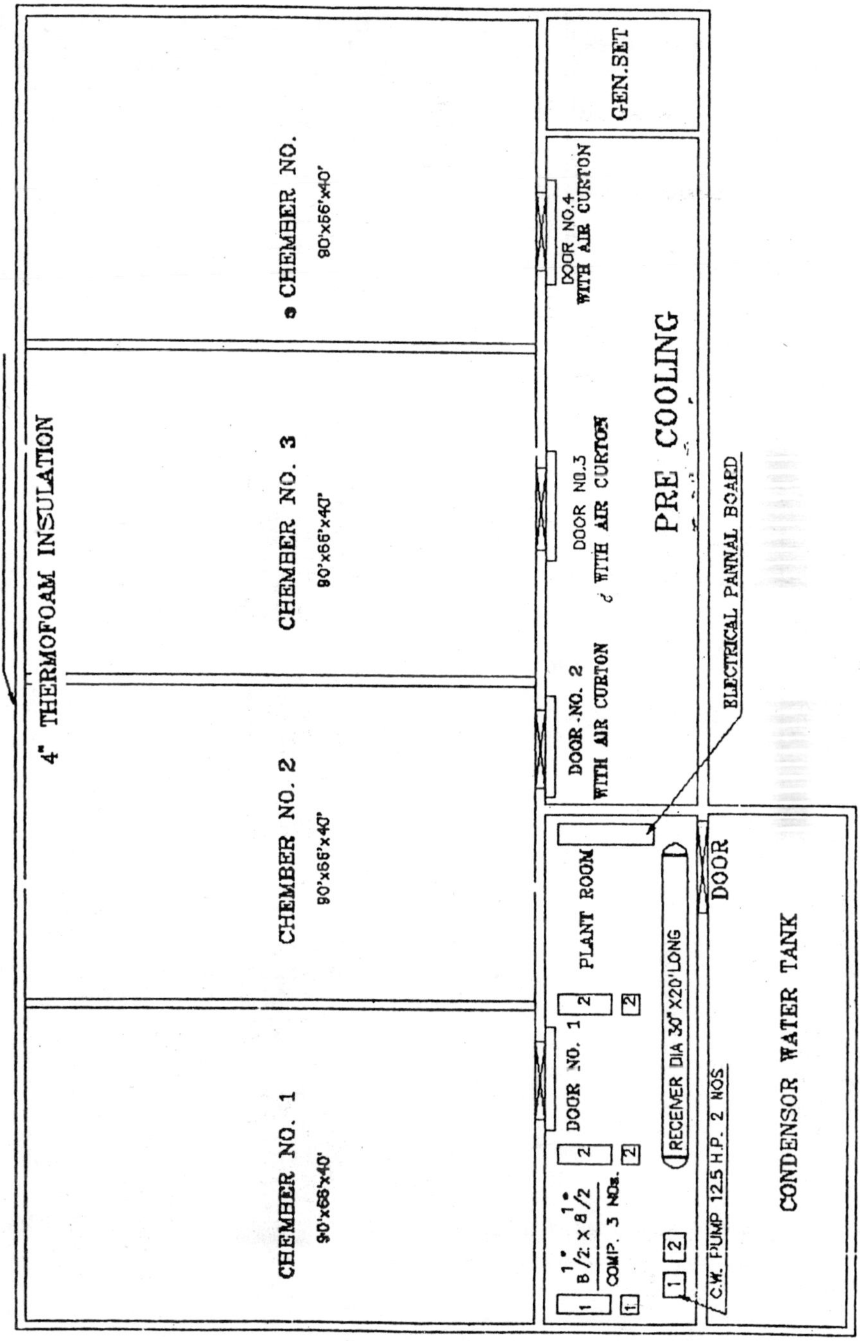
4" THERMOFOAM INSULATION
CHEMBER NO. 1
90'x68'x40'
CHEMBER NO. 2
90'x66'x40'
CHEMBER NO. 3
90'x66'x40'
CHEMBER NO.
90'x56'x40'
GEN.SET
DOOR NO.4
WITH AIR CURTON
DOOR NO.3
WITH AIR CURTON
DOOR NO. 2
WITH AIR CURTON
DOOR NO. 1
PRE COOLING
ELECTRICAL PANNAL BOARD
PLANT ROOM
COMP. 3 NOs.
RECEIVER DIA 30"X20'LONG
C.W. PUMP 12.5 H.P. 2 NOS
DOOR
CONDENSOR WATER TANK

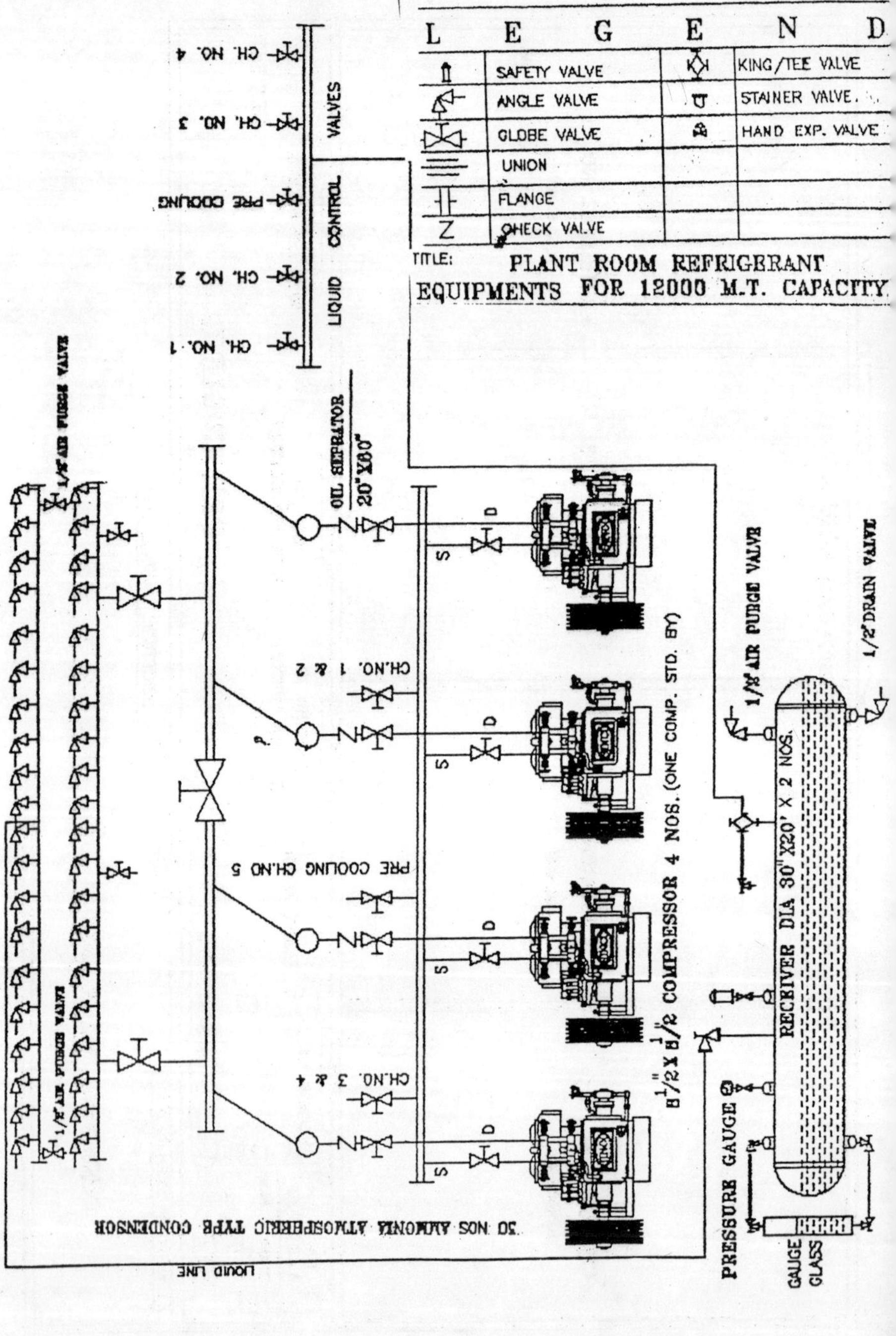
LEGEND
SAFETY VALVE
ANGLE VALVE
GLOBE VALVE
UNION
FLANGE
CHECK VALVE
KING/TEE VALVE
STAINER VALVE.
HAND EXP. VALVE
TITLE: PLANT ROOM REFRIGERANT EQUIPMENTS FOR 12000 M.T. CAPACITY
LIQUID CONTROL VALVES
CH. NO. 1
CH. NO. 2
PRE COOLING
CH. NO. 3
CH. NO. 4
OIL SEPRATOR 20"X80"
CH.NO. 1 & 2
PRE COOLING CH.NO 5
CH.NO. 3 & 4
1/2" AIR PURGE VALVE
30 NOS AMMONIA ATMOSPHERIC TYPE CONDENSOR
LIQUID LINE
8 1/2 X 8 1/2 COMPRESSOR 4 NOS. (ONE COMP. STD. BY)
1/2" AIR PURGE VALVE
1/2" DRAIN VALVE
RECEIVER DIA 30"X20' X 2 NOS.
PRESSURE GAUGE
GAUGE GLASS

11

REFRIGERATED COLD STORAGE DESIGN

Refrigerated Cold Storage is any building or Section which control storage condition using refrigeration. The basic storage facilities are as under :-

1. Evaporative Temperature that protect the commodities at 0^0C.
2. Prevent spoilage or extend Product life.

The conditions within a closed Refrigerated Chamber must be maintained to preserve the stored commodities. This refers particularly to seasonal, self life and long-term storage. Specific items for consifderation as under :-

1. Uniform Temperatures.
2. Length of Air blow and impingment on stored product.
3. Effect of Relative Humidity.
4. Effect of Air movement.
5. Controlling Ventilation System, if necessary.
6. Product Entering Temperature.
7. Expected Duration of Storage.
8. Required Product outdoor Temperature.
9. Transportation in and out of Storage area.

The *Association of Food and Drug* officials development a guide of establishing standards for all phases of handling frozen foods. The code treats receiving, handling, freezing, storage and transporting Frozen Foods and calls for sanitary measures, as well as temperature required for any frozen foods -20^{0}C. The standards must be recognised in the design and operation of the Refrigerated Cold Storage. *Regulation of the Occupational Safety and Health Act* (OSHA), *Envirorenmental Protection Agency* (EPA), U.S. *Department of Agriculture* and other standards must also be incorporated in cold storage operation and procedures. The Private Cold Storage of their own Products or as a Public Facility whereby storage services are offerred to many concerns, or for both. Important location for Cold Storage, Public private are :-

1. Point of Processing.
2. Intermediate points for general commodities.
3. Final Distribution Point.

The five category for the classification of Refrigerated Storage for preservation of food qualities are :-

1. Controlled Atmosphere for long term storage of Fruits and Vegetables.
2. High Temperature Freezer at -2^0 to -3^{0}C.
3. Low Temperature Storage at -20^0 to -40^{0}C with a surplus of refrigeration of Freezing product received like Ice Cream etc. at -20^{0}C.
4. Evaporative Temperatures of 0^{0}C and above.
5. Low Temperature Storage generally for Frozen Foods usually maintain -18^0 to -30^{0}C.

INITIAL BUILDING CONSIDERATIONS :

Generally Public/Private cold storage adjacent their product according building and their operations of commodities.

1. Convenient Location for Procedure shippers and distributors, considering the present tendency.
2. Good transportation facilities either the Road or Rail which is profitable.
3. Location with reasonable land cost.
4. Adequate power and water supply.
5. Provision of Waste and Sanitary Water disposal.
6. Location that avoid residential areas.

7. Taxes and Insurance to be investigated.
8. Equipments Security.
9. Favourable under soil, bearing conditions and good Surface drainage.

Refrigeration plants are generally located away from the congested areas or outside from the city limits for the better plant layout possibilities, a better Road network, better or lower price labour supply and other economic of operation.

SIZE DETERMINATION :

Cold Storage Buildings are generally determined by the following factors :-

1. Is the receipt of shipment of goods to be primarily by Rail or Truck? Shipment Practice will be affected the platforms areas and internal traffic pattern.
2. What RH percentage for Freezer storage? Product requiring specially controlled conditions such as fresh fruits and vegetables may justifying or demand several individual rooms. e.g. Sea foods, Butter and Nuts also require special treatment.
3. What RH percentage is anticipated for long term storage?
4. Will the Product be primarily in small or large lots? The drive through racks system or a combination of pallet racks and a mezzanine have proved effective in achieving efficient operation.

BUILDIGN DESIGN :

Mostly Cold Storages are single storied structures. Small columns on wide centres permit pallatized storage with minimum lost space. These type of buildings provides additional highway truck and unloading space. The single storied design has a following characteristics that must be considered.

Cold Storage layout incorporating facilities that comply with current practice.

1. Plant Room.
2. Refrigerated Shipping Docks with seal-Cushion closures on the doors.
3. Automatic Doors.

5. Low Temperature Storage at -20^{0}C or lower.
6. Pallet Racks system to be facilitate the handling of small lots and to comply with regulation of first in first out which is required for some products.
7. A blast Freezer or separate Freezer room for isolation of products being frozen.
8. Space for brokerage offices and for distributors.
9. Space for empty pallet storage and repair.
10. Space for Shop and battery charging.
11. Automatic Sprinklers in accordance with NFPA regulation.

Other Areas that must be included in the complete operatable facility under a single roof.

1. Electrical areas.
2. Shipping Office.
3. Administration Office.
4. Personal Welfare facilities.

A modification single storey design is sometimes used to reduce horizontal distance and land cost. An alternative is to be located non-productive service, on a second floor level, usually over the truck platform work area to permit full use of the ground floor for production work and storage. However, potential vibration of the second floor from equipment must be considered. Such type of buildings gave a maximum capacity per unit of investment, Refrigeration, and labour. Mechanisation must be considered as well. Such designs that give minimum over all cost restricts office facilities and utility areas to the minimum.

SPECIALISED STORAGE DESIGN :

Cold Storage requirement decades many design on the many commodities. Automated materials handling with the cold storage, particularly, high stack pilings, may be an integral part of the structure system or required special structural treatment. Controlled Atmosphere and minimum Air Circulation require special building design and mechanical equipment to required conditions. In general, Cold storage may be classified as follows :

1. Public Refrigeration Cold Storage design to handle all commodi

ties with several chamber to control temperature from 0^0 to 15^0C with their humidity controls.

2. Public Cold Storage serving several production manufacturers, storing and inventorying products in lots and assembling out shipments for commercial carrier pickup and delivery or for delivery service offerred by the Public Cold Storages.

3. Specialized mechanized Cold Storage with stacker cranes, racks infeed and outfeed conveyors, and special conveyor vestibules. In the design of such a facility, which may be 18 to 24 M high, the cooling units must be mounted in the highest internal area to pick up moisture infiltration. They must also be mounted to prevent condensation from dripping on the stored product and mechanical equipment below.

CONTROLLED ATMOSPHERE STORAGE ROOMS :

Controlled Atmosphere storage rooms may be required for specialized storages, particularly those handling apples. In addition to refrigeration apparatus to control temperature, these storages also include special gastight seals to facilitate the maintenance of an atmosphere that is lower in oxygen and higher in nitrogen and carbon dioxide than normal atmosphere. These storage rooms require apparatus to control the CO_2 concentration and, in many cases, use nitrogen-generating or oxygen-consuming devices.

The desired atmosphere must be experimentally determined for the commodity as produced in the specific area that the storage is to serve.

Commercial application of Controlled Atmosphere storage has been limited to fresh fruits and vegetables that respire in storage, consuming Oxygen and producing Carbon Dioxide.

JACKETED STORAGES :

Mechanically cooled walls, floors and ceilings may be economical for long-term storage duty, such as bin storage, Controlled Atmosphere storage, and for products that deteriorate with active air movement. Embedded pipe coils or air spaces through which refrigerated air is recirculated can provide the cold surface. With this method, leakage is absorbed in the jacket and prevented from entering the refrigerated space.

The following must be considered in the initial design of the storage :

1. Initial cool-down of the product, which can impose short-term peak loads.
2. Service loads when loading product in and out.
3. Odor contamination from products that are not compatible.
4. Product heat of respiration in cooler spaces.

Supplementary refrigeration or conditioning units in the refrigerated spare, which would be operated only as required, can usually alleviate these problems.

CONSTRUCTION METHODS :

Cold Storages, more than most construction, require correct design, quality materials, good workmanship, and close supervision. Design should ensure that proper installation can be accomplished under various adverse job-site conditions. Materials must be compatible with each other. Installation must be made by careful workers directed by an experienced, well-trained superintendent. Close co-operation between the general, roofing, insulation, and other contractors increases the possibility of a successful installation.

FLOOR CONSTRUCTION :

Refrigerated facilities held above freezing need no special under-floor treatment. A below-the-floor vapour barrier is needed in facilities held below freezing, however. In these facilities, the subsoil eventually freezes, and any moisture in this soil will also freeze and cause floor frost heaving. In moderate climates, underfloor tubes vented to ambient air are sufficient to prevent heaving. Artificial heating either by air circulated through underfloor ducts or glycol circulated through plastic pipe is the preferred method to prevent frost heaving. Electric heating cables installed under the floor can also be used to prevent frost formation. The choice of heating method depends on energy cost, reliability, and maintenance requirements.

Future facility expansion must be considered when underfloor heating systems are being designed. Therefore, a system including artificial heating methods that do not require building exterior access is preferred.

ELECTRICAL WIRING :

Electrical wiring should be brought into a refrigerated room through as few locations as possible (preferably one), piercing the wall vapour barrier and insulation only once. Plastic-coated cable is recommended for this service where codes permit. If codes require conduit, the last fitting on the warm side of the run should be of the explosion-proof type, sealed to prevent water vapor from entering the cold conduit. The light fixtures in the room should not be vapour-sealed but should allow free passage of moisture. Care should be taken to maintain the vapour seal between the outside of the electrical service and the cold room vapour barrier.

TRACKING :

Cold Room meat tracking, wherever possible, should be erected and supported within the insulated structure, entirely independent of the building itself. This places all the mass of the tracking on the cold room floor, eliminates flexure of the roof structure or overhead members, and simplifies maintenance.

COLD STORAGE DOORS :

Doors should be strong and, at the same time, light enough for easy opening and closing. Hardware should be of good quality, so that it can be set to compress the gasket uniformly against the casing. All doors to rooms operating below freezing should be equipped with heaters.

In-fitting doors are not recommended for rooms operating below freezing, unless they are provided with heaters, and they should not be used at temperatures below -18^{0}C with or without heaters.

REFRIGERATION SYSTEM SELECTION :

The selection of the refrigeration system for a refrigerated Cold Storage must be established in the early stages of planning. If it is a single-purpose, low-temperature storage building, almost any type of system can be applied. However, if commodities to be stored require different temperatures and humidities, a system must be selected that may require the use of several isolated rooms and conditions.

Using factory-built package unitary equipment may have merit for the smallest structures and also for a multiroom facility that requires a variety of storage conditions. Conversely, the central compressor room has been the accepted standard for larger installations, especially where energy conservation is important.

Direct refrigeration, either a flooded or pumped recalculation system serving can coil units, is a dependable choice for a central compressor room. Screw compressors, programmable logic controllers, and microprocessor controls complement the central engine room refrigeration equipment.

LOAD DETERMINATION :

The refrigeration loads of warehouses of the same capacity vary widely. Many factors, including building design, indoor and out-door temperatures, and most important, the type and flow of goods expected, plus the daily freezing capacity, contribute to the load. Therefore, no simple design rules apply. Experience from comparable buildings and operations is valuable, but an analysis of any projected operation should be designed for maximum daily requirements, which will be well above any monthly average.

The factors to be considered include :

1. Heat transmission through insulated
2. Heat and vapour infiltration load from warm air passing into refrigerated space.
3. Heat from pumps or fans circulating refrigerated brine or air, power equipment, personnel working in refrigerated space, product moving equipment, and lights.
4. Heat removed from goods in reducing them from receiving to storage temperatures.
5. Heat produced by goods in storage.
6. Heat to be removed infreezing goods received unfrozen.
7. Other loads, such as office air conditioning, car precooling, or special operations inside the building.
8. Refrigerated shipping docks.
9. Heat released from automatic defrost units from the fan motors and defrosting, which increases overall refrigerant system requirements.
10. Blast freezing or process freezing extra.

Areas subject to high humidity, warm temperatures, or manual product handling may dramatically effect the design, particularly the refrigerating system.

AIR COOLING UNITS AND COILS :

Fan and Coil Units :

These units may have either direct expansion, flooded, or recirculating liquid evaporatorsv with either primary or finned coil surfaces or a brine spray coolant. Storage temperature, packaging method, type of product, etc., must be considered when selecting a unit. The coil surface area, temperature difference between the refrigerant coil and return air, and airflow volume depend on the particular application. If air units must be located above the entrances to a refrigerated space, they will draw in warm, moist air from the adjacent space, which will increase the frequency of defrosting.

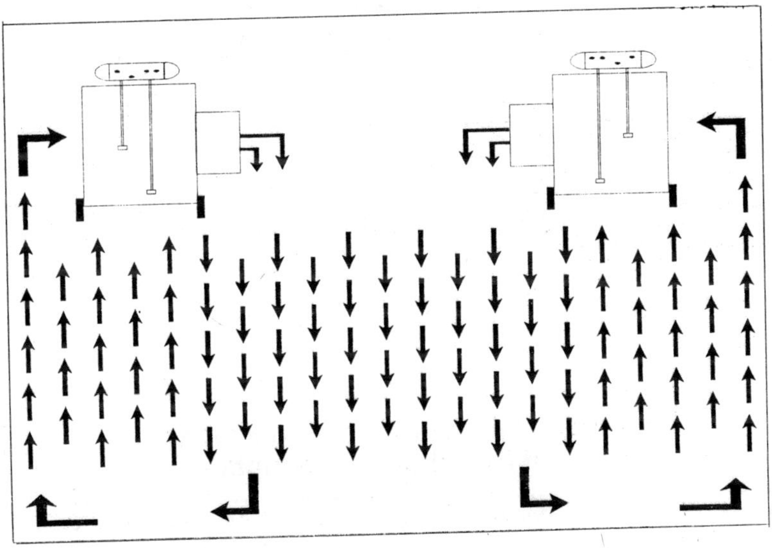

FIN TYPE AIR COOLING UNITS

Fin type air cooling units are Ceiling Mounted and are available in following models :

Model	Capacity	Motor H.P.
S.F.U. 35	6000 Maunds.	2X0.75 H.P. = 1.5 H.P.

AUTOMATIC DEFROSTING :

Properly engineered and installed system can be automatically defrosted successfully with hot gas, water, electric, or continuously sprayed brine. The sprayed brine system has the advantage of producing the full refrigeration capacity at all times; however, it does not require a supply and return pipe system with a means of boiling off the absorbed condensed moisture.

Refrigeration Design Load Factors for Typical 10,000-m^2 Single Floor Freezer :

	Long-Term Storage		Short-Term Storage		Distribution Operation	
	Cooling Capacity		Cooling Capacity		Cooling Capacity	
Items of Refrigeration Load	**KW**	**Percent**	**KW**	**Percent**	**KW**	**Percent**
Transmission Losses	343	49	343	43	343	36
Infiltration	35	5	70	9	140	15
Internal Operation Loads	175	25	196	24	217	22
Cooling of Goods received	25	3	53	6	105	11
Other factors	122	18	143	18	158	16
Total design capacity	700	100	805	100	963	100

Storage Requirements and Properties of Perishable Products

Commodity	**Storage Temperature °C**	**Relative Humidity %**	**Approximate Storage Life**	**Water Contend %**
Potatoes Early	3 to 4 °C	85 to 95 %	4 to 5 Months	81%
Late Crop	3 to 4°C	85 to 95 %	5 to 8 Months	78%
Onions Green	0°C	85 to 95 %	3 to 4 Weeks	89%
Dry Onions	10°C	50 to 60%	1 to 8 Months	86%

DESIRABLE TRANSIT FOR VARIOUS VEGETABLES

VEGETABLE	Desirable Transit Temp.°C	Suggested Thermostat Setting°C	Highest Freezing Point Temp.°C
Onions Dry.	0 to 4°C	1.7°C	-0.8°C
Onions Green.	0°C	1°C	-0.9°C
Potatoes Early Crop.	10 to 16°C	10°C	-0.6°C
Late Crop.	4 to 10°C	4.4°C	-0.6°C
For Chipping Early Crop.	18 to 21°C	18 to 21°C	-0.6°C
Late Crop.	10 to 16°C	10 to 16°C	-0.6°C

ONIONS (10°C AND 50 TO 60 RH%) :

A Comparatively low RH is essential in the successful storage of dry onions. However, humidities as high as 60% and forced-air circulation have given satisfactory results. At higher humidities, at which most other vegetables keep best, onions are disposed to root growth and decay; at too high a temperature, sprouting is encouraged. Storage at 10°C with 60% RH is recommended to keep them dormant.

Onions should be adequately cured either in the field, in open sheds, or by artificial means before or in storage. The most common method of curing in northern areas is by forced ventilation in storage. Onions are considered cured when the necks are tight and the outer scales are dried until they rustle. If not cured, onions are likely to decay in storage.

Onions are stored in 20 Kg. bags, in crates, in pallet boxes that hold 500 Kg. of loose onions, or in bulk bins. Bags of onions are frequently stored on pallets. Bagged onions should be stacked to allow proper air circulation.

In the northern onion-growing states, onions of the globe type are generally held in common storage because average winter temperatures are sufficiently low. They should not be held after early March unless they have been treated with maleic hydrazide in the field to reduce sprout growth.

Refrigerated storage is often used to hold onions for marketing late in the spring. Onions to be held in Cold Storage should be placed there immediately after curing. A temperature of 10°C will keep onions dormant and reasonably free from decay, provided the onions are sound and well cured when stored. Sprout growth indicates too high a storage temperature, poorly cured bulbs, or immature bulbs. Root growth indicates the relative humidity is too high. Hence, Globe onions can be held for 6 to 8 months.

Ammonia Gas Discolouration :

Exposure of onions to 1% ammonia in air for 24h causes the surface of yellow onions to turn brown, red onions to turn deep metallic black, and white onions to turn greenish yellow. Control : Ventilate storage rooms as soon as possible after exposure.

POTATOES (TEMPERATURE, SHOWN BELOW; 80 TO 90% RH) :

The proper Storage environment for potatoes might be defined as that environment which will promote the most rapid healing of bruises and cuts, reduce rot penetration to a minimum the deleterious quality changes that might occur during storage.

Early crop potatoes are usually not stored except during congested periods. They are more perishable and cannot be expected to keep as well or as long as late-crop tubers. Refrigerated storage at 4°C following a curing period of 4 or 5 days at 21°C is recommended; or they can be stored for about 2 months at 10°C without curing. If early-crop potatoes are to be used for chipping or French frying, storage at 21°C is recommended. Holding these potatoes in cold storage even at moderate temperatures of 10 to 13°C for only a few days causes excessive accumulation of reducing sugars, which results in production of dark-coloured chips.

Late-crop potatoes produced in the northern half of the *United States* are usually stored. The greater part of the crop is held in non-refrigerated commercial and farm storages, but some potatoes are held in refrigerated storages.

Late-crop potatoes should be cured immediately after harvest by being held at 10 to 16°C and high relative humidity for about 10 to 14 days to permit suberization and wound periderm formation (healing of cuts and bruises). If properly cured, they should keep in sound dormant condition at 3 to 4°C with 90% RH for 5 to 8 months. A temperature below this is not desirable, except for seed stock for late planting. For this purpose, 3⁰C is best. At 3⁰C or below, Irish potatoes tend to become sweet, for ordinary table use, potatoes stored at 4⁰C are satisfactory, but they probably will be unsatisfactory for chipping or Frency frying without being desugared or conditioned at about 18 to 21⁰C for 1 to 3 weeks prior to use. However, conditioning may be costly, and good results are often uncertain.

Potatoes will remain dormant at 10⁰C for 2 to 4 months; and since tubers from this temperature are more desirable for both table use and processing than those from 4⁰C, late crop potatoes intended for use within 4 months should be stored at 10⁰C and those for later use at 4⁰C. All potatoes should be stored in the dark to prevent greening.

A storage temperature of 10 to 13⁰C is recommended for most cultivars of potatoes intended for chip manufacture. At these temperatures, they usually remain in satisfactory condition if their reducing-sugar content is low enough when they are initially stored. Storage at 16 to 18⁰C is less desirable because shrinkage, internal and external sprout growth and decay are greater at these temperatures than at 10 to 13⁰C. *Russet Burbank* potatoes for table stock or for chipping are stored at 7⁰C with 95% RH.

Potatoes usually do not sprout until 2 to 3 months after harvest, even at 10 to 16⁰C. However, after 2 to 3 months of storage, sprouting can be expected in potatoes stored at temperatures above 4⁰C and particularly at temperatures around 10⁰C. Although limited sprouting does not affect potatoes for food purposes, badly sprouted stock shrivels and is difficult to handle and market.

12

QUOTATION FOR 50,000 BAGS COLD STORAGE PLANT

Three	Heavy duty, industrial type, double cylinder, vertical, reciprocating Ammonia Compressors. Size 6-1/2"X6-1/2". (One Compressor Stand by.)
Three	Flywheel.
Three	Pulley. (Including Excise Duty.)
Three	Suction & Discharge Stop valve.
Three	Set other items.
16 No.	Fin type ammonia air cooling unit model SFU-35 made of steel tube and M.S. wound fins, spray galvanised. Complete with propeller fan, fan motor and galvanised steel sheet casing with Accumulator.
Eight	Atmospheric type ammonia condensers made of M.S. Pipe size 2"X20'X12 with M.S. angle iron stand. Set of gas header, liquid header, valves and fittings for above condensers. (Including Excise Duty.)
One	Ammonia receiver size 20'X24" made of M.S. plate welded & hydraulically tested. Inlet & outlet valves, safety valve, purge drains, gauge glass, gauge glass valve & stands for receiver.
Three	Ammonia oil separator size 16"X42" made of M.S. plate welded & hydraulically tested with companion flanges and drain connections.

Three Set of ammonia pressure gauges (Set of three)
Erection charges of refrigeration machinery only.

PART B :

One Lot of ammonia, water pipe & pipe fitting for the interconnection of ammonia refrigeration machinery & cooling of compressor water jacket and condenser.

First charge of ammonia gas & oil.

Four Dry & wet thermometer.

Five Cold storage doors.

One Lot of electric motors & starters :-

3-50 H.P. S.P.D.P. slipring A/c induction motor, 1440 RPM, 3 phase, 50 cycles 400, 440 volts, 3-50 H.P. stator/rotor starter for the above motor, 3-5 H.P. monoblock centrifugal pumpset suitable for 400/440 volts, 50 cycles, A/c supply with D.O.L. starter, with switches, starters, amp. meter, rails, V-belt, belt guard and pannel board etc.

One Lot of aluminium electric wires & cables for the wiring of electric motors only.

Wiring charges of electric motors only

Total Cost of Plant & Equipments : Rs. 30,10,955.00

Courtesy : Sunder Singh & Co. Pvt. Ltd.

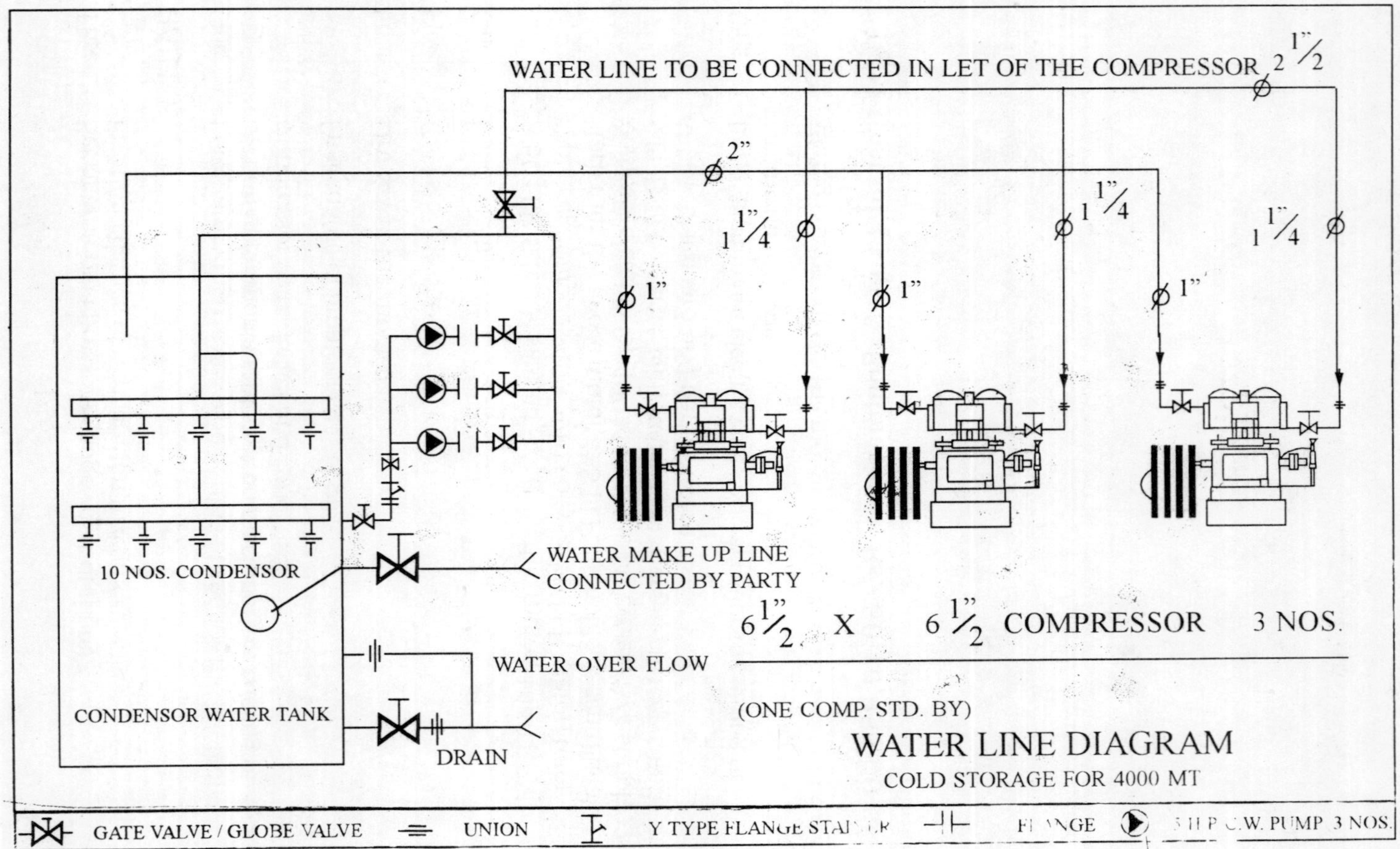

WATER LINE TO BE CONNECTED IN LET OF THE COMPRESSOR
Ø 2 1"/2
Ø 2"
1 1"/4 Ø
Ø 1"
Ø 1 1"/4
Ø 1"
1 1"/4 Ø
Ø 1"
10 NOS. CONDENSOR
WATER MAKE UP LINE
CONNECTED BY PARTY
6 1"/2 X 6 1"/2 COMPRESSOR 3 NOS.
WATER OVER FLOW
(ONE COMP. STD. BY)
CONDENSOR WATER TANK
DRAIN
WATER LINE DIAGRAM
COLD STORAGE FOR 4000 MT
GATE VALVE / GLOBE VALVE
UNION
FLANGE
C.W. PUMP 3 NOS.

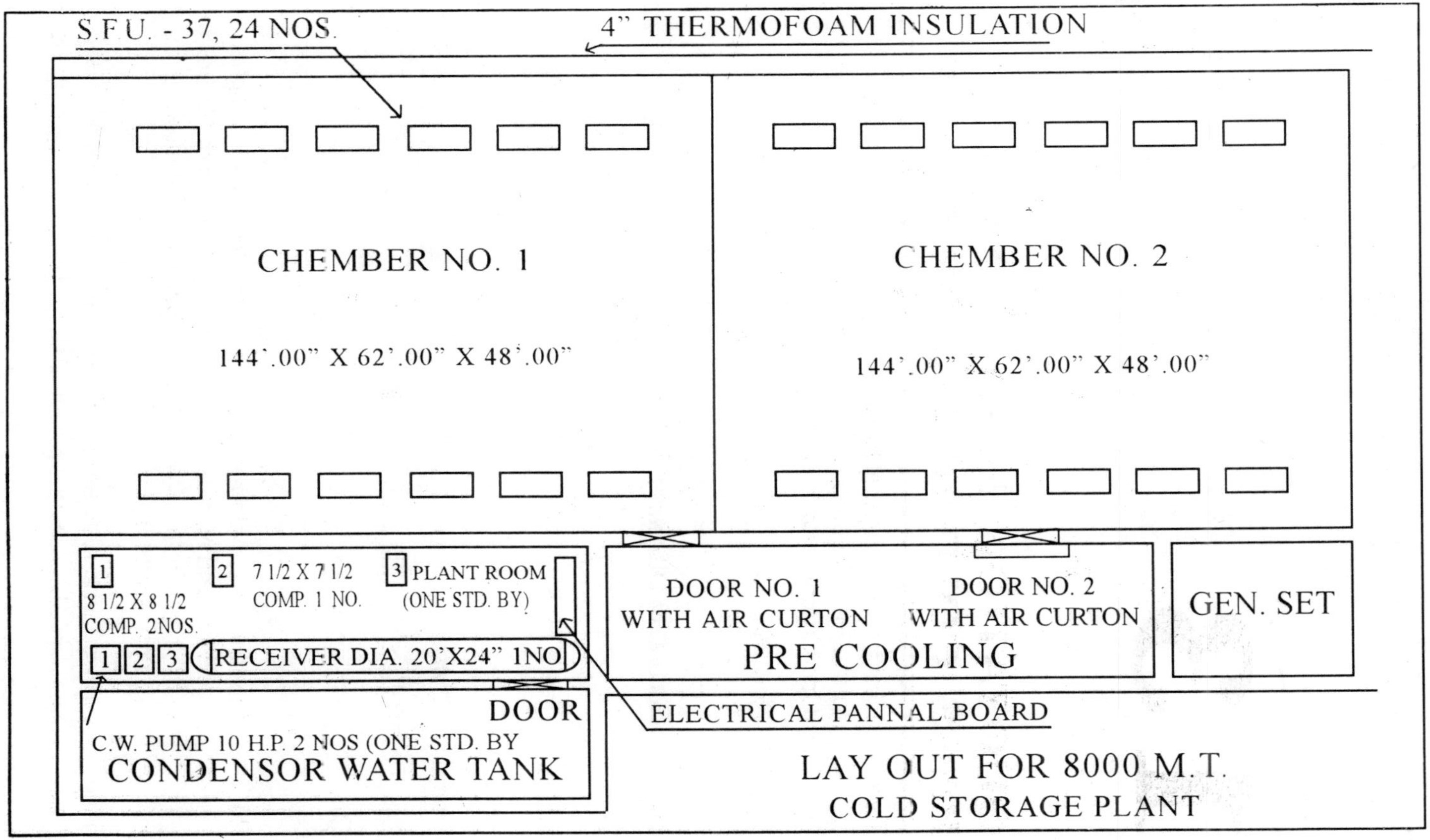

LAY OUT FOR 8000 M.T.
COLD STORAGE PLANT

13

QUOTATION FOR 1,00,000 BAGS COLD STORAGE PLANT

Two	Heavy duty, industrial type, double cylinder, vertical, reciprocating Ammonia Compressors. Size 8-1/2"X8-1/2". (One Compressor Stand by.)
Two	Flywheel.
Two	Pulley. (Including Excise Duty.)
Two	Suction & Discharge Stop valve.
Two	Set other items.
One	Heavy duty, industrial type, double cylinder, vertical, reciprocating Ammonia Compressors. Size 7-1/2"X7-1/2". (One Compressor Stand by.)
One	Flywheel.
One	Pulley. (Including Excise Duty.)
One	Suction & Discharge Stop valve.
One	Set of other items.
24	Fin type ammonia air cooling unit model SFU-37 made of steel tube and M.S. wound fins, spray galvanised. Complete with propeller fan, fan motor and galvanised steel sheet casing with Accumulator.
16	Atmospheric type ammonia condensers made of M.S. Pipe size 2"X20'X12 with M.S. angle iron stand. Set of gas header,

liquid header, valves and fittings for above condensers. (Including Excise Duty.)

One Ammonia receiver size 20'X24" made of M.S. plate welded & hydraulically tested. Inlet & outlet valves, safety valve, purge drains, gauge glass, gauge glass valve & stands for receiver.

Three Ammonia oil separator size 16"X48" made of M.S. plate welded & hydraulically tested with compansion flanges and drain connections.

Three Set of ammonia pressure gauges (Set of three)

Erection charges of refrigeration machinery only.

PART B :

One Lot of ammonia, water pipe & pipe fitting for the interconnection of ammonia refrigeration machinery & cooling of compressor water jacket and condenser.

First charge of ammonia gas & oil.

Four Dry & wet thermometer.

Four Cold storage doors.

One Lot of electric motors & starters :-

2-100 H.P. S.P.D.P. slipring A/c induction motor, 1440 RPM, 3 phase, 50 cycles, 400/440 volts, 2-100 HP stator/rotor starter for the above motor, 1-75 H.P. S.P.D.P. slipring A/c induction motor, 1440 RPM, 2 phase, 50 cycles, 400/440 volts, 1-75 HP stator/rotor starter for the above motor, 2-10 HP monoblock centrifugal pumpset suitable for 400/440 volts, 50 cycles, A/c supply with D.O.L. starter, with switches, starters, amp. meter, rails, V-belt, belt guard and pannel board etc.

Lot of aluminium electric wires & cables for the wiring of electric motors only.

Wiring charges of electric motors only

Total Cost of Plant & Equipments : Rs. 50,13,345.00

Courtesy : Sunder Singh & Co. Pvt. Ltd.

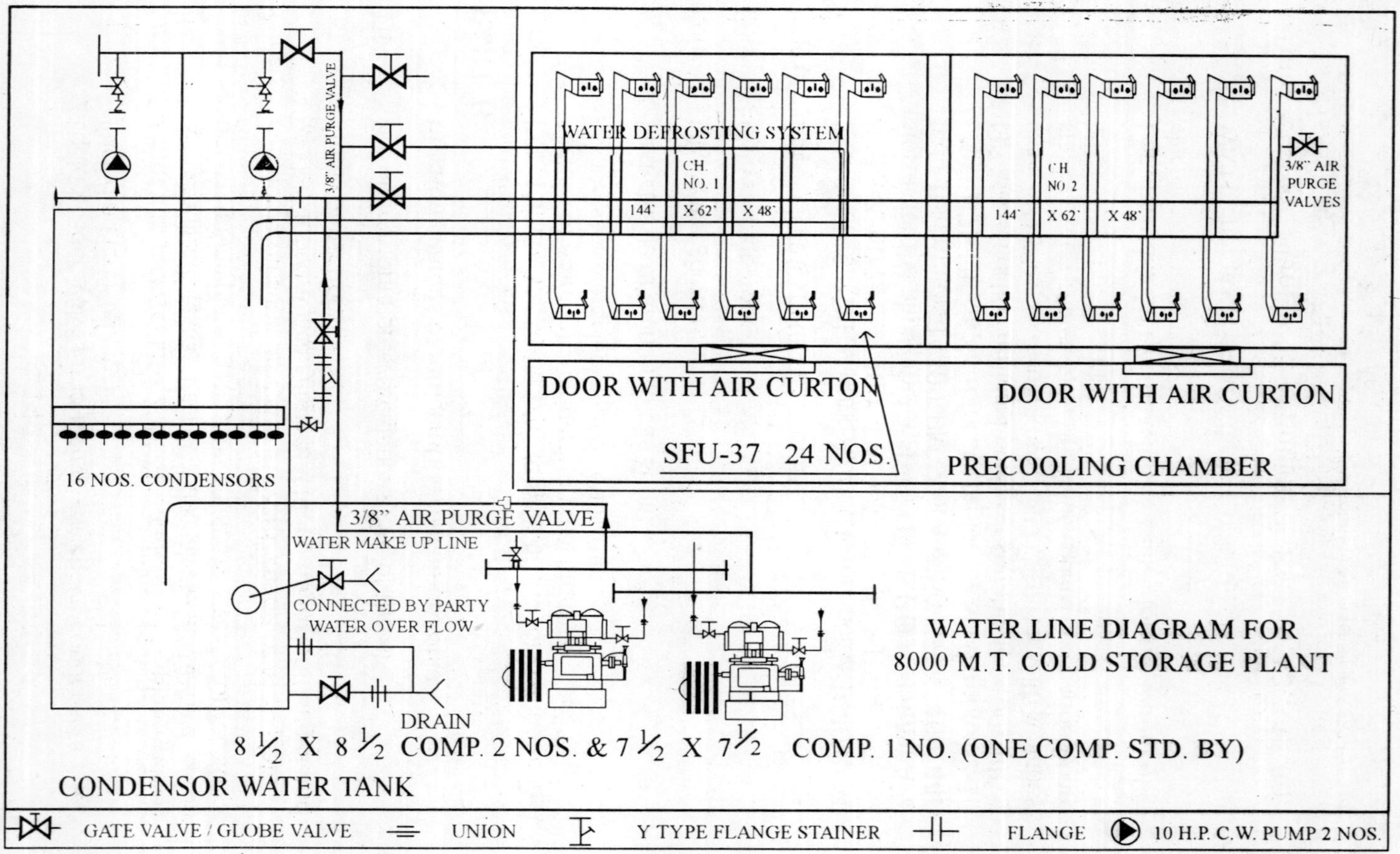

3/8" AIR PURGE VALVE
WATER DEFROSTING SYSTEM
CH. NO. 1
144' X 62' X 48'
CH NO. 2
144' X 62' X 48'
3/8" AIR PURGE VALVES
DOOR WITH AIR CURTON
DOOR WITH AIR CURTON
SFU-37 24 NOS.
PRECOOLING CHAMBER
16 NOS. CONDENSORS
3/8" AIR PURGE VALVE
WATER MAKE UP LINE
CONNECTED BY PARTY
WATER OVER FLOW
DRAIN
WATER LINE DIAGRAM FOR
8000 M.T. COLD STORAGE PLANT
8 1/2 X 8 1/2 COMP. 2 NOS. & 7 1/2 X 7 1/2 COMP. 1 NO. (ONE COMP. STD. BY)
CONDENSOR WATER TANK
GATE VALVE / GLOBE VALVE
UNION
Y TYPE FLANGE STAINER
FLANGE
10 H.P. C.W. PUMP 2 NOS.

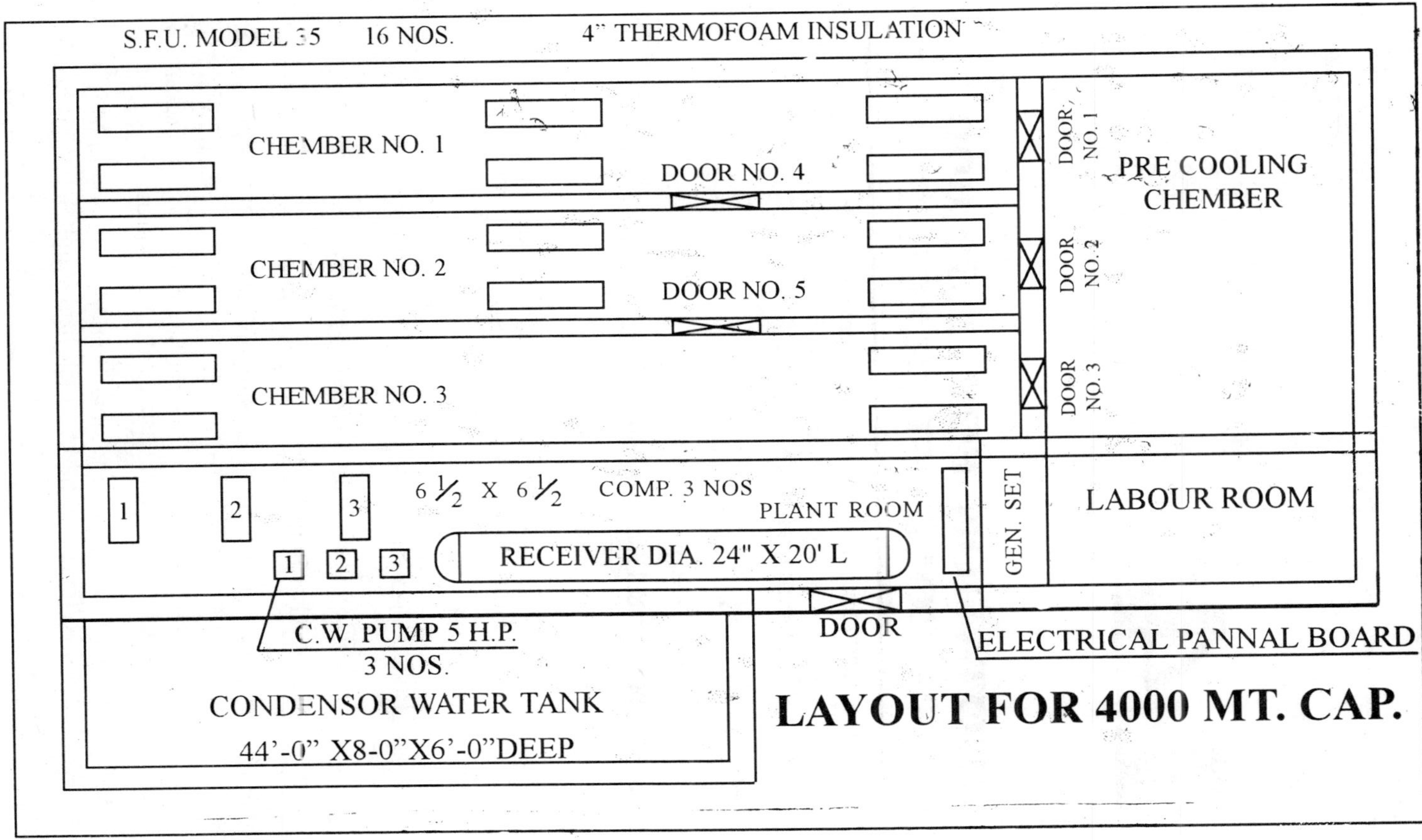

LAYOUT FOR 4000 MT. CAP.

14

QUOTATION FOR 1,50,000 BAGS COLD STORAGE PLANT

Two	Heavy duty, industrial type, double cylinder, vertical, reciprocating Ammonia Compressors. Size 8-1/2"X8-1/2". (One Compressor Stand by.)
Two	Flywheel.
Two	Pulley. (Including Excise Duty.)
Two	Suction & Discharge Stop valve.
Two	Set of other items.
One	Heavy duty, industrial type, double cylinder, vertical, reciprocating Ammonia Compressors. Size 9-1/2"X9-1/2".
One	Flywheel.
One	Pulley. (Including Excise Duty.)
One	Suction & Discharge Stop valve.
One	Set of other items.
38	Fin type ammonia air cooling unit model SFU-37 made of steel tube and M.S. wound fins, spray galvanised including excise duty. Complete with propeller fan, fan motor and galvanised steel sheet casing with Accumulator.
24	Atmospheric type ammonia condensers made of M.S. Pipe size 2"X20'X12 with M.S. angle iron stand. Set of gas header,

liquid header, valves and fittings for above condensers. (Including Excise Duty.)

One — Ammonia receiver size 20'X24" made of M.S. plate welded & hydraulically tested. Inlet & outlet valves, safety valve, purge drains, gauge glass, gauge glass valve & stands for receiver.

Three — Ammonia oil separator size 16"X48" made of M.S. plate welded & hydraulically tested with compansion flanges and drain connections.

Three — Set of ammonia pressure gauges (Set of three)

Erection charges of refrigeration machinery only.

PART B :

One — Lot of ammonia, water pipe & pipe fitting for the interconnection of ammonia refrigeration machinery & cooling of compressor water jacket and condenser.

First charge of ammonia gas & oil.

Four — Dry & wet thermometer.

Four — Cold storage doors.

One — Lot of electric motors & starters :-

2-100 H.P. Screen protected slipring induction motor, 1440 RPM, Suitable to operate on 400/440 volts, 3 phase, 50 cycles, A/c supply, 2-100 HP stator/rotor starter for the above motor, 1-150 H.P. Screen protected slipring induction motor, 1440 RPM, Suitable to operate on 400/440 volts, 3 phase, 50 cycles, A/c supply, 1-150 H.P. stator/rotor starter for the above motor, 2-10 H.P. centrifugal monoblock pumpset with D.O.L. starter, with switches, starters, amp. meter, rails, V-belt, belt guard and pannel board etc.

Lot of aluminium electric wires & cables for the wiring of electric motors only.

Wiring charges of electric motors only

Total Cost of Plant & Equipments : Rs. 71,10,235.00

Courtesy : Sunder Singh & Co. Pvt. Ltd.

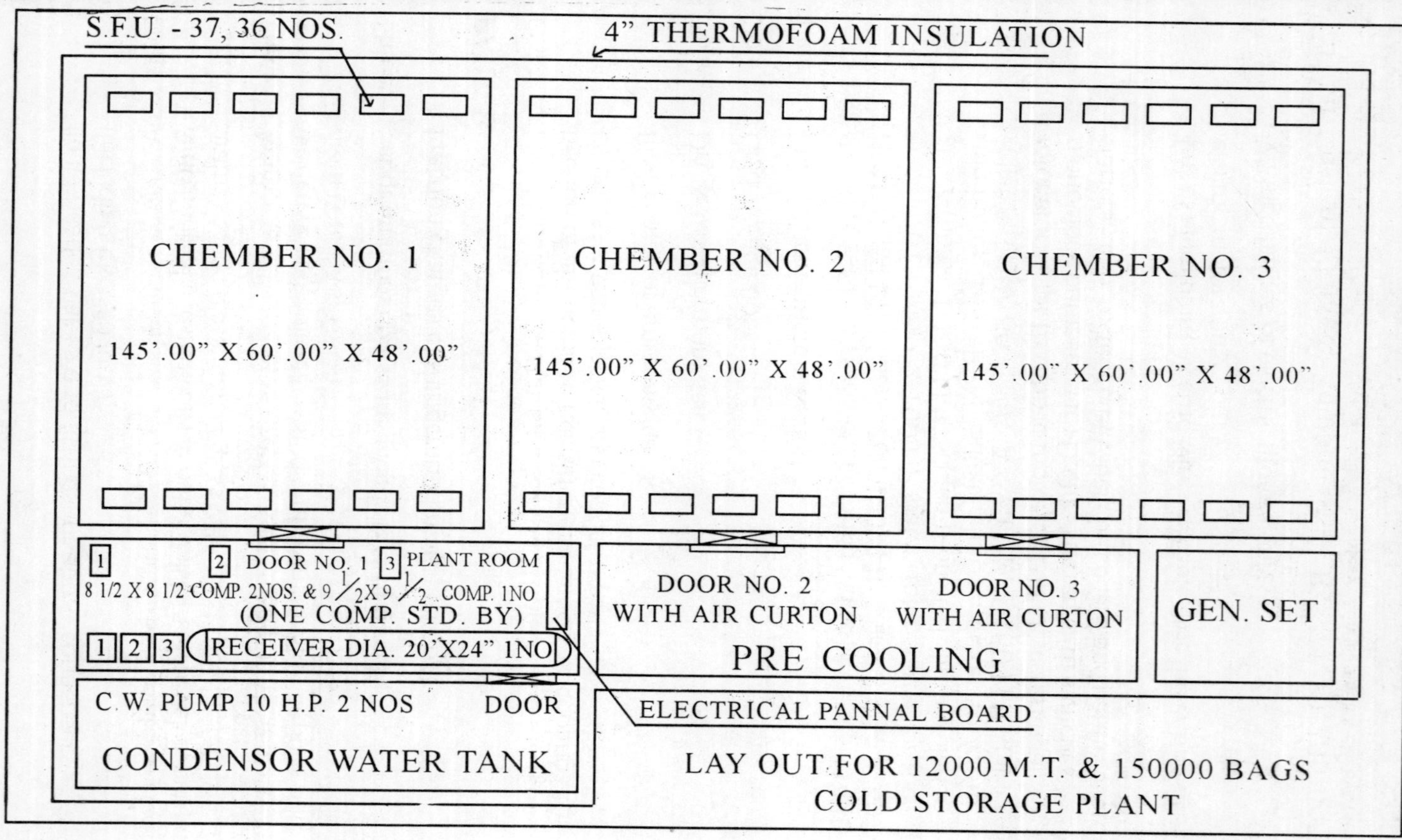

LAY OUT FOR 12000 M.T. & 150000 BAGS
COLD STORAGE PLANT

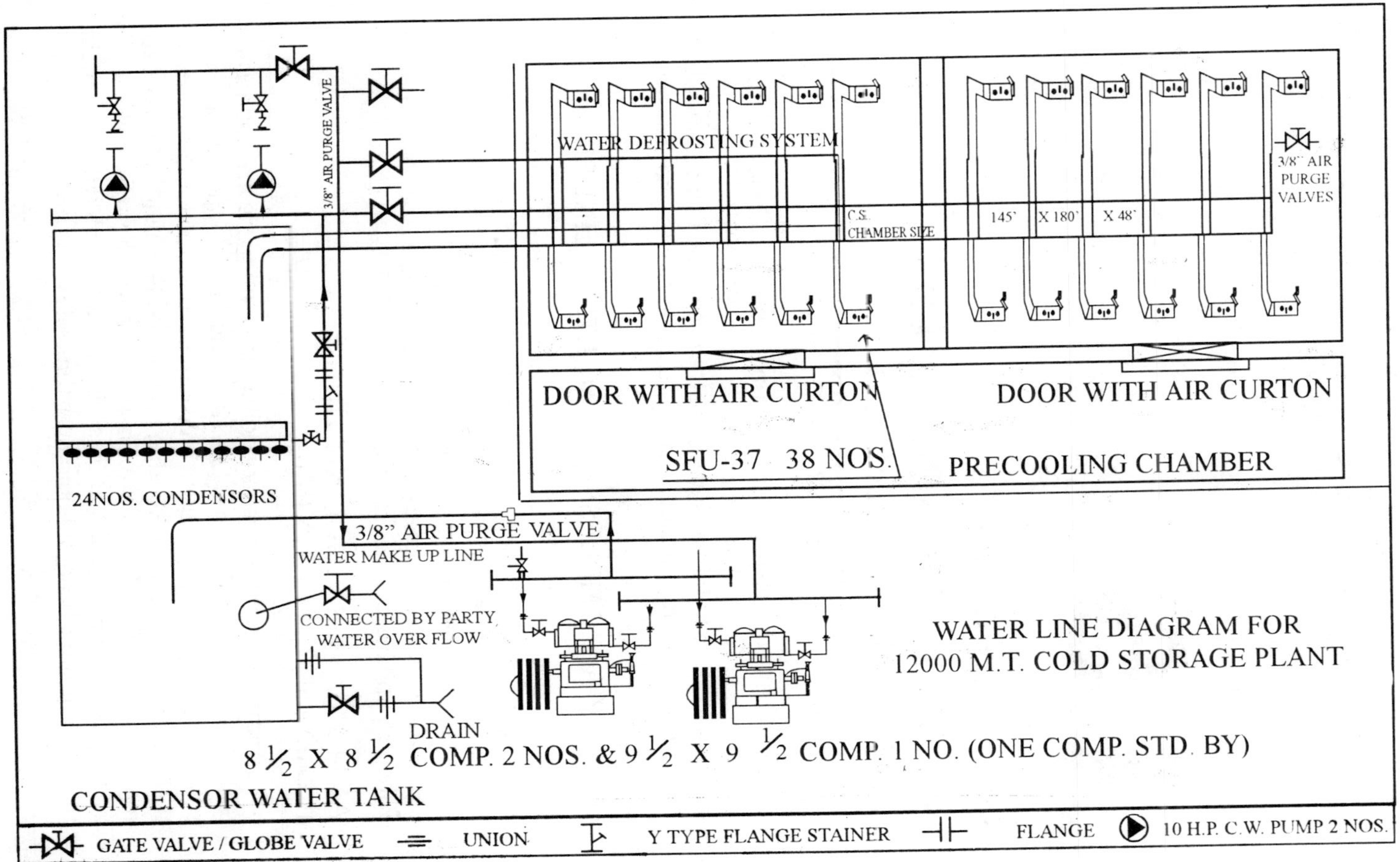
3/8" AIR PURGE VALVE
WATER DEFROSTING SYSTEM
3/8" AIR PURGE VALVES
C.S. CHAMBER SIZE
145' X 180' X 48'
DOOR WITH AIR CURTON
DOOR WITH AIR CURTON
SFU-37 38 NOS.
PRECOOLING CHAMBER
24NOS. CONDENSORS
3/8" AIR PURGE VALVE
WATER MAKE UP LINE
CONNECTED BY PARTY
WATER OVER FLOW
DRAIN
WATER LINE DIAGRAM FOR
12000 M.T. COLD STORAGE PLANT
8 ½ X 8 ½ COMP. 2 NOS. & 9 ½ X 9 ½ COMP. 1 NO. (ONE COMP. STD. BY)
CONDENSOR WATER TANK
GATE VALVE / GLOBE VALVE
UNION
Y TYPE FLANGE STAINER
FLANGE
10 H.P. C.W. PUMP 2 NOS.

15

DETAILS OF PLANT EQUIPMENTS AND MACHINERIES

AMMONIA COMPRESSORS DOUBLE CYLINDER :

Slow speed, vertical, reciprocating, double cylinders, Ammonia Comprerssors are made in sizes 3½"3½" to 9½"X9½". The compressors are working to the satisfaction of the customers in India and abroad in ice plants, cold storages, dairies, chilling plants and fish freezing plants.

AMMONIA COMPRESSORS MULTI CYLINDER :

High speed, multi cylinder, reciprocating ammonia compressor are manufactured in four models SO2, SO3, SO4 and SO6 having 2,3,4, and 6 cylinders respectively. These compressors can be used as a high stage compressors, booster compressors and two stage compressors. These compressors are used for cold storages, ice plants, dairies, fisheries, chilling plants, freezing plants upto -40 deg.C.

AMMONIA AIR COOLING UNITS (PLAIN SURFACE TYPE) :

Ammonia plain surface air cooling units are made in 4 models i.e. SAU 1 - SAU 2 - SAU 3 and SAU4 having 1, 2, 3, and 4 multi blade rotary type air blowers. These are suitable for cold storages of fruits, meat or vegetables, blast freezing rooms and for many other air cooling purposes. These units are made in 3 parts dip tray, coil section and blower section. Accumulator is supplied with each diffuser to maintain the constant head of liquid over the coil.

FIN TYPE AMMONIA AIR COOLING UNITS (FLOOR & CEILING MOUNTED TYPE) :

Fin type ammonia air cooling units are made in two models SFU-35 & SFU 37. These are made of steel pipe with aluminium fins, tightly pressed over the coils. The pipes are spray galvanised/hot dip galvanized, the casing of the coil is made from G.P. sheet. Two propellor type blowers are fitted at front of the unit for air circulation to increase the heat transfer. These units are more efficient, light in weight, have more air cooling capacity and require less space and save energy.

AMMONIA CONDENSING UNIT :

Ammonia condensing unit is very compact and require very small space. It consists of compressor, shell tube condensor, oil separator, check valve, motor, starter, V-belt & belt guard. It is most suitable for small chilling plants, ice candy plants and cold storages. It is manufactured in two models SCU-4 and SCU-9.

FIN TYPE AMMONIA AIR COOLING UNIT (WALL MOUNTED/CEILING SUSPENDED TYPE :

Fin type wall mounted/ceiling suspended type/ammonia air cooling units are made of 3/4" M.S. pipe and fins are wound on the pipes. All the pipes and fins are hot dip galvanized for firm contact with each other. Propellor type fans are fitted at the back of the coil which throws air on the coil for cooling. Water pan is fitted under the coils. The defrosted water collects in the pan and flows in to the drain. These are made in 6 models of capacities 0.75 T.R., 1.0 T.R., 1.5 T.R., 2 T.R., 3 T.R. and 4 T.R.

ICE CANS :

Ice cans are made from 16 gauge G.P. sheet by welding. Steel ring of M.S. flat is rivetted on the top of the cans in which the lifting pin holes are made. The ring reinforce the top and prevent from damaging. Each can is tested against leakage to ensure its qualities. These are made according to the requirement of the customers.

INSULATED DOORS :

Insulated cold storage doors are manufactured from the seasoned teak-wood and are insulated with expanded polystrene which is fixed between the inner and outer sides. The door is covered with aluminium sheet to prevent from any damage.

HAND HOIST :

Hand hoist is made very strong to lift the ice cans if any size. The drum of the hand hoist is made of cast iron on which the chain is wound is engaged with a small gear. The small gear is operated by a shaft on which a large size of hand wheel is fitted which require less manual power to operate.

AGITATORS :

Vertical and horizontal agitators are made heavy duty to circulate the brine water in the ice tank. The vertical agitators are available in two models i.e., 'V' belt driven or direct coupled. The size of the agitators are made according to the requirement of the customers.

VALVES :

Ammonia valves and fittings are manufactured in all sizes from¼" to 4". These are made from special cast iron alloy to withstand high and low pressure and temperature of ammonia refrigerant. All the valves & fittings are tested at 400 PSKIG for any leakages

AMMONIA COMPRESSORS

Heavy duty ammonia compressors are designed for industrial and commercial refrigeration applications such as air-conditioning, cold storages, ice plants, chemical industries. Fisheries, etc. These are available in sizes 3½"X3½" through 9½"X9½". and cover the capacity range of 3 TR to 104 TR.

Ammonia compressors have two cylinders and are of vertical design. Because of their low speed operation, they are known in the industry for unfailing, troublefree, continuous long operation. These compressors are suitable for V-belt drive.

Each ammonia compressor consists of by-pass valves assembly, forced feed lubrication system, fly-wheel for compressor, motor pulley, special tools, foundation bolts, etc.

CONSTRUCTION DETAILS

COMPRESSOR :

Two cylinder single acting, high efficiency, quiet operation and long life attained by accurate machining and close inspection of each part. Cylinders are diamond bored and honed resulting in absolutely round, accurately alinged bores with mirror-like finish.

PISTONS :

Highest grade cast iron pistons accurately machined and balanced. These are equipped with 5 rings including two oil scraper rings to remove excess oil.

CRANK SHAFT :

Heavy forged steel with ground and lapped bearings surface and drilled oil passages to all bearings, statically balanced.

CONNECTING RODS :

Made from high quality steel with bearings & oil passage for free movement of oil.

COMPRESSOR SHAFT SEAL :

Compressor shaft seal is easily accessible. Simple design and easy to assemble.

WATER JACKET :

To provide more effective cooling, the water jacket completely surrounds the cylinder heads.

All compressors are equipped with ring plate suction and discharge valves which are light in weight and are more efficient.

MANIFOLD :

Consists of four valves - suction, discharge and two by-pass valve which are manually operated. By-pass valves equalize the pressure between high and low side of the compressor for easy starting.

SPECIFICATIONS : AMMONIA COMPRESSORS

MAXIMUM COMPRESSOR SIZE CMS (IN.) SQ.IN.)	NO. OF CYLINDER	BORE X STROKE CMS. (IN.)	SWEPT VOLUME CU. M/HR (CU. FT./HR.)	CONNECTION SIZE SUCT.	DISCH.	WEIGHT INCLUDING FLYWHEEL	SPEED RPM MIN	NOR	MAX	DISCHARGE PRESSURE KG./SQ.CM (LBS./
8.89 X 8.89	2	8.89 8.89	27.9	2.54	2.54	200	375	400	450	17.58
(3½" X 3½")		(3½" X 3½")	(987)	(1")	(1")					(250)
11.43 X 11.43	2	11.43 X 11.43	58.5	3.17	3.17	540	375	400	450	17.58
(4½" X 4½")		(4½" X 4½")	(2066)	(1¼")	(1¼")					(250)
13.97 X 13.97	2	13.97 X 13.97	108.6	3.81	3.81	1015	375	400	450	17.58
(5½" X 5½")		(5½" X 5½")	(3839)	(1½")	(1½")					(250)
16.51 X 16.51	2	16.51 X 16.51	169.6	5.08	5.08	1260	360	375	400	17.58
(6½" X 6½")		(6½" X 6½")	(5994)	(2")	(2")					(250)
19.05 X 19.05	2	19.05 X 19.05	249.7	6.35	6.35	1800	360	375	400	17.58
(7½" X7½")		(7½" X7½")	(8822)	(2½")	(2½")					(250)
21.59 X 21.59	2	21.59 X 21.59	379.0	7.62	7.62	2900	360	375	400	17.58
(8½" X 8½")		(8½" X 8½")	(13387)	(3")	(3")	2900	360	375	400	(250)
24.13 X 24.13	2	24.13 X 24.13	529.5	10.16	7.62	3700	360	375	400	17.58
(9½" X 9½")		(9½" X 9½")	(18700)	(4")	(3")					(250)

BHP AND CAPACITY RATINGS : AMMONIA COMPRESSORS

Suction Pressure Psig	BHP at Discharge Pressure		Capacity TR	BHP at Discharge Pressure		Capacity TR	BHP at Discharge Pressure		Capacity TR
	180	200		180	200		180	200	
	SIZE 3½" X 3½"								
	375 RPM			400 RPM			450 RPM		
15	4.3	4.3	3.0	4.7	5.0	3.2	5.1	5.4	3.7
20	4.6	4.9	3.6	5.1	5.3	3.8	5.5	5.8	4.3
25	4.9	5.1	4.2	5.3	5.6	4.5	5.8	6.1	5.0
30	5.0	5.3	4.7	5.5	5.8	5.0	5.9	6.3	5.7
35	5.1	5.4	5.1	5.6	5.9	5.5	6.0	6.5	6.2
	SIZE 4½" X 4½"								
	375 RPM			400 RPM			450 RPM		
15	9.1	9.7	6.4	9.7	10.3	7.0	10.9	11.5	7.6
20	9.8	10.3	7.6	10.4	11.0	8.2	11.7	12.3	8.9
25	10.3	10.8	9.0	11.0	11.6	9.7	12.3	13.0	10.5
30	10.6	11.2	10.0	11.2	12.0	11.0	12.7	13.5	11.9
35	10.7	11.5	11.0	11.4	12.3	12.0	12.8	13.8	13.0
	SIZE 5½" X 5½"								
	375 RPM			400 RPM			450 RPM		
15	16.5	17.5	11.8	17.6	18.7	12.5	19.9	21.0	14.1
20	17.8	18.8	13.8	19.0	20.0	14.7	21.4	22.6	16.6
25	18.8	19.8	16.4	20.0	21.0	17.4	22.6	23.8	19.6
30	19.3	20.5	18.4	20.5	21.8	19.6	23.2	24.7	22.1
35	19.5	21.3	20.1	20.8	22.4	21.2	23.5	25.2	24.1

Suction Pressure Psig	BHP at Discharge Pressure		Capacity TR	BHP at Discharge Pressure		Capacity TR	BHP at Discharge Pressure		Capacity TR
	180	200		180	200		180	200	
	SIZE 6½" X 6½"								
	360 RPM			375 RPM			400 RPM		
15	26.3	27.8	18.7	27.4	29.0	19.5	29.2	30.9	21.0
20	28.2	29.8	22.0	29.5	31.0	22.4	31.4	33.1	24.7
25	29.8	31.4	26.0	31.0	32.7	27.0	33.1	34.9	29.2
30	30.6	32.5	29.2	31.9	33.9	30.4	34.0	36.2	32.8
35	30.9	33.3	31.7	32.3	34.7	33.3	34.4	37.0	35.9
	SIZE 7½" X 7½"								
	360 RPM			375 RPM			400 RPM		
15	40.2	42.6	28.7	41.9	44.4	30.0	44.6	47.3	32.0
20	43.2	45.6	33.7	45.0	47.4	35.2	48.0	50.6	37.7
25	46.5	48.0	39.9	47.5	50.0	41.6	50.6	53.3	44.6
30	46.8	49.8	44.8	48.7	51.9	46.7	51.9	55.3	50.0
35	47.4	51.0	49.0	49.4	53.0	51.1	52.6	56.6	54.5
	SIZE 8½" X 8½"								
	360 RPM			375 RPM			400 RPM		
15	58.7	62.2	41.8	61.2	64.8	43.5	65.3	69.2	49.4
20	62.4	66.6	49.0	65.7	69.4	51.3	70.2	74.0	61.7
25	66.6	70.0	58.0	69.4	73.0	60.4	74.0	78.0	68.8
30	68.3	72.7	65.2	71.2	75.8	67.8	76.0	80.9	77.1
35	69.2	74.5	71.3	72.1	77.6	74.3	78.0	83.3	86.1

Suction Pressure Psig	BHP at Discharge Pressure		Capacity TR	BHP at Discharge Pressure		Capacity TR	BHP at Discharge Pressure		Capacity TR
	180	200		180	200		180	200	
				SIZE 9½" X 9½"					
	360 RPM			375 RPM			400 RPM		
15	82.0	87.0	59.0	85.5	90.6	60.9	92.5	97.9	69.0
20	88.2	93.1	68.6	91.9	97.0	71.5	97.2	103.4	86.3
25	93.1	98.0	81.1	97.0	102.0	84.5	103.4	108.8	96.2
30	95.5	101.7	91.1	99.5	105.9	95.0	106.1	112.9	107.7
35	96.8	104.1	99.7	100.8	108.5	103.9	107.4	115.6	120.4

16

PROJECT PROFILES

PLANT ECONOMICS OF COLD STORAGE & ICE MAKING

Rated Plant Capacity = Potato Cold Storing of 8500 MT

Ice Slab 3000 MT

LAND & BUILDING

Land required 2.25 acres

TOTAL	Rs. 39,75,000.00

PLANT & MACHINERY

Total plant and machinery for Cold Storage.
Total plant and machinery for Ice Making Plant.
Miscellaneous equipment and material handling equipment.

TOTAL	Rs. 25,75,000.00

FIXED CAPITAL

Land & Building
Plant & Machinery
Other Fixed Assets

TOTAL	Rs. 71,00,000.00

WORKING CAPITAL REQUIREMENT/ANNUM

RAW MATERIALS

Potato 100000 bags (85 kgs/per bag)

Salt 60 tonnes
Miscellaneous ammonia gas

TOTAL	Rs. 1,02,000.00

TOTAL WORKING CAPITAL/ANNUM

Raw Material
Salary & Wages
Utilities & Overheads

TOTAL	Rs. 16,62,500.00

TOTAL CAPITAL INVESTMENT

TOTAL FIXED CAPITAL
TOTAL WORKING CAPITAL FOR 3 MONTHS

TOTAL	Rs. 75,15,625.00

TURN OVER/ANNUM

By doing the Job work of Potato Cold Storing of 8500 MT/Annum

By sale of Ice Slab 3000 MT

TOTAL	Rs. 45,20,500.00

PROFIT = RECEIPTS - COST OF PRODUCTION = 7,68,921.88

PROFIT SALES RATIO = Profit/Sales x 100 = 17.01 %

RATE OF RETURN = Operating profit/T.C.I x 100 = 10.23 %

BREAK EVEN POINT (B.E.P) = 77.92

PLANT ECONOMICS OF COLD STORAGE

Rated Plant Capacity = Cold Storing of 1000 MT (Potato)

LAND & BUILDING

Land required 1000 sq.mts

TOTAL	Rs. 8,35,000.00

PLANT & MACHINERY

TWO FRICK Model 5x5 slow speed heavy duty industrial type double cylinder compressor complete wsith suction and discharge valves, suction scale trap, safety value, high; low and oil pressure gaugre, gauge board, flywheel, motor pulley , V-belts, tools, wrenches, anchor bolts.

ONE FRICK ammonia oil seperator size 12" dia X 3' long complete with flanged connections with companion flanges and oil drain valve.

FOUR Stands of FRICK atmospheric type ammonia condenser each having single row of 12 pipes high x 20' long made of 50 mm dia. Pipe complete with liquid and gs valves, water sprinkling header, gas and liquid headers.

ONE FRICK ammonia receiver size 20" dia. x 9' long complete with liquid inlet and outlet valve, puruge glass with valve.

ONE Set of G.I pipe and pipe fittings for condenser water circulation as per our design and bsed on the assumption that the condensers shall be placed at a distance of not more than 5m from the plant room.

ONE Set of ammonia pipe and pipe fittings to interconnect high and low side equipment based on close hook up of the equipment.

LOT Suction line insulation..

First charge of ammonia gas and compressor oil.

TWO FRICK model ATR-56ceiling suspended frigid coil air cooling unit complete with finned cooling coil hot dip galvanised after fabrication, fans, motors, drain pan, accumulator.

ONE 25HP SPDP slipring induction motor suitable for operation on 400/440 Volts, 3 phase, 50Hz, A/C supply with slide rails.

ONE Oil immersed manual operated stator rotor starter.

ONE 3 HP monobloc centrifugal pumpset for condenser water circulation suitable for operation on 400/440 Volts, 3 phase, 50Hz, AC supply.

ONE Direct on line starters.

LOT Electrical wiring material comprising of cables, wires, conduits, switches, switch board, ammeter, voltmeter. Insulation material of expanded polystrene 100 mm thick for ceiling, 80mm thick for walls 40mm thick for partition walls, 50mm thick for floor. Cold sticker, Chicken wire mesh.

ONE FRICK cold storage doors made out of wooden frame GI sheet metal cladded with latches, hinges, push-bars.

JOB Erection, testing and commissioning of the plant.

Packing, forwarding, freight, insurance charge (5%)

Sales tax, octroi tax etc. (8%)

Miscellaneous as Gas Cylinders, tools, material Handling equipments

TOTAL	Rs. 14,41,875.00

FIXED CAPITAL

LAND & BUILDING
PLANT & MACHINERY
OTHER FIXED ASSETS

TOTAL	Rs. 24,26,875.00

WORKING CAPITAL REQUIREMENT/ANNUM

RAW MATERIALS

Potato 11765 bags (85 kgs/per bag)
Miscellaneous ammonia gas 1000 kgs

TOTAL	Rs. 11,000.00

TOTAL WORKING CAPITAL/ANNUM

RAW MATERIAL
SALARY & WAGES
UTILITIES & OVERHEADS

TOTAL	Rs. 6,61,000.00

TOTAL CAPITAL INVESTMENT

TOTAL FIXED CAPITAL
TOTAL WORKING CAPITAL FOR 3 MONTHS

TOTAL	Rs. 25,92,125.00

TURN OVER/ANNUM

By doing the Job work of Potato Cold Storing of 1000 MT/Annum

TOTAL	Rs. 20,00,000.00

PROFIT = RECEIPTS - COST OF PRODUCTION = 3,53,238.75

PROFIT SALES RATIO = Profit/Sales x 100 = 17.66 %

RATE OF RETURN = Operating profit/T.C.I x 100 = 13.63 %

BREAK EVEN POINT (B.E.P) = 77.91 %

PLANT ECONOMICS OF COLD STORAGE

Rated Plant Capacity = Cold Storing of 100 MT Frozen Vegetables

LAND & BUILDING

Land required 2079 sq.mts

TOTAL	Rs.	21,19,000.00

PLANT & MACHINERY

2 No.Units consisting of compressor Condenser Coils & Cooling Coils to work as refrigeration plant including excise S.T. packing forwarding installing at site and commissioning. Insulation: 6"thickness of PU Rigid Foam including water vapour barrier of installation & commissioning

TOTAL	Rs.	14,00,001.00

FIXED CAPITAL

LAND & BUILDING
PLANT & MACHINERY
OTHER FIXED ASSETS

TOTAL	Rs.	36,69,001.00

TOTAL WORKING CAPITAL/ANNUM

SALARY & WAGES
UTILITIES & OVERHEADS

TOTAL	Rs.	4,43,350.00

TOTAL CAPITAL INVESTMENT

TOTAL FIXED CAPITAL
TOTAL WORKING CAPITAL FOR 3 MONTHS

TOTAL	Rs.	37,79,838.50

TURN OVER/ANNUM

By doing the Job work of Cold Storing of 100 MT/Annum Frozen Vegetables

TOTAL	Rs.	20,00,000.00

PROFIT = RECEIPTS - COST OF PRODUCTION = 3,34,750.28

PROFIT SALES RATIO = Profit/Sales x 100 = 16.74 %

RATE OF RETURN = Operating profit / T.C.I x 100 = 8.86 %

BREAK EVEN POINT (B.E.P) = 80.69 %

PLANT ECONOMICS OF COLD STORAGE

Rated Plant Capacity = 10000 MT of fruits & Vegetables

LAND & BUILDING

Total Land Area. 10,000 Sq. mtrs.

TOTAL	Rs. 1,61,00,000.00

PLANT & MACHINERY

Ammonia Compressor heavy duty 8.5"x 8.5"(8 1/2)double cylinder vertical type,with flywheel,pully, suction & discharge stop value with accessories, Ammonia Cooling coil size 12.5'x3' made of 3/4"pipe with blower fitted with for rotors 18"x18", Ammonia Receiver size 15"x24" (M.S.plate) with accessories, Ammonia Condensers of MS pipe size (2"x20'x12) with all accessories, Ammonia oil separator size 16"x48" (M.S. plate) with accessories, Ammonia Pressure gauge, Water reservir (PVC Tank), Electric Motor for compressor 100HP with 440 V, 3 Phase, 50 cycle, Electric motor for air cooling 10HP, motor, 440V 3 Phase, 50 cycles, Condenser water pumping set with 10 H.P. motor for 18000 glns, Pipes, pumps, valves, fittings & miscellaneous structures, Electric Panels, control Boards, wirings & other accessories, Fire safety equipments, Weighing Bridge platform types, Laboratoy equipments, Conveyor belt, (2 set), Insulation for walls, various-equipments electrical accessories etc., Miscellaneous equipments and accessories

TOTAL	Rs. 92,67,000.01

FIXED CAPITAL

LAND & BUILDING
PLANT & MACHINERY
OTHER FIXED ASSETS

TOTAL	Rs. 2,81,97,000.01

WORKING CAPITAL REQUIREMENT/MONTH

RAW MATERIALS

Liquid Ammonia,Miscellaneous chemicals.

TOTAL — Rs. 90,000.00

TOTAL WORKING CAPITAL/MONTH

RAW MATERIAL
SALARY & WAGES
UTILITIES & OVERHEADS

TOTAL — Rs. 12,29,375.00

TOTAL CAPITAL INVESTMENT

TOTAL FIXED CAPITAL
TOTAL WORKING CAPITAL FOR 3 MONTHS

TOTAL — Rs. 3,18,85,125.01

TURN OVER/ANNUM

Return By Rental charges for 10000MT of fruits & Vegetables

TOTAL — Rs. 3,50,00,000.00

PROFIT = RECEIPTS - COST OF PRODUCTION = 1,18,73,204.37

PROFIT SALES RATIO = Profit/Sales x 100 = 33.92 %

RATE OF RETURN = Operating profit/T.C.I x 100 = 37.24 %

BREAK EVEN POINT (B.E.P) = 53.83 %

PLANT ECONOMICS OF COLD STORAGE

Rated Plant Capacity = Cold Storing 1000 Tons Vegetables & Fruits

LAND & BUILDING

Land Area 5,000 Sq. Ft. Total

TOTAL	Rs. 3,50,001.00

PLANT & MACHINERY

Industrial compressor receiver condensor and cooling coil, Electric Motor 25 H.P. and starter Electric Motor 5 H.P. Blower, Humidifier Air Handling system, Pump and 2 H.P. Motor Cold Storage Door, Ducting Ammonia Gas and Valve, Thermocol Insulation, Steel and Wooden Rack, Fire Extinguishers, Weighing Machine etc.

TOTAL	Rs. 5,84,750.00

FIXED CAPITAL

LAND & BUILDING
PLANT & MACHINERY
OTHER FIXED ASSETS

TOTAL	Rs. 9,34,751.00

WORKING CAPITAL REQUIREMENT/MONTH

RAW MATERIALS

Ammonia Gas, Ammonium Sulphate, and Jute Bardana

TOTAL	Rs. 5,500.00

TOTAL WORKING CAPITAL/MONTH

RAW MATERIAL
SALARY & WAGES
UTILITIES & OVERHEADS

TOTAL	Rs. 64,700.00

TOTAL CAPITAL INVESTMENT

TOTAL FIXED CAPITAL		
TOTAL WORKING CAPITAL FOR 3 MONTHS		
TOTAL	Rs.	11,28,851.00

TURN OVER/ANNUM

By doing the job work of 1000 Tons Vegetables & Fruits		
TOTAL	Rs.	15,00,000.00

PROFIT = RECEIPTS - COST OF PRODUCTION = 5,29,489.90

PROFIT SALES RATIO = Profit/Sales x 100 = 35.05 %

RATE OF RETURN = Operating profit/T.C.I x 100 = 46.66 %

BREAK EVEN POINT (B.E.P) = 38.32 %

PLANT ECONOMICS OF COLD STORAGE

Rated Plant Capacity = Cold Storing of 600 MT Frozen Vegetables

LAND & BUILDING

Land required 9950 sq.yds.

TOTAL	Rs. 50,22,250.00

PLANT & MACHINERY

4 No.Units consisting of compresso Condenser Coils & Cooling Coils to work as refrigeration plant including excise S.T. packing forwarding installing at site and commissioning.

3. Insulation:6"thickness of PU Rigid Foam including water vapour barrier of installation & commissioning

TOTAL	Rs. 32,50,001.00

FIXED CAPITAL

LAND & BUILDING
PLANT & MACHINERY
OTHER FIXED ASSETS

TOTAL	Rs. 84,22,251.00

TOTAL CAPITAL INVESTMENT

TOTAL FIXED CAPITAL
TOTAL WORKING CAPITAL FOR 3 MONTHS

TOTAL	Rs. 88,99,955.50

TURN OVER/ANNUM

By doing the Job work of Cold Storing of 600 MT/Annum Frozen Vegetables

TOTAL	Rs. 1,20,00,000.00

PROFIT = RECEIPTS - COST OF PRODUCTION = 71,13,103.54

PROFIT SALES RATIO = Profit/Sales x 100 = 59.28 %

RATE OF RETURN = Operating profit/T.C.I x 100 = 79.42 %

BREAK EVEN POINT (B.E.P) = 34.20 %

17

VACCINE COLD CHAIN

The "Cold Chain" is the system of transporting and storing vaccines within the temperature range of 35°F (2°C) to 45°F (8°C). The cold chain begins when vaccine is manufactured, moves through to the state distribution center and ends with the local immunization provider at the time of administration.

Cold Chain Management

Anyone handling vaccines is responsible for their potency, at each step in transport, storage and administration of vaccines. Vaccines are delicate biological substances that can become less effective or destroyed if they are:

- Frozen
- Allowed to get too hot
- Exposed to direct sunlight or fluorescent light

Vaccines should be maintained within the recommended temperature range of 35°F (2°C) to 45°F (8°C). The loss of vaccine effectiveness is cumulative and cannot be reversed.

Equipment for Transporting and Storing Vaccines

The essential cold chain equipment needed to transport and store vaccines within a consistent safe temperature range include:

- A refrigerator for storing vaccines
- A digital, electronic or mercury/maximum thermometer and chart for recording daily temperature reading
- Cold boxes for transporting and storing vaccines
- Ice packs to keep vaccines cool
- Material to separate ice packs from the vaccines when using cold boxes (e.g. shredded paper, cardboard, bubble wrap or Styrofoam).

Refrigerators and Freezers

It is recommended that one refrigerator should be dedicated to store vaccines. Points to consider when purchasing a refrigerator. Estimate the amount of vaccines required for your clinic's supply period, and choose a refrigerator that can store this amount in the middle and upper shelves with out crowding. At least 50% of the space needs to be filled at all times to allow for adequate circulation of cold air, and to stabilize the refrigerator temperature. [Vaccines should be maintained with the recommended temperature range of 35°F (2°C) to 45°F (8°C)]. Safe vaccines storage is possible with refrigerators if the following procedures or modifications are carried out.

Maintenance of the vaccine refrigerator

- Report breakdowns immediately so repairs can be made
- Regularly check refrigerator seals to ensure cold air cannot leak out. If they are brittle or torn arrange for replacement
- Defrost refrigerators are required to prevent ice build up which reduces efficiency.
- Ensure the area around (including behind and under) the refrigerator is clean and dust free
- Arrange for regular maintenance inspections by the manufacturer or technician. Inspections may need to be more frequent as the refrigerator ages.

Defrosting or Cleaning

When defrosting or cleaning the refrigerator, move the vaccines to second refrigerator. This temporary storage refrigerator must also be monitored to ensure the correct temperature 35°F (2°C) to 45°F (8°C) is maintained. If you don't have a storage refrigerator, store the vaccines in a pre-cooler insulted container with icepacks. Continue to monitor the temperature inside the container until the normal vaccine refrigerator is ready for use again.

Power Failures

During a power failure of 4 hours or less, the refrigerator door should be kept closed. If the power failure continues for more than 4 hours, store vaccines in an insulted container with ice packs. If power failures are a common occurrence consider purchasing a portable power generator, or, vaccines could be transferred to another site with power.

Maintaining and Monitoring Refrigerator Temperatures

The thermometer needs to measure the refrigerator temperature close to the vaccine vials. Choosing a thermometer to monitor the vaccine refrigerator. Digital-type thermometers or mercury minimum-maximum thermometers are the reliable and easiest to read.

Ordering Vaccines

Keep vaccine stock to a minimum by regularly ordering only the quantity of vaccine required for the period until the next scheduled delivery. Should always have at least 14-day supply of vaccine in the refrigerator when you are reordering. Storing excess vaccines supplies in the refrigerator can increase the risk of wastage from vaccines.

Equipment for Transporting Vaccines

A number of issues should be considered when choosing equipment to transport vaccines. They should include:

- Space required for the amount of vaccine transported
- Number of icepacks needed to keep the vaccines at less than 50°F
- The length of time in transit
- How the cold box will be handled

Criteria for Selecting a Cold Box

- It needs to be large enough to store vaccines and icepacks during transport
- External surface material needs to be durable and robust
- Lid needs to be tight fitting
- Strong handles for carrying the cold box

Icepacks, Freezer Blocks, Ice Blocks

Icepacks are used to cool insulated containers or cold boxes. Icepacks are flat plastic containers that are filled with water and froze. Some commercial icepacks contain a chemical product that ensures the icepack remains colder than 23°F (0°) longer than water-filled icepacks.

Unpacking Vaccines after Transport

Unpack vaccines from the transport container and store them in their packaging regardless of their bulkiness. Removing vaccines from the original packaging exposes vaccines to room temperature and light. Check the temperature to ensure the vaccines have not been exposed to temperatures above 35°F or below 32°F.

Placing Vaccines in Refrigerator

- Store IPV, MMR on the top shelf
- If diluent accompanies MMR, Hib vaccine within vial packaging, the diluent must be removed and stored on the middle or next lower shelf
- All freezer sensitive vaccines should be stored on the middle shelves
- Diluent and emergency drugs can be stored on the lower shelves

Vaccines should remain in the refrigerator until immediately before they are administered. They should be returned to the refrigerator immediately after drawing up each recommended dose.

18

CONTROLLED ATMOSPHERE STORAGE

The concept "Controlling the atmosphere"

Cold stores alter the temperature inside an enclosed chamber through the use of refrigeration. To save operating costs of the refrigerating equipment, insulation as a thermal barrier is used during construction to minimise external heat ingress. Depending on the product types stored, the cooling is distributed inside the chambers using fans which circulate cool air – in case of frozen temperature goods, the cold air need only shield the cargo, to isolate it from exterior peripheral walls and other heat ingress. In the case of living fresh produce, the cold air must additionally envelope each individual piece and penetrate interstitial space in storage to evacuate other gases & heat produced due to respiration. This is ordinary storage and does not involve any change to the base atmospheric composition.

Controlled atmospheres are essentially those which deviate from the normal air composition of 21% oxygen, 78% nitrogen and 380ppm of carbon dioxide. Other gases are also present but normally in too small a concentration to have a prime effect on stored produce.

Controlled Atmosphere cold stores

Controlled Atmosphere cold stores are understood as cold storages designed and fitted with additional equipment such as to actively control the atmospheric content inside the closed chamber. The concept involves forcibly purging the mass of air in a closed room with other 'inert' gas, to quickly obtain a low level of oxygen inside the chamber. Low oxygen levels (in tandem with controlled temperature) have been observed to further reduce the physiological rates of living tissue stored in such an environment. Controlled atmosphere technology benefits by reducing produce respiration, slowing ethylene production, inhibiting pathogen reproduction, and killing insects.

The most common inerting gas used is natural Nitrogen (abundant in plenty in earth's air). Special generator units are employed to extract the atmospheric Nitrogen (reducing O^2 content). The resulting air mixture is then pumped into the cold store chamber, purging the existing mass of air. The atmosphere content in the chamber is controlled to preset levels (depending on produce) and CA requirements complied with.

The main added cost component for building a controlled atmosphere store is the nitrogen generator with controls and associated fan blowers. The equipment regularly samples air parameters inside the target chamber to stop the system and to replenish with fresh air when needed.

Globally a lot of research has been conducted in quantifying the benefits from controlling the atmosphere when storing fruits and vegetables. The most commonly beneficial products accepted for commercial storage in CA are apples, pears, kiwifruits for long term and for temporary storage or transport of strawberries, cherries, bananas and lettuce. Research has continued on various other produce types.

In either case, the intent of CA storage is to extend the shelf life of fresh produce, wherein price realisation is possible through sale in their original non-processed condition.

When used for long term storage, CA storage is deployed as farm-gate infrastructure and designed to suit batch wise dispatch as per market requirement.

It is notable that CA conditions (low oxygen contents) are harmful to living produce when delayed after harvest, cannot be tolerated by produce which is in later stage of shelf life and must be enforced within first few days of harvest. If CA conditions cannot be operationally achieved within first 36 to 96 hours of initiation, the process is annulled and normal cold storage parameters are to be maintained. Once a produce has been removed from CA environment, it reverts to normal physiological activity and reintroducing into CA is harmful and causes tissue demise.

Cold storage Status in India

The Indian government promotes the development of cold-chain infrastructure. This includes cold storage infrastructure, transport infrastructure and point of production infrastructure. Development so far has manifested in the storage space, largely stemming from earlier successes with storing potato on an annual basis. For other horticultural crops, point of production infrastructure in form of pre-coolers and packhouses are required to serve as the base initiators of cold-chain movement. It is noted that food processing units as a point of production for food items have been successfully implemented. Without such production units, the goods cannot enter the cold-chain and hence instead of domestic produce transiting through our cold storages, we have imported produce that is effectively serviced.

In case of cold storages, two primary types persist. The first is farm gate infrastructure that is deployed close to producing regions for long term storage of farm produce. These storage types are designed for single commodity bulk storage where the produce is intended for subsequent sale over an extended period over its marketable life. These stores are predominated by potato stores and those for spices and specific crops like carrots, apples, oranges, onions, etc. CA stores, due to their base intent of extending shelf life over long term, fall under this category. Produce stored in such cold storage is not intended for repetitive handling and these stores can serve as initiating points for subsequent market links.

The second type of cold stores, are more transient in their nature of service. These are the distribution hubs close to market, those that are at point of consumption (retail outlets and fridges at homes), consolidation hubs (eg. for grapes and those appended to pack-houses), etc. The integrity of the coldchain largely depends on this transit infrastructure including logistics. The goods handled in these stores are those with shorter shelf life, those that have exited bulk storage, and those that are enroute to market or final consumption. The majority of horticultural crops have a limited shelf life even when in the cold-chain and cannot be stored across seasons. Additionally, all products towards the end of their storage life, need to transit to market through such cold-chain facilities. Such storage infrastructure has only recently been developed in India.

Amongst laymen all cold storages seem to be the same but farm gate cold storage infrastructure must not be confused with the other types of cold storage, especially when correlating with the integrated cold supply chain that links farm to markets.

As per recent reports there are approximately 6000 cold stores in India, predominantly the farm gate long term storage type, designed originally for single commodity storage. In the last decade, more of the market linked transit type storage facilities have developed. Without these facilities, the chain breaks as soon as the produce exits farm-gate production units if there is no close to market facilities.

Pack-houses with pre-coolers with appended staging stores are not sufficiently present in India. Reefer transportation that links the primary processing units to the cold-chain service facilities are present to service existing trade in the must-have category (ice-creams, dairy, meats and imports in the cold-chain).

Use of Controlled Atmosphere (CA) Cold Storage

Apples are the major commodity stored in Controlled Atmosphere (CA) cold stores worldwide. The reason for limited commercial use of CA to relatively few products, despite experimented benefits on quality of many others, is related to cost benefit ratios. Like ordinary cold stores, CA structures must not only be air tight and refrigerated, but require added investment in equipment to modify and maintain the desired atmospheres. The volumetric size of these storage rooms is also optimised to maximize the value of the added equipment. Typically, adding CA equipment can increase the cost of a cold store by x1.8 to x3.0 times depending on various factors.

Therefore, the return on investment requires long lived horticultural products that are stored for months and not days or even weeks. In addition, the extension of storage life is often too small to warrant added investment. If the storage potential of a particular product is a week, for example, then adding on a few days extra, is often not commercially significant.

However, newer tent-based CA based cold storage systems, with lower cost oxygen and carbon dioxide control monitors, are now available, and maybe more useful for shorter lived products. The tents and controllers are placed in cold storage rooms and have been used successfully for local market strawberries for example. Similarly, Modified Air Packaging which allows the produce's own respiration to alter the air composition inside the package, is considered more viable in case of short storage life products. CA is also used for long term storage of dry grains. Ripening rooms are examples of short term controlled atmosphere storage – in this case ethylene and CO_2 are the parameters controlled.

Since nitrogen is the most commonly used gas in controlling the atmosphere, special human safety aspects must also be deployed in CA cold stores. These include personnel O_2 monitoring instruments to safeguard inadvertent asphyxiation and nitrogen related hazards (one whiff of pure nitrogen can cause brain death). Nitrogen is generated by separating it from normal atmospheric air (78% Nitrogen) through special equipment. Alternately, gas injection from cylinders and CO_2 generators are also used in some facilities.

Additionally, since the internal atmosphere of a chamber is forcibly flushed, the chambers are fitted with pressure relief valves to avoid excess pressure build up inside the chamber which can cause the insulating walls to bulge outwards. CA cold stores maintain a positive internal pressure to avoid ingress of external air which is detrimental to controlled status. Monitoring equipment to record and control the CA conditions are also installed. Usually, once CA parameters are achieved – usually within 5 days of harvest – the gas generator can be switched off as natural respiration then continues to lower the oxygen level and effect CO_2 and other gases. At predetermined limits, outside air is then vented into the rooms to effectively maintain the desired levels – feed and bleed approach. Such cold stores also deploy CO_2 scrubbers and optionally ethylene scrubbers. Before sale of the stored produce, the entire chamber is flushed with fresh air with venting blowers to bring the atmosphere back to normal conditions and to make it safe for human access.

The most capital intensive component added to a cold store (with CA facility) is the Nitrogen generator with associated controls. The common N^2 generators are swing adsorption type and pressure membrane type (like reverse osmosis tubes). The capacity of the CA generator (in M^3 or litres per hour), is matched to ensure that the entire broken space in the cold store can be purged in 36 to 72 hours. If CO2/O2 parameters cannot be achieved in this critical initial duration, the space must be reverted to normal atmosphere condition and the produce should be maintained as in an ordinary cold store.

CA Cold Storage in India

Controlled Atmosphere storage in India has been well developed in case of apples, a model that is one of the most commercially accepted globally. In India, the single season produce, apple is selectively stored in CA cold stores with the intention to safely store the crop, while drip feeding the consuming market for the whole year, until the next harvest comes due, when the cycle is repeated.

The costs involved for building a controlled atmosphere Cold store are highly subjective and will depend on a variety of factors – source of equipment, design parameters, number of chambers under controlled atmosphere, type of utility, capacity etc. CA cold stores are used for storing of fresh produce over extended duration but in some cases, food processors may use CA stores to safeguard produce like peaches intended for canning purpose over short durations to counter canning line capacity restraints. Reference to NHB Guidelines and Standards (CS3); these also refer guidance to WFLO for use of CA storage, which is notably only for Apples and Pears.

Components: differentiating technology of a cold storage

1. The Normal component costs applicable to a cold store, such asa. Thermal structural barriers (Insulating wall, ceiling, floor, doors, air curtains)

   b. Refrigeration designed to produce type and capacity.

      i. Evaporators/Air handlers

      ii. Compressors/Condensers

   c. Humidifiers

   d. Energy efficiency controls

      i. PLC controls

      ii. Temperature monitors

      iii. RH monitors

      iv. Air Ventilation systems.

e. Safety and structural components

   i. Emergency door release

   ii. Gas leak detectors

   iii. Fire Detection, fighting equipment

   iv. Effluent and waste treatment

f. Handling and Storage components

   i. Docks – staging and receiving

   ii. Ante-rooms

   iii. Racking, bins, crates

   iv. Material handling equipment (Forklifts, pallet lifts, conveyor, etc.)

2. Add-on cost components specific to Controlled Atmosphere componentsa.

   a. Gas generator – nitrogen generator – by unit capacity.

   b. Additional piping to supply gas to chambers

   c. Pressure relief valves or pressure equalisers

   d. Gas analysing/sensing instruments

   e. Added air ventilation systems

   f. CO_2 & ethylene scrubbers (where needed)

   g. Human safety – oxygen analysers

   h. Gas tightening walls etc with resin, coating/cladding

   i. Specialised Gas tight doors

   j. Storage Bins and special high reach trucks

While the CA components are an added cost to capital, the overall cost of these additional components is not a direct factor to the storable ton capacity of a cold storage. This is more so, in cases where only some compartments and chambers are designed for CA use. The remaining cold chamber space created is for use as normal temperature controlled storage.

Not understanding the technology or its application, many projects are reported with nominative compliance with technical CA parameters from regions far distant from the established commercially tested norm (in desert regions, more than 8 hours distance from farms, in ports with intent to store imported produce, etc).

In such cases, where target intent is not the prevalent or commercially established norm, partial capacity for CA may be considered for trial pilot projects.

Nitrogen Generators

What is MEMBRANE TECHNOLOGY

Compressed air enters one end of a permeable membrane. The membrane is comprised of many hollow fibres. The N_2 travels the length of the fibres and exits at the other end of the membrane. The O_2 in the air passes through the sidewall of the fibres and exits the side of the membrane. Prior this basic process, the air mixture is treated to remove contaminants, moisture, etc. Nitrogen generated on demand and is directly pumped into enclosed chambers.

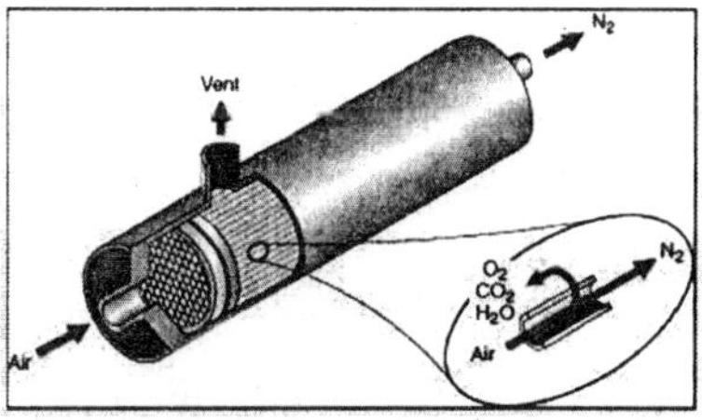

This technology is more modular for expansion, is mobile and similar to membrane sieve technology used in water purification (reverse osmosis) designs. It has a much reduced foot-print (a 10 feet by 20 feet container can house capacity to serve 15000MT of produce).

What is PSA TECHNOLOGY

Compressed air enters one end of two absorber tubes . . . filled with carbon molecular sieve (CMS). While the smaller oxygen molecules are absorbed by the CMS, the larger nitrogen molecules pass through and are stored. Upon saturation, the first adsorber releases the oxygen, which the second adsorber repeats the process over again for further purification for N_2 levels.

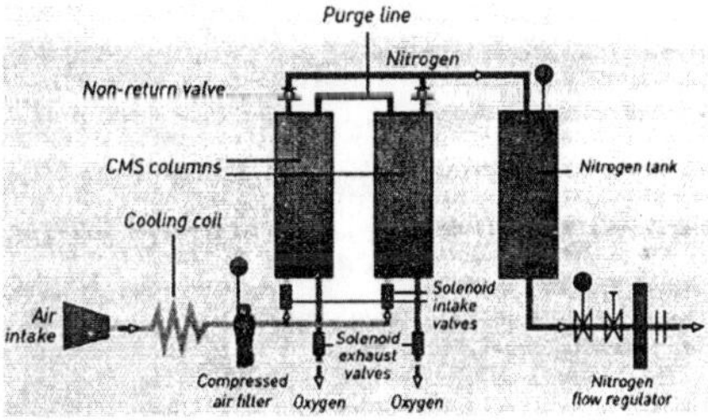

After about one minute adsorption in one adsorption tower the process controller is switching over to the second tower and the first one is regenerated. Nitrogen generated is stored in tanks for subsequent use. This technology is more commonly used in India and requires larger area to install.

Other methods involve stored nitrogen in cylinders (usually used for air transport) or in case of small storage options.

Importance of Controlled Atmosphere

CA storage has been the subject of an enormous number of biochemical, physiological and technological studies, in spite of which it is still not known precisely why it works. The actual effects that varying the levels of O_2 and CO_2 in the atmosphere have on crops varies with such factors as:

a. The species of crop
b. The cultivars of crop
c. The concentration of the gases in the store
d. The crop temperature
e. The state of maturity of the crop at harvest
f. The degree of ripeness of the. climacteric fruit
g. The growing conditions before harvest
h. The presence of ethylene in the store

There are also interactive effects of the two gases, so that the effects of the CO_2 and O_2 in extending the storage life of a crop may be increased when they are combined. The practical advantages of storage under CA can be summarized as follows:

1. A considerable decrease in respiration rate, with a reduction in climacteric maximum, accompanied by an expansion of both pre-climacteric and post-climacteric periods
2. A reduction in the effect of ethylene on metabolism due to the interaction of O_2 with ethylene, with a consequent delay of appearance of senescence symptoms
3. An extension in storage life, which can even be doubled, in as much as the over ripening is delayed

4. The preservation of an excellent firmness of flesh, due to effect of CO_2 concentration on the enzymes acting on cellular membranes
5. A high turgidity is achieved, such that fruits are more juicy and crisp
6. A smaller loss of acidity, sugars and vitamin C, so that the nutritional and sensory quality is higher
7. A limited degradation of chlorophyll, with a consequent higher stability of color.
8. CA is also used for long term grain storage where it reduces wastage due to infestation by pests, insects, etc.

These benefits manifest commercially when storage span is longer than 3 months or where quality benefits are similarly realised in consumption markets. Partial in-transit benefits are also targeted as in case of cross continent ocean transport where an added week in special CA transport containers allows for longer times to new markets at added distances.

Commercial viability from controlling the atmosphere, either actively or passively ranges from product to product. In storage it is mostly used for long term storage at production end. For produce with short term storage it is used in transportation in specially designed refrigerated modes and by use of Modified Air packaging.

Modified Air Packing

Modified Atmosphere Packaging is a way of extending the shelf life of fresh and other food products. The technology allows modification to the atmospheric air inside a package.

The simplest form of this technology is the application of a wax coat to the surface of the fruit. Similarly, selectively permeable plastics can be used to package fresh produce. In effect, the packaging serves like a molecular sieve and allows for normal respiratory process of fruit to alter the atmosphere inside the packaging within specified limits.

In some cases including meat, fish and processed foods, forcible flushing of the package with gas can be used to counter microbial build up and preserve the product longer. CO_2 in carbonated drinks is the most common example.

19

COLD STORAGE (Controlled Atmosphere, Apple)

Introduction

Controlled atmosphere (CA) storage may he used to extend the storage life of apples. Varieties such as McIntosh are CA stored at 36°F (2°C) to control flesh browning and physiological flesh breakdown caused by chilling injury which develops in storage. Chilling insensitive varieties, such as Delicious and Rome, are CA stored at 30 to 32°F (-1 to 0°C). State Agricultural Experiment Station or cooperative extension specialists should be consulted for recommended concentrations of carbon dioxide (1 to 5%) and oxygen (1 to 3%) because recommended gas mixtures vary with the variety and the geographic area in which the variety is grown. In general, temperatures are increased 1-2°F or oxygen is decreased. CA recommendations for apples grown in one area may cause injury to the same variety grown in another area.

Lowering the Oxygen Concentration

An air-tight door is sealed in place after the air-tight CA room has been filled with apples. The oxygen in the room is lowered to the desired concentration generally by flushing the room with nitrogen gas from an external tank or from an air separator (hollow-fiber-membrane or pressure-swing-adsorption), which separates the oxygen from the nitrogen air. Most apple growing areas report that the more quickly the low oxygen atmosphere is attained after harvest and cooling, the better will be the condition of the CA apples after storage. Rarely, oxygen is lowered by fruit respiration by a fossil fuelled atmosphere generator.

Maintaining the Desired Gas Concentrations

The desired oxygen concentration is maintained by adding some air to the CA room each day, if the atmosphere is analyzed manually, or several times each day if atmospheres are automatically analyzed and controlled by a computer. Excess carbon dioxide is removed from the atmosphere by chemical reaction with lime, adsorption onto activated carbon, permeation through silicone elastomer or hollow fiber membranes, or by slow flushing of the CA room with nitrogen gas. Removal of ethylene gas from the storage atmosphere by chemisorption or by catalytic oxidation has found limited commercial application for firmness retention of Empire apples and control of storage scald on Bramley's Seedling apples.

Technology

The technology for establishing and maintaining the desired atmospheres is changing rapidly. There has been a rapid increase in the use of air separators for quick establishment of the low oxygen atmosphere. Systems for automatic analysis and computer control of oxygen and carbon dioxide are currently in use in North America, Europe and elsewhere. Before proceeding with construction of a new CA warehouse facility, the latest advances in CA technology should be appraised by visiting the nearest state-of-the-art CA facility.

Precautions

Only apples of good quality and long storage potential should be cold-stored in controlled atmospheres. Immature or over mature apples should not be held in this manner. Rapid cooling and quick filling of the room are essential. Use storage scald control methods practiced in your area. The atmospheres used in CA apple storage will not support human life. If inspection or repair is needed, aerate the room and then quickly reestablish the atmosphere after making the inspection and/or repairs.

CO_2 Injury	Irregular, sunken, dry, pebbly patches of brown on the green skin of apples indicates the carbon dioxide was too high early in the CA season. This skin injury is aggravated by the presence of water on the fruit. There are also three forms of flesh carbon dioxide injury. One often begins as a discrete milk-chocolate browning between the core and the skin. The brown tissue is firm, but not necessarily moist. Another form of carbon dioxide injury appears as cavities, sometimes surrounded by patches of discolored tissue. Finally, in Delicious apples there is often very premature mealiness without tissue browning. Control: Follow recommendations of the local State Agricultural Experiment Station because varietat susceptibility to carbon dioxide injury varies with the fruit growing region and the recommended oxygen concentration used in CA.
Low Oxygen Injury	Symptoms of low oxygen injury include: skin lesions which are similar in appearance to soft scald; a purplish or bluish cast to red areas of the skin; clearly defined chocolate brown areas in the flesh; apples become very soft and split open. If the tainted flavor associated with low oxygen injury is not present, it may be difficult to distinguish low oxygen injury from high carbon dioxide injury. **Control**: Follow recommendations of the local State Agriculture! Experiment Station because varietal susceptibility to low oxygen injury varies with the fruit growing region and the recommended CA temperature.

NOTE: CO_2 - related disorders have caused severe commercial losses in Braeburn and Empire apples when kept under poor circulation (e.g., in packed cartons) within a few days.

Storage Conditions

Temperature	30-32°F (-1 to 0°C), with exceptions
Relative Humidity	90% - 95%
Freezing Point Approximately	29°F (-1.7°C)

Most apples maintain their quality best when held between 30 and 32°F (-1.8 and 0°C), although some varieties are cold-sensitive at this lower temperature and have to be held at 38 to 40°F (3.3 to 4.4°C). Internal browning of the flesh is the most common indication of cold sensitivity. The local State Agricultural Experiment Station will usually have data on what varieties in the area are cold-sensitive.

Maintaining the proper relative humidity around stored apples is very important. Apples have approximately 84% moisture at the time of harvest, and to maintain this water content and prevent shriveling of the skin, the storage relative humidity should be 90% or higher. With good air circulation, a higher relative humidity (95 to 98%) may be maintained without mold formation.

The freezing point of apples varies considerably, but most types will not freeze until the flesh is below 29°F (-1.7°C). Freezing discolors the surface and browning can occur internally. To prevent unnecessary injury, apples should not be handled while frozen.

Storage with Other Commodities

Other temperate climate tree fruits can be stored with apples if they have the same temperature requirements. Odor from celery, cabbage, carrots, potatoes and onions will be absorbed by apples and should therefore not be stored in the same room with apples. Also, odors from apples are readily absorbed by meat, eggs and dairy products, which should be stored in other rooms.

Apples produce ethylene gas as a natural product. Commodities sensitive to ethylene at 32° F (0°C) should not be stored with apples. Commodities that are adversely affected by ethylene at 32°F (0°C) include: asparagus, cabbage, carrots, lettuce and other salad greens, watermelons, kiwifruit, nursery stock, and some kinds of cut flowers, potted plants and florist greens. When an apple storage room and other storage rooms holding ethylene sensitive commodities open onto a common corridor, it may be necessary to continuously flush the corridor with outside air to prevent transfer of the ethylene from the apple storage room to the other rooms.

Ammonia Damage

Ammonia fumes that have escaped from the refrigeration plant can cause damage to apples exposed to a low concentration foe a long time or a high concentration for a short time. The first visible symptoms occur at the lenticles (dots) on the skin. Red changes to blue-black and yellow or green changes to brown. Normal skin color will be restored when the ammonia has been removed from the room, if the exposure has not been long and the concentration of ammonia has not been high. Prolonged exposure to low concentrations or short exposure to high concentrations will cause death of the tissue adjacent to the lenticles (dots). The dead tissue turns brown, becomes sunken and is likely to be infected with fungus diseases.

The human nose is very sensitive to ammonia. It detects less than 20 ppm (μl/1) ammonia in the air. 100 ppm (μl/1) ammonia is hazardous to humans exposed for 8 hours or longer. More than 8 hours is required for permanent damage to apples to occur when exposed to 500 ppm (μl/1) ammonia.

Electronic ammonia detectors should be installed in warehouses which use ammonia as the refrigerant, if 24-hour human surveillance is not practised.

An ammonia leak should be isolated by shutting valves and then the escaped ammonia fumes can be removed from the building by aeration and water washing of the ammonia from the air. Refrigeration coils should be deiced, because ammonia dissolved in ice will be slowly released into the room over a long period of time.

Storage Period

The good quality storage life of apples is influenced by fruit maturity when picked, delays before cold storage, storage temperature, and the presence of other foods in the room. Varieties differ widely in their inherent length of keeping. Some, such as McIntosh, ripen quite rapidly at 32°F (0°C) and therefore have a relatively short storage life. Others, such as Rome, ripen more slowly at 32°F (0°C) and therefore keep longer. Some varieties are susceptible to storage diseases and disorders and therefore have a short storage life.

Orchard culture and climate influence storage "life. Less than ideal soil conditions influence the composition of apples and thus their storage life. Cool, cloudy growing seasons result in a shorter life.

Fruit size and prehandling procedures also influence storage life. Large, over-sized fruit have a shorter life than normal ones. Rough handling shortens the expected storage period.

Storage Period in Air

Variety	Potential months of storage — 32°F (0°C)	Potential months of Air storage — CA*
Cortland	2 to 3	4-6
Delicious	3	8-12
Empire	2 to 3	5-10
Fuji	4	8-10
Gala	2 to 3	5-6
Golden Delicious	3 to 4 1	L 8-10
Ida red	3-4	7-9
Jonagold	- 2 1	5-7
Jonamac	2	3
Law Rome	3-4	7-9
Macoun	3	I 5-7
McIntosh	II 2-3	5-7

*The potential months for storage are for rapid CA and range from those obtained with standard CA to those obtained with low oxygen storage.

Prestorage Treatment

Apples may be stored "orchard run" or packed in boxes or cartons. Some storages supply a service of treating the orchard run apples with diphenylamine for prevention of storage scald. This is done by drenching bulk bins with the storage scald inhibitor. Packed boxes or cartons should have already had some such treatment if the variety is scald susceptible.

Some varieties, such as Golden Delicious, are very subject to water loss. The fruit boxes or bulk bins may be covered with polyethylene film. These covers should not be sealed or the fruit may develop an off flavor.

The tops of bins should be covered with film after field heat has been removed. Many apples are waxed after storage and before packing for market. The wax is applied to improve the cosmetic appeal of the apples.

Diseases, Disorders, and Injuries

Diseases in stored apples are caused by fungi, which penetrate the fruit in the orchard and/or after harvest. Diseases may frequently be distinguished from disorders and injuries by the presence of fungal spores which usually develop on the surface of the fruit at the center of the lesion.

Disorders develop over a period of time when the normal biological processes are changed by conditions which may be present in the orchard or in storage.

Injuries are caused by a single traumatic event in the orchard or after harvest. Colored pictures of many apple diseases, disorders, and injuries have been printed in two publications. Market Diseases of Apples, Pears, and Quinces, Agricultural Handbook No. 376, may be obtained from the Superintendent of Documents, US Government Printing Office, Washington, DC 20402. Postharvest Disorders of Apples and Pears, Publication 1737/E, may be obtained from Communications Branch, Agriculture Canada, Ottawa, K1A OC7, Canada.

Diseases

Alternaria Rot	Universal, small, firm, slightly sunken spots, brown around the edges but mostly with a rough black rust. At higher temperatures, spots may enlarge to brown or grayish rotted areas. Often develops by mid-season in cold storage on apples showing sun-scald, bruising or chemical injury and frequently follows storage scald, soft scald and Jonathan Spot. Rot does not spread from one fruit to another. **Control**: Careful handling and prevention of mechanical injury or storage disorders; prompt cooling and storage.
Bitter Rot	Occurs in areas east of Great Plains, especially in hot, humid districts. Appears in orchard but may also affect apples in storage and after

removal. Firm and uniform brown color, somewhat sunken and often shows wet pink or cream-colored spores; does not spread from one fruit to another, dormant below 50°F (10°C).

Control: Nothing that a warehouseman can do. Orchard control involves removing old bitter rot mummified apples and spray program; cold storage at 32°F (0°C) will check, but rot resumes growth on removal.

Black Rot

East of Rocky Mountains. Brown, irregular spots, later dark brown or black, firm with scattered black pimples containing spore masses; on removal from storage rotted areas become soft and mushy. Control: Nothing that a warehouseman can do. Spray program in orchard. Prevention of insect and mechanical injuries to fruit and proper storage and transit refrigeration will hold it in check.

Blotch

Middle West. Mostly on McIntosh, Maiden, Blush, North-Western Greening, Rome Beauty, Yellow Newtown and Yellow Transparent; light-brown fan-shaped areas with fringed margins, later nearly black and markedly sunken, subsequently cracking.

Control: Nothing that a warehouseman can do. Spray program in orchard.

Blue Mold Rot

Universal and very common: soft watery spots sharply defined from sound tissue, rotted portion can readily be scooped from sound tissue; in a moist environment white fungus and later blue spore masses appear, accompanied by musty odor and flesh tastes musty.

Control: Nothing that a warehouseman can do except maintain proper storage temperatures, careful handling, packinghouse sanitation, avoiding chemical injury during washing, use of approved fungicides such as benomyl or thiabendazole (TBZ) in wash water, and prompt refrigeration.

Bull's Eye Rot

Primarily in the Pacific Northwest. Rot develops slowly in cold storage from spores on apples when harvested, does not spread from one fruit to another; most frequent on Winesap, Yellow

Newtown, and Delicious. Spots of various sizes, singly or in groups, may be pale yellowish or brown, but often spot is brown with a pale center. Rotted tissue is firm and somewhat mealy and does not separate readily from healthy tissue, shallow or deep.

Control: Usually worse after rainy harvest period and if fruit cooling is delayed. Best control is orchard spray.

Core Rot

Sometimes apples that seem sound externally are found to be internally decayed, following infection through an open calyx tube. This infection may occur in the orchard and has been known to occur when apples were submerged during washing.

Control: Nothing that a warehouseman can do.

Fisheye Rot

In Pacific Northwest, resembles Bull's Eye Rot, spongy and stringy; infected tissue does not separate easily from healthy tissue. This disease is associated with wet harvest seasons. It can develop at 30 to 32°F (-1 to 0°C) but is usually found late in season in stored apples; does not spread.

Control: Nothing that a warehouseman can do.

Brooks Fruit Spot

Usually in Northeast United States. Deep red or black on red areas and dark green on green or yellow areas; spot later becomes black in center; later slightly sunken and in over-ripe fruit, surrounded by brown band. Fruit looks speckled. Affected areas are shallow, change little in cold storage.

Control: Nothing that a warehouseman can do. Controlled by spray program.

Gray Mold Rot

Quite universal. Initially pale, translucent, watery appearing but firm with light brown to brown areas; later softening and with freckled appearance. Spreads from decayed to healthy apples, causing "nests" in stored fruit. Gray mold develops faster in cold storage than any other decay.

Control: Source of infection is in the orchard. Orchard sanitation and fungicides like benomyi or thiabendazole (TBZ) in fruit wash or drencher help control.

Scab

Occurs widely in areas where there is considerable rainfall during growing season. Development in storage is due to large infections in orchard. Irregular circular dark spots with definite borders, sometimes smooth, but also roughened or russeted surface; can enlarge slightly in cold storage.

Control: Nothing that a warehouseman can do. Controlled by spray program in orchard.

Flyspeck

Appears as clusters of small, slightly raised, black specks on the fruit surface, This superficial fungus disease is present on the fruit at harvest.

Control: Controlled by orchard sprays, only.

Sooty Blotch

Common in Central and Eastern United States. Irregular sooty patches or spots, easily removed by scraping or moistening and wiping fruit; does not develop or spread in transit or storage.

Control: By orchard spray program.

Orchard Related Storage Disorders

Bitter Pit

Sunken spots often distributed over calyx end of apple, resembling small bruises or hail injury, initially appearing water-soaked, with intensified green or red color, finally becoming brown, gray or sometimes black. When fruit is peeled or cut, numerous brown areas appear, mostly just beneath skin but also may be deep in flesh. Affected tissue sometimes has a bitter taste. Appearance varies somewhat on different varieties. Spots may increase in numbers and intensity upon removal from cold storage. Worse on large fruit from light crops and young trees.

Control: Related to orchard practices, especially irregular heavy irrigation or rainfall or heavy nitrogen fertilization. Calcium deficiency, light cropping and early harvest aggravate it. A prestorage drench with 2 to 4% calcium chloride will reduce its development during storage.

Cork Spot

Widely distributed and often confused with other disorders producing corky spots. Due to boron deficiency in soil; usually fruit lacks characteristic shape, ripens earlier with dull color. Irregular corky spots frequently in core tissue. Present on fruit at harvest. Any corky-type disorder on apples should be diagnosed by a fruit specialist if there is any claim against the warehouse

Control: Nothing that a warehouseman can do.

Water Core

Water-soaked areas in flesh, more often near core and around core "dots. When only core area is involved, disorder cannot be detected without cutting fruit. Visible water often accompanies sunburn, caused by high heat and intense sunshine. Does not develop or spread in transit or storage and if slight in degree, may actually disappear in apples while in storage. When large portions of apple are involved, especially in Delicious, Jonathan, Rome Beauty and Stayman, internal breakdown may follow. Fuji appears relatively resistant to damage from water core.

Control: Harvest before extensive water core develops. Most susceptible varieties are Delicious, Fuji, Winesap, and Stayman.

Water Core Breakdown

If water core in apples is serious it may eventually cause breakdown of the flesh. With this type of breakdown remnants of the severe water core or water soaked flesh can often be seen. However, some studies indicated that water core breakdown may appear even though the water cored areas have disappeared. Slight water core usually, if not always, disappears in storage. In the late stages of this breakdown, affected fruit may have a dull skin and the fruit is spongy. Severely affected fruits may smell and taste fermented. When the breakdown is near the surface of the fruit, the soft area can be detected by touch of the points at the calyx end of Delicious. Control: It is-worse in large, late picked fruit and is aggravated by delayed storage. The problem is delayed by CA storage. Among the susceptible cultivars are: Delicious, Stayman, Jonathan, Winesap, Cox's Orange Pippin, Miller's Seedling, James Grieve, Bramley Seedling, Worcester, Braeburn and Holstein Cox.

Storage Chilling Disorders

Brown Core

Occurs principally on apples from New York and New England. Most serious on McIntosh, but also found on Empire, Idared, and others. No external symptoms. When fruit is cut, core is first brown between seed cavities, then in whole core area and brown streaks may extend into flesh. Associated with too low storage temperature, appearing late in season and increases after fruit is removed from storage. Tendency to brown is in fruit before it is stored. Cloudy, rainy weather, when apples are maturing, aggravates disorder. Control: Hold apples with brown core tendency at 36°F (2°C) and market in 2-3 months, or put them in controlled atmosphere storage at 36°F (2° C).

Internal Browning

Affects only certain apples ir; certain regions, notably Yellow Newtown and Bellflower grown where weather is cool and foggy, as in the Watsonville area of California. Detected only by cutting fruit. Mostly browning in the core; worse on larger fruit; tendency is inherent in fruit but is aggravated by storage at 30 to 32°F (-1 to 0°C) and increases with longer storage period. Control: Store at 38 to 40°F (3 to 4°C) in CA storage.

Low Temperature Breakdown

(Tissue affected by this disorder is likely to be firmer and more moist than tissue affected by senescent breakdown. In the earlier stages fruit must be cut for the discolored areas to be seen. There are a variety of symptoms, even in one sample of fruit. The normal syndrome is markedly brown vascular bundles ("core dots"), browning of the flesh and a clear halo of unaffected tissue beneath the skin. Low temperature breakdown develops before the apples are senescent. Jonathan may show the trouble within 12 weeks at 30°F (-1°C) and Cox's Orange Pippin sooner at 32°F (0°C). The disorder is found in Twenty Ounce, Northern Spy, Jonathan, Cox's Orange Pippin and Bramley Seedlingand several others.

Control: Store at 38 to 40°F (3 to 4°C) in CA. With Jonathan it has been reduced by postharvest calcium treatments.

Soft Scald

Distinguished by roundish or ribbon-like browned areas of skin and possibly underlying flesh with sharp line of separation of healthy and diseased tissue. Becomes progressively worse when apples removed from storage. Most common on Jonathan, but also on other varieties, such as Honeycrisp; favored by storage below 36°F (2°C) during early part of storage season. Possibly an expression of Soggy Breakdown.

Control: Avoid storage at low temperatures (30-32°F/-1 to 0°C) during first 2 months of storage.

Soggy Breakdown

Different from internal breakdown. Light brown areas in outer fleshy part of apple, sharply defined from healthy tissues, initially moist and soggy. Adjacent sound areas have fermented taste, fruit may seem to be spongy, more prevalent in apples stored at 30 to 32°F (-1 to 0°C), generally increased greatly by delaying storage of fruit.

Control: Store at 36 to 40°F (2 to 4°C) or store at 32°F (0°C) in CA storage. Varieties most susceptible are Golden Delicious, Grimes Golden, Jonathan, Northwest Greening and Wealthy. Soggy breakdown doesn't appear in CA storage with Jonathan even when the temperature is this low.

Senescent Breakdown Disorders

Senescent Breakdown

With slight variations among varieties, symptom development is usually: flesh becomes very soft, first on one side then on entire fruit; apple is easily punctured with thumb and is easily bruised; flesh becomes dry, mealy and lacks aroma and flavor; browning of the fruit flesh and vascular strands in the flesh; skin becomes dull, dark, or water-soaked in appearance; fruit splits open. Although it is most common on McIntosh, almost all apple varieties are susceptible to some type of senescent breakdown. Senescent breakdown has been aggravated by low calcium levels in the fruit, very hot and dry weather before harvest, delayed harvest, slow cooling in storage, delayed establishment of low O_2 in CA, high storage temperature, prolonged storage, and for McIntosh, CA. storage with low CO_2 (1% or lower).

Control: Senescent breakdown can be controlled or alleviated by drenching the apples with 2 to 4% food grade calcium chloride, rapid cooling, rapid establishment of the proper CA atmosphere, and sale of the apples soon after CA rooms have been opened.

Other Storage Disorders

Superficial Scald (syn. Storage Scald

Very common, widespread and serious disease, affects the skin of the apple, mostly on the green side. Superficial browning of skin, but in severe cases, decay follows. Usually not severe while apples are in storage. When moved out of storage, scald develops rapidly. Worse on fruit that was immature at harvest and after a warm harvest period.

Control: Prestorage drenching of bins of apples with diphenylamine. Varieties most seriously affected are Cortland, Delicious, Law Rome, Granny Smith, Stayman, Winesap, and York Imperial. McIntosh develops scald in some seasons.

Jonathan Spot

Initially appears as bluish-black circular spots in the skin, then becomes brown and sharply sunken, later becoming lobed and more sunken. Spots may be irregular in outline on Idared. Tends to develop in transit or storage on fruit that seemed to be sound when shipped. It is aggravated by late harvest, delayed storage, high storage temperature, and CO_2 levels below 1% in CA.

Control: Prompt refrigeration after harvest, avoiding delays at ordinary temperatures. Store in CA with adequate CO 2 .

Injuries

Braising

Bruises on fruit at harvest time, in the packing operation and in transit, may influence adversely the storage life of apples. While the warehouseman has no control over such bruising, he should be aware of the significance of mechanical injury on the ripening and deterioration of apples in storage, especially if some claim is made regarding the condition of the apples while in storage. One of the types of bruises that may be confused with freezing injury is that found in apples at the lower side of the bottom layer of boxes in a reefer car or trailer. If such bruises are not detected when the fruit is accepted for storage, claims may be made later that the apples were frozen in the warehouse. This type of bruise is flat, water-soaked and darkened in appearance, generally firm. In cross section, the bruise is usually water-soaked and glassy and may be shallow or deep and wedge-shaped. Hence, a glassy, water-soaked bruise is not necessarily a sign that freezing has occurred. The transit bruises are caused by pressure and the jolting of the transport vehicle in motion. Bruise breakdown, which is seen as brown tissue radiating into the flesh from a bruise may develop on any apple variety, but is most common on soft fleshed varieties as McIntosh and Golden Delicious.

Chemical Injury

Reference will be made merely to the fact that chemical injury may occur from orchard sprays, postharvest drenches with storage scald inhibitors and calcium chloride, during the washing of apples before packing, and when fruit comes in contact with salt or fertilizer. If fruit delivered to the warehouse is suspected to be chemically injured, the diagnosis is best made by a fruit inspector or qualified pathologist.

Freezing Injury

Slight freezing injury may not be noticeable externally, or even internally, although such apples will be softer and not keep as well after defrosting. But, if severe, the surface is discolored and darkened in irregular-shaped areas, and is water-soaked. In frozen condition, apple skins show network of wrinkles and, of course, apple has "hard feel." Best indication of freezing found is when defrosted apples are cut. Core "dots" will be brown as well as strands in flesh if freezing has been severe. In extreme cases, flesh has solid discoloration, shades of brown or even black with watersoaked appearance. Frozen apples usually decay if left in storage. Slightly frozen apples will defrost with no apparent after-effect except slight softening, if thawed slowly. It is best not to move or handle apples when frozen because bruising injures frozen apples severely. Sometimes internal breakdown is mistaken for freezing injur.'. If there is any question about cause where claims are made, a fruit inspector or qualified pathologist should diagnose the problem. Control: Prevent cold "pockets" in storage by air movement and do not allow temperature to drop below 30°F (-1°C).

Hail Injury

Usually on one side of fruit, sunken spots with brown, corky, dry tissue beneath which do not tend to decay. Fruit may grow distorted. Injury near harvest may result in increased decay incidence.

Control: None.

Heat Injury

On slightly injured apples, isolated spots of brown spongy tissue; if severe, whole apple may seem to be baked due to excessively high temperatures in orchard. Skin may look sunburned, even if not brown, with collapsed tissue beneath, which may lead to fruit becoming distorted. Sun scald cannot be controlled by diphenylamine.

Control: Surround™ is being used in the northwest to reduce sun scald.

20

COLD STORAGE OF PEARS

Storage Conditions

	Temperature		Relative Humidity	Freezing Point	
	°F	°C		°F	°C
Storage	30-32	-1to0	90-95%		
Ripening	60-72	16-22	85-95%	29	-1.5

Storage Period*

Anjou	6-7 month
Bartlett	2-3 month
Bosc	3-4 month
Cornice	4-5 months
Hardy	2-3 months
Kieffer	2-3 months
Packham's Triumph	5-6 months
Seckel	3-3.5 months
Winter Nelis	7-8 months

*These storage times allow for additional time for transportation and subsequent marketing. The storage life ofAnjou, Cornice, and Bosc can be extended 1-2 months by packaging in polyethylene liners or storage incontrolled atmospheres (1-2% oxygen + less than 1% carbon dioxide, balance nitrogen).

For best storage quality, pears should be cooled rapidly after harvest. Fruit temperatures should be brought down to 32°F (0°C) within 48 hours. The storage life may be 33% longer at 30°F (-1.1°C) than at 32°F (0°C). At 30°F (-1.1°C), precise temperature control is needed to prevent freezing. Pears low in solids may be damaged by freezing when stored below 30°F (-1°C). Intermediate temperatures of 36.5-50°F (2.5-10°C) are harmful to some cultivars of pears; Bartletts stored in this temperature range are dry textured.

The time that pears can be held safely in storage at 30-32°F (-1.1 to 0°C) varies with cultivar as shown above. If held beyond their normal storage life, some cultivars may not ripen properly and attain good flavor. Even though they may appear in good condition, the flesh will not soften, the skin "scalds" or turns brown, and breakdown occurs.

Pears lose weight rapidly by evaporation, so relative humidity in storage rooms should be carefully maintained.

When weight loss is a problem in the top bins of a stack in a commercial storage, the addition of polyethylene covers will reduce weight loss and visible shrivel. Most pears for long storage are packaged in folded-over polyethylene liners with needle point or 1/4 inch (6 mm) perforations. The liners are opened when pears are removed from cold storage. For ripening purposes, the relative humidity can be lower, at 85-90%. Some winter pears require a period of cold storage before they will ripen normally at room temperature. Anjou, for example, need to be held at 30-31°F (-1 to -0.6°C) for at least 30 days before they will ripen with good quality.

Pears are good candidates for controlled atmosphere (CA) storage (1.0-2.0% 02 + less than 1.0% CO 2). Storage period of some varieties can be extended by several months with CA storage. However, fruit maturity and growing district are important factors in determining storage potential.

Disorder and Diseases

Superficial Scald (Anjou Scald)	This brown to black discoloration of the skin of Anjou and Packham's [Triumph pears does no harm other than marring appearance. It may occur even in fruit held under good refrigerated storage conditions for long durations.

Control: Ethoxyquin (antioxidant) applied as dip, spray, or wrap.

Alternaila Rot

Occurs usually late in the storage season, usually at punctures. Decayed tissue is gray to black, dry in center, gelatinous at edge, and easily removable as a core from surrounding flesh. Control: Prevent skin breaks and remove from storage promptly when noted. Blue Mold Rot Frequently appears on pears as scattered spots. This is the most common and most destructive rot of pears in storage. Affected areas have a straw to brown color and soft, watery tissues. One phase of the disease develops when the fungus [Penicillium expansum) grows down the stem and rots the tissues of the neck.

Control: Prevent skin breaks and lower fruit temperature to 30-31°F (-1 to -0.5°C). Use of approved fungicides, along with good housekeeping practices to prevent infection during packing.

Core Breakdown

Often accompanies pear scald. Soft, brown breakdown in core area, accompanied by disagreeable odor. Due primarily to over-maturity before harvest, or to holding pears too long at low storage temperatures.

Control: Harvesting at optimum maturity should largely eliminate this problem.

Cork Spot

Primarily on Anjou pears. Has small, brown corky regions in the flesh which cause surface pitting if near the skin.

Control: It is due to growing conditions, not storage conditions, although it may first be observed in storage. Fruit with cork spot can be stored almost as long as normal fruit, although market value is depreciated.

Gray Mold Rot

Characterized by firm, dull brown, water-soaked decay with bleached borders and, when more advanced, by dirty white to gray masses or "nests" of decayed fruits.

Control: Use approved fungicides; cool promptly to 30-31°F (-1.0 to -0.5° C)

Senescent Scald

This brown to black discoloration of the skin,

which is frequently accompanied by softening of the underlying tissues, is associated with fruit that is not fully mature at harvest and is stored at temperatures above optimum.

Control: Harvest at optimum maturity for long storage and cool promptly to desired storage temperature.

Freezing Injury

Symptoms are a glassy, water-soaked external appearance, with a tan, pithy region around the core. Pears frozen severely may break down completely or show marked sunken areas where slightly bruised while frozen.

Control: For pears with low soluble solids content, hold at 30-31°F (-1 to -0.5°C). Even severely frozen pears will recover if thawed gradually at temperatures not exceeding 36°F (2°C).

21

COLD STORAGE FOR POTATO AND OTHER HORTICULTURE PRODUCTS

FREON BASED REFRIGERATION PLANT

Description

Refrigeration systems are operated on the "vapor compression" principle. This term simply means that the heat being removed and transported to another location is accomplished by the alternate evaporation and condensation of a refrigerant usually referred to as a Freon. This type of refrigerant plant is controlled by a compressor which varies the pressure on the refrigerant. The Freon gas which transfers heat in a refrigerating machine or heat pump, has the ability to absorb heat when it changes state from a liquid to a gas. Similarly, when the Freon changes back into a liquid it releases its heat much like wringing out the sponge. It is this process that allows us to absorb heat from ground water, concentrate it through the heat pump system, and deliver it to the home in the form of warm air.

Freon Refrigeration System

Can be used R404a, R507 and R22, just replace the refrigeration oil and use any refrigerant.

Applicable to all kinds of cold storage and frozen equipment: Use the advanced single with double-stage compressors and special cooler, heat exchanges, low evaporation temperature of up to -70°C~-25°C.

Chillers with high cooling capacity (25hp~111hp) and the lowest energy consumption, meanwhile, it use parallel unit technology and energy control can reach 33% ,66%,100% optional.

PLANT ECONOMICS

Rated Plant Capacity	=	5000 Mt. Cold Storage
Land & Building (Land Area 2.47 Acre)	=	Rs. 2,92,17,000.00

PLANT & MACHINERY

1. Potato Grading and sorting equipments
2. Super freeze refrigeration compressors
3. Freon gas charging type
4. Freon receiver
5. Freon/Ammonia air cooling units
6. Humidity control system
7. Oxygen Sensor
8. Water Accumulator
9. Freon Detector
10. Air Cerculating fans
11. Fumigation Equipment
12. Steel Racks
13. Wooden Ballay
14. Miscellaneous
15. Lighting Equipment
16. Safety Equipments
17. Handling equipments/Lifting/Unloading
18. Generator
19. Insulation
20. Depolluting Equipments
21. Tube well & Water Supply

22. Pipe Fitting
23. Miscellaneous

FIXED CAPITAL

1.	Land & Building	Rs.	2,92,17,000.00
2.	Plant & Machinery	Rs.	1,99,00,000.00
3.	Other Fixed Assets	Rs.	14,00,000.00
	TOTAL	Rs.	5,05,17,000.00

RAW MATERIALS

1. Freon
2. Chemicals
3. Miscellaneous

TOTAL WORKING CAPITAL/MONTH

1.	Raw Material	Rs.	4,00,000.00
2.	Salary & Wages	Rs.	4,08,310.00
3.	Utilities & Overheads	Rs.	2,39,915.00
	TOTAL	Rs.	10,48,225.00

TOTAL CAPITAL INVESTMENT

Total Fixed Capital	Rs.	5,05,17,000.00
Total Working Capital For 6 Months	Rs.	62,89,354.00
TOTAL	Rs.	5,68,06,354.00

TURN OVER/ANNUM

Return by Rental charges for 5000 MT. (1,00,000 Bags Potatoes & others Horticulture Products)	Rs.	3,60,00,000.00

PROFIT SALES RATIO = Profit / Sales x 100 = 32%

RATE OF RETURN = Operating profit / T.C.I x 100 = 20%

BREAK EVEN POINT (B.E.P) = 57%

Note: *Above figures are just assumptions and entrepreneurs are requested to please update while entering into the business/industry.*

22

PLANT ECONOMICS OF COLD STORAGE (Controlled Atmosphere or CA)

INTRODUCTION

Controlled Atmosphere (CA) Storage

Controlled atmosphere storage is a system for holding produce in an atmosphere that differs substantially from normal air in respect to CO_2 and O_2 levels. Controlled atmosphere storage refers to the constant monitoring and adjustment of the CO_2 and O_2 levels within gas tight stores or containers. The gas mixture will constantly change due to metabolic activity of the respiring fruits and vegetables in the store and leakage of gases through doors and walls. The gases are therefore measured periodically and adjusted to the predetermined level by the introduction of fresh air or nitrogen or passing the store atmosphere through a chemical to remove CO_2.

There are different types of controlled atmosphere storage depending mainly on the method or degree of control of the gases. Some researchers prefer to use the terms "static controlled atmosphere storage" and "flushed controlled atmosphere storage" to define the two most commonly used systems. "Static" is where the product generates the atmosphere and "flushed" is where the atmosphere is supplied from a flowing gas stream, which purges the store continuously. Systems may be designed which utilize flushing initially to reduce the O_2 content then either injecting CO_2 or allowing it to build up through respiration, and then maintenance of this atmosphere by ventilation and scrubbing.

Importance of Controlled Atmosphere

CA storage has been the subject of an enormous number of biochemical, physiological and technological studies, in spite of which it is still not known precisely why it works. The actual effects that varying the levels of O_2 and CO_2 in the atmosphere have on crops varies with such factors as:

a. The species of crop

b. The cultivars of crop

c. The concentration of the gases in the store

d. The crop temperature

e. The state of maturity of the crop at harvest

f. The degree of ripeness of the climacteric fruit

g. The growing conditions before harvest

h. The presence of ethylene in the store

What is Controlled Atmosphere Storage

- Altering and maintaining atmospheric composition that is different from air composition of N_2 78%, O_2 21% and CO_2 0.03%
- Low O_2 and higher CO_2, within range tolerated, help reduce respiration and ethylene generation
- Helps increase storage life of fresh produce like apples, pears, kiwis, cabbage, etc.

Requirements of CA

- Chambers of size 50 250 MT. Loading of a chamber should normally complete in 3 days
- Capacity in the plant to bring optimum CA conditions within 5 7 days of harvest
- Automatic regulation of O_2 & CO_2 levels

- Maintenance of required temperature and humidity levels
- Pre cooling of produce helps in achieving optimum results
- Storage of fruit in bins / crates / cartons
- Single storey design or with mezzanine floor

Requirements of CA II

- Temperature should normally vary only up to +1°C
- Humidity (RH) should remain 90 95% for long term storage
- Coil size should be large enough to operate at 2.2 to 4.4°C cooler than the room temp.
- Air circulation should be more than 165 cmh per MT of fruit for rapid cooling. After temp. stabilization, reduce air circulation to 33 66 cmh
- Reduce air circulation after reaching required temp., by variable frequency drive and control system
- Lighting condition: dark during storage

There are also interactive effects of the two gases, so that the effects of the CO_2 and O_2 in extending the storage life of a crop may be increased when they are combined. The practical advantages of storage under CA can be summarized as follows:

1. A considerable decrease in respiration rate, with a reduction in climacteric maximum, accompanied by an expansion of both pre-climacteric and post-climacteric periods
2. A reduction in the effect of ethylene on metabolism due to the interaction of O2 with ethylene, with a consequent delay of appearance of senescence symptoms
3. An extension in storage life, which can even be doubled, in as much as the over ripening is delayed
4. The preservation of an excellent firmness of flesh, due to effect of CO_2 concentration on the enzymes acting on cellular membranes
5. A high turgidity is achieved, such that fruits are more juicy and crisp

6. A smaller loss of acidity, sugars and vitamin C, so that the nutritional and sensory quality is higher
7. A limited degradation of chlorophyll, with a consequent higher stability of colour
8. Some physiological alterations, such as chill injuries, spot, decay, browning, water core and scald are prevented, or greatly limited
9. Moulds can be reduced, in particular under low O_2, high CO_2 atmospheres
10. A longer shelf life in the post storage trading, which can even be trebled thanks to theprotraction of the effects on respiration and on the other metabolic activities.

CA Cold storage industry is a very important and essential industry. In India, fruits and vegetables are produced in plenty. A large number of fruits and vegetables are exported to other countries and even in India itself fruits and vegetables are transported from one place to another. This transportation business takes some time. So, it is desirable that fruits should be kept at a place where they can remain safe, other wise a lot of its will be wasted. For this purpose, Cold Storage is used.

CA Cold Storage is a special kind of room the temperature of which is kept very cold with the help of machines and instruments. The temperature is maintained low with the help of precision instruments. In deciding the scale of a cold storage plant, all the external condition location conditions stored, object etc. must be considered. When the scale of plant is larger however running costs would generally be less and automation would become more exact.

PLANT ECONOMICS

Rated Plant Capacity = 5000 MT. Cold Storage (Potatoes)

Land & Building (Land Area 2 Acre) = Rs. 2,52,84,000.00

PLANT & MACHINERY

1. C.A. System
2. Nitrogen Generators
3. Prism Pressure
4. Oxygen Sensor

5. Water Accumulator
6. Room Breather Bags
7. Ammonia Detector
8. Dual Gas Analyzer
9. Ammonia Refrigerating System
10. Ammonia Condensers
11. VSPA O_2 Scrubber
12. CO_2 Scrubber
13. Combi Systems
14. Air Cerculating fans
15. Fumigation Equipment
16. Steel Racks
17. Wooden Ballay
18. Miscellenous
19. Lighting Equipments
20. Safety Equipments
21. Handling Equipments/Lifting/unloading
22. Water filteration system
23. Generator
24. Insulation
25. Depolluting Equipments
26. Tube well & water supply
27. Pipe Fitting
28. Miscellaneous

FIXED CAPITAL

1.	Land & Building	Rs.	2,52,84,000.00
2.	Plant & Machinery	Rs.	3,26,40,000.00
3.	Other Fixed Assets	Rs.	11,80,000.00
	TOTAL	Rs.	5,91,04,000.00

RAW MATERIALS

1. Liquid Ammonia
2. Chemicals
3. Miscellaneous

TOTAL WORKING CAPITAL/MONTH

1.	Raw Material	Rs.	4,50,000.00
2.	Salary & Wages	Rs.	4,14,000.00
3.	Utilities & Overheads	Rs.	2,39,915.00
	TOTAL	Rs.	11,03,915.00

TOTAL CAPITAL INVESTMENT

Total Fixed Capital	Rs.	5,91,04,000.00
Total Working Capital For 1 Month	Rs.	11,03,915.00
TOTAL	Rs.	6,02,07,915.00

TURN OVER/ANNUM

Return by Rental charges for 5000 MT of Potatoes (1,00,000 Bags Potatoes storing)	Rs.	3,75,00,000.00

PROFIT SALES RATIO = Profit / Sales x 100 = 19%

RATE OF RETURN = Operating profit / T.C.I x 100 = 12%

BREAK EVEN POINT (B.E.P) = 74%

Note: *Above figures are just assumptions and entrepreneurs are requested to please update while entering into the business/industry.*

23

REFRIGERATED COLD STORAGE EQUIPMENTS & ALLIED EQUIPMENT SUPPLIERS

Om Metals And Engineers
Mr. Raju Baravkar (CEO)
S. R. No. 5, Ekata Housing Society, Bapujibuwa Nagar, Thergaon, Pune - 411033, Maharashtra, India
Mobile: +(91)-9272228397
+(91)-9850846493
+(91)-8888827833
Phone: +(91)-(20)-65300457

New Life Steel Structures
Mr. Sunil Shrivastava (Director)
1, Shiv Darshan, Radhabai Mahatre Road, Near Vithal Mandir, Dahisar West, Mumbai - 400068, Maharashtra, India
Mobile: +(91)-9324633330
+(91)-9324623558
+(91)-9022232788
Phone: +(91)-(22)-28923558
+(91)-(22)-28933330
Fax: +(91)-(22)-28933330

Premier Refrigeration Limited
Mr. Suraj Shah (Sales & Marketing Department)
1, Akurli Industrial Estate, Akurli Road, Next to Big Bazar, Kandivli East, Mumbai - 400 101, Maharashtra, India

Mobile: +(91)-9323398233
Phone: +(91)-(22)-28870304
+(91)-(22)-28874298
+(91)-(22)-28868974
Fax: +(91)-(22)-28841275

Advance Agro Ripe Pvt. Ltd
Mr. Sunil Bhat
(Managing Director)
Survey No. 30/8, Block No. 7,
Saraswati Industrial Estate,
Near Prabhat Press, Dhayari
Narhe Road, Pune - 411041,
Maharashtra, India
Mobile: +(91)-9226115747
+(91)-9225137161
+(91)-9225137165
Phone: +(91)-(20)-60121967
Fax: +(91)-(20)-60121967

Master Food Tech
Mr. Ibrahim Pathan (Manager)
S. No. 232/2, Pune Nasik Road,
Atlas Compound, Opposite
Rupee Co. Operative Bank,
Bhosari, Pune - 411039,
Maharashtra, India
Mobile: +(91)-9822027910

Unique Air Tech
Mr. Jigar Shah / Satnam Singh
(Partner)
H - 2 - 44, Aastha Avenue,
Beside Anandvan Flats,
Subhanpura Main Road,
Subhanpura,
Vadodara - 390023,
Gujarat, India
Mobile: +(91)-9825911618,
+(91)-9879486710
Phone: +(91)-(265)-2635890
Fax: +(91)-(265)-2635890

Bombay Ammonia Refrigeration Company
Mr. Deep Dua / Mrs.Yogita Dua
(Partner)
No. 9/47, Industrial Area, Kirti
Nagar, New Delhi - 110015,
Delhi, India
Mobile: +(91)-9312839577
+(91)-9810045792
+(91)-9250023606
+(91)-9999785792
Phone: +(91)-(11)-46254660
+(91)-(11)-25927524
Fax: +(91)-(11)-25927524

Datacone Engineers Pvt. Ltd.
271, `Samrajya',
Near Sangliwadi High School,
Sangliwadi,
Sangli - 416416,
Maharashtra, INDIA.
Tel. No. : +91 - 233 - 2535197,
2535759, 2535841, 2850851,
Fax : +91 - 233 - 2535769,
Mobile : + 91- 98231 44099,
98231 65787
www.dataconeequip.com
www.icenginelaboratory.com

Sri Sai Tech Refrigeration Pvt. Ltd.
Mr. Ravindra Kumar
(Managing Director)
3-A, Numbal Road,
Velappanchavadi,
Chennai - 600077,
Tamil Nadu, India

Mobile: +(91)-9841731335
Phone: +(91)-(44)-64554447
+(91)-(44)-48868662
Fax: +(91)-(44)-26495335

Freezo Tec India
Mr. Prem Kumar
Champapet, Hyderabad,
Andhra Pradesh, India
Phone : +91-40-24072467
Mobile : +91-9396983699
Web Site : http://
www.freezotecindia.com

Mech Air Industries
3/16-A, BIDC Industrial Estate,
Gorwa, Vadodara,
Gujarat, 390016, INDIA
Fax: 2291613
Phone: +(91)-(265)-2285751,
+(91)-(265)-2290728
Mobile: +(91)-9426416803

Bright International Bright Freezer (India)
Unit No. 4, K.A. Kamal Estate,
Opp. Ruby Coach Factory
Marol Naka, Andheri (E),
Mumbai - 400 059.
Tel.: 022-2852 4572
Mob: +91-9820700411,
+91-9820199791
Fax: 022-2850 1466
Email:bintl@mtnl.net.in

ALL FOLLOWING PROJECT REPORTS ARE READILY AVAILABLE

- Steel Furnitures And Electrical Appliances
- Steel Furniture And Fire Fighting Equipments
- Steel Furniture And Room Cooler
- Steel Wire Drawing And Galvanizing
- Steel Wire/Rod
- Steel Wool
- Ston Scrusher And Screening Plant
- Submerged Arc Welded Pipes
- Submersible Pump Manufacturing
- Super Enamelled Copper Wire
- Super Enamelled Copper Wire (From Copper Cathode Rod)
- Three Wheelers
- Tie-Rod Ends
- Tin Containers
- Toolroom And Sheet Metal Products
- Trolley (Shopping) For Carrying Of Stores At Super Market And Ware Houses
- Tractor Trailers
- Transmission Power Fitting
- Tubular Poles
- Tyre Retreading By Cold Process
- Super Enamelled Copper Wires
- Trolley (Shopping) For Carrying Of Stores At Super Market & Ware Houses
- Tmt Bars
- Tubular Poles For Electrical Transmission (By Fabrication Process)
- Tubular Poles Of M.S. & High Tensile Steel
- V- Belt
- Vacuum Cleaners
- Vacuum Flask (Stainless Steel)
- Valves For Refrigeration And Air-Condition
- Vehicle Welding & Painting
- Venetion Blind
- Washing Machines (Automatic & Computerised)
- Water Controller (Automatic)
- Watch Straps/Chains/ Bracelets/Belt Brass & Stainless Steel
- Water Coolers
- Welded Wire Mesh
- Welding Electrodes
- Wheel Barrow
- Wick Stoves
- Wind Mill Window Frame (Ferrous & Non-Ferrous)
- Wrist Watch

CHEMICALS (ORGANIC & INORGANIC) WITH PETROLEUM PRODUCTS

- Acetic Anhydride
- Acetic Acid (Glacial)
- Acetic Acid From Ethanol
- Acetone
- Acetylene Black
- Acetyl Chloride
- Acetylene Gas
- Acetylene Gas & Oxygen Gas (Integrated Unit)
- Acid Black Dye
- Acid Slurry
- Activated Alumina
- Activated Bleaching Earth (Activated Fullers Earth)
- Activated Carbon From Cashewnut Shell
- Activated Carbon From Rice Husk
- Activated Carbon From Rice Husk, Coconut Shell & Coconut Powder
- Activated Carbon From Wood
- Activated Carbon Powder & Granules From Coconut Shell
- Activated Carbon & Sodium Silicate From Paddy & Rice Husk
- Alcohol From Broken Rice
- Alum For Water Treatment
- Adhesive (Fevicol Type)
- Aerosol Insecticides Spray (Baygon, Hit, Mortein Type)
- Agarbatti Synthetic Perfumery Compounds
- Alcohol From Potato
- Alcohol From Rice Grains
- Alcohol From Rice Husk
- Alcohol From Molasses
- Alcohol, Beer, Starch, Liquid Glucose, Dextrose, Sorbitol, Vitamin-C,
- Alcoholic Beverages And Vinegar From Coconut Water
- Germ Oil, Cattle Feed Etc. From Maize
- Alkyd Resin
- Alkylated Phenol Likenonyl Phenol, Dodecyl Phenol
- Alum (Non Ferric)
- Alum (Ferric)
- Aluminium Chloride From Aluminium Ore
- Alum Cake
- Alum From Aluminium Hydrate
- Aluminium Ingot By Bauxite
- Aluminium Phosphide
- Aluminium Phosphate
- Aluminium Sulphate (Non Ferric Alum) 17% - 18% Alumina Content In Granules (2 Mm To 4 Mm) And Flakes
- Amines & Allied Products
- Amino Acid
- Ammonia Gas
- Ammonia Gas Bottling
- Ammonia Liquor
- Ammonium Nitrate
- Ammonium Chloride (Pure & Technical)
- Ammonium Sulphate
- Annato Seed Extraction And Processing
- Anti Corrosion Chemicals
- Anthranilic Acid From Phthalic Anhydride
- Anesthesia (All Types) Used In Hospitals
- Aniline
- Argon Gas
- Ariel Type Detergent Powder
- Anthraquinone
- Antimony Trioxide
- Atenolol
- Auramine "O"
- Azodicarbonamide
- Baking Soda From Ash
- Barium Carbonate
- Barium Compounds
- Barium Nitrate
- Barium Peroxide
- Barium-Thio-Sulphate Banzene
- Baryte Powder
- Bar Soap (All Varieties) Using Soap Noodles
- Beer Plant
- Belt Paste
- Beneficiation Of Chromite Ore Processing Charge Chrome
- Benzyl Acetate, Benzyl Benzoate, Benzyl Alcohol
- Beta Naphthol
- Bentonite Powder
- Benzoic Acid
- Benzidine
- Biofertiliser From Mother Culture
- Bio Oil For Power Generation From Coffee Husk
- Bio Gas Plant
- Bio Gas Filling In Cylinder
- Bio Tech Unit
- Bi-Chromate Of Sodium, Potassium & Ammonium
- Bi-Functional Black Mfgr.Reactive Dye (Dye From Cotton Yarn Dyeing)
- Bio-Fuel (Jatropha Cultivation And Extraction)
- Bituminous Roademulsion
- Black Phenyl
- Black Sulphur
- Bleaching Powder (Stable)
- Blue Detergent Powder
- Bone Crushing Plant
- Bone Meal (Calcined) Enrichment With Calcium & Phosphorus
- Boric Acid
- B.O.N. Acid
- Bromine Gas Plant
- Brandy
- Butanol
- Butyl Rubber For The Manufacture Of Tubes For Truck And Car Tyres
- 1,4, Butanediol
- Butyl Acetate
- Caffein From Tea Waste
- Calcined Lime (Dead Burnt Dolomite)

Market Survey Cum Detailed Techno Economic Feasibility Report on all Projects are available Contact.
"ENGINEERS INDIA RESEARCH INSTITUTE". 4449, Nai Sarak (D), Main Road, Delhi-110006 (India)
Ph. : 09811437895, 91-11-23918117, 23916431, 45626431, 64727385 Fax : 91-11-23916431
E-mail : eiriprojects@gmail.com, eiribooks@yahoo.com • website: www.eiri.in, www.eiriindia.org

ALL FOLLOWING PROJECT REPORTS ARE READILY AVAILABLE

- Calcined Petroleum Coke
- Calcining Of Magnesite & Dead Burnt Magnesite
- Calcium Aluminate
- Calcium Based Grease
- Calcium Carbide
- Calcium Carbonate
- Calcium Carbonate (Precipitated) From By Product (Lime Slurry & Carbon Dioxide)
- Calcium Carbonate (Activated & Precipitated)
- Calcium Chloride
- Calcium Gluconate
- Calcium Nitrate
- Calcium Silicate Bricks
- Calcium Stearate By Fusion Process
- Camphor Powder (Synthetic)
- Construction Chemicals (With Detailed Market Survey And Formulae Etc.)
- Carbon Dioxide
- Carbon Black From Fertilizer Waste
- Carbon Black (Petroleum Based)
- Carboxy Methyl Cellulose (Cmc)
- Casein And By Products
- Casein From Milk
- Cationic Softner (Stearic Acid Based)
- Caustic Soda
- Caustic Soda From Soda Ash By Soda Lime Process
- Caustic Soda (Liquid) By Electrolytic Process
- Caustic Soda From Trona
- Caustic Soda, Chlorine And Hydrogen Gas By Electro-Lysis Of Brine Solution
- Cellulose Acetate Moulding Powder
- Cellulose Powder & Micro Crystalline Cellulose Powder
- Cement Admixture
- Cement Colour
- Cement Water Proofing Compound
- Cement From Fly Ash & Lime
- Cement Tiles (Glazed)
- Chlorinated Paraffin Wax (Cpw)
- Citric Acid From Lemon
- Citric Acid From Molasses
- Double Firing (Heating)
- Chelated Zinc (Zn Edta)
- Chemicals From Prawn Head
- Chitin & Chitosan From Prawn Shell Waste
- Chloral Hydrate
- Chloramphenicol
- Chromic Acid (With Pollution Control)
- Chromic Acid (Oxide) & Blue Oxide
- Chlorinated Paraffin Wax (Cpw)
- Chromic Acid
- Cement Paint & Distemper
- Citric Acid From Lemon
- Citric Acid From Molasses
- Cleaning Of Cooling System And Boiler
- Coal Tar Distillation
- Coal Washing Plant
- Cobalt Octoate

- Compost For Mushroom
- Construction Chemicals
- Copper Oxychloride
- Coolant (Engine)
- Copper Phthalocyanine Blue & Green
- Correction Fluid
- Cupric Chloride
- Crude Oil Bleaching For Petroleum Jelly
- Cutting Oil
- Cyanuric Chloride
- Cyanoacrylate Adhesive
- Cutting Oil
- Defoaming Agent For Paper Industry
- De-Nickeling (Electrolytic Process)
- Detergent Cake & Powder
- Detergent Powder
- Detergent Concentrate (Idet 10)
- Dextrose Monohydrate & Dextrose Anhydrous Powder From Tapioca Starch
- Di-Basic Lead Stearate
- Di Calcium Phosphate
- Diclofenal Sodium Slow Release (Sr) Tables 100mg.
- Di Ethyl Oxalate
- Di Methyl Orthophthalate
- Di-Methyl Phthalate
- Diclofenac Gel
- Dioctyl Phthalate (Dop)
- Di Phenyl Glycerine
- Di Phenyl Oxide
- Dinitro-Chloro Benzene
- Distillery
- Distilled Water
- Dodecyl Benzene Sulphonate
- Dustless Chalk
- Edta & Its Salts
- Electroless Nickel Plating On Plastics
- Electrolyte (Like Sulphuric Acid) For Lead Acid Dry Rechargable 5.5.Ah. Battery
- Electropolishing On Gold Jewellery
- Electropolishing On Various Metals
- Endosulfan
- Enzyme Based Detergent Powder
- Ephedrine Hydrochloride
- Epoxy Resin Based Compound
- Ethanol (Biofuel)
- Ethyl Alcohol From Molasses
- Ethyl Acetate
- Ehtyl Ether
- Ethyl Alcohol (Potable Liquor)
- Ethyl Hexanol
- Extra Temperature Lubricating Grease
- Extraction Of Essential Oils By Sugar Critical Fluid (Carbon Dioxide) Method From Flowers, Herbal & Spices
- Fabric Stain Remover
- Fatty Acid
- Ferric Alum
- Ferric And Non Ferric Alum (Aluminium Sulphate)
- Ferro Chrome Ligno Sulphonate
- Ferro Manganese
- Ferro Silicone

Contact **EIRI** for required Project report apart from this list.

- Ferro Vanadium From Vanadium Sludge
- Ferrous Silicate
- Ferrous Sulphate
- Ferrous Sulphide
- Fertilizer From Animal Blood & Leather Waste
- Fluorescent Tube Light Powder
- Foamed Pvc Compounding & Its Products
- Formaldehyde
- Food Grade Grease Or Lubricant
- Fractional Distillation Of D.M.O (Dementholized Oil)
- Fractional Distillation Of Essential Oil & Medicinalplant Extract
- Friction Dust (Liquid & Powder) From Cnsl
- Fruit Flavours
- Furfural From Rice Husk
- Fumaric Acid
- Gas Filling Of Lpg Cylinder
- Garlic Acid
- Ginger And Garlic Paste
- Ginger Processing
- Gasket Shellac Compound
- Gear Oil
- Gibberellic Acid
- Glass Putty
- Gluconic Acid
- Glucose D- Powder
- Glycerine
- Gossypol (Poly Phenol) From Cotton Seed Oil
- Greases (Lithium Based)
- Guar Gum Powder
- Hair Fixer (Hair Gel Type)
- High Temerature Grease
- Hard Grease
- H - Acid
- Henna Paste Making
- Henna Powder Repackaging
- Heptal Dehyde
- Herbal Beer
- High Carbon Ferro Chrome
- Humid Acid
- Hydrated Calcium Silicate Brick
- Hydrated Lime From Sea Shell
- Hydrochloric Acid
- Hydro Fluoric Acid
- Hydrogen Peroxide (By Auto-Oxidation Process)
- Ice Packs (Solutions Type, White Gel Type, Violet Semi Solid Polymer Type)
- Improving Drop Point Paraffin Wax From 45-50°c To 75-80°c
- Industrial Alcohol

Market Survey Cum Detailed Techno Economic Feasibility Report on all Projects are available Contact.
"ENGINEERS INDIA RESEARCH INSTITUTE". 4449, Nai Sarak (D), Main Road, Delhi-110006 (India)
Ph. : 09811437895, 91-11-23918117, 23916431, 45626431, 64727385 Fax : 91-11-23916431
E-mail : eiriprojects@gmail.com, eiribooks@yahoo.com • website: www.eiri.in, www.eiriindia.org

ALL FOLLOWING PROJECT REPORTS ARE READILY AVAILABLE

- Alluminium Printing Plate For Offset Printing Machine
- Aluminium Foils
- Aluminium Wire And Rods
- Brass And Aluminium Hinges
- Hard Anodizing On Aluminium
- Pilfer Proof Caps
- Piston Assembly (Aluminium Alloy)
- Pressure Die Casting (Aluminium)
- Paper Coated Aluminium Wire
- Pressure Cooker

FISH FARMING AND FISHERY PRODUCTS

- Aquaculture Prawn Farming (Fresh Water)
- Chitin & Chitosan From Prawn Shell Waste
- Chemicals From Prawn Fish Head
- Developing Trout Fish Preservation & Storage And Marketing Infrastructure
- Fish Farming
- Fish Canning And Pouching
- Fish Processing (Blast Freezing Process)
- Fish Net
- Fish Oil Soap
- Fish Meal
- Hdpe Fishing Net
- Plastic Milk Crate And Plastic Fish Crate
- Trout Fish Farming, Canning & Preservation With Aqua Feed Manufacturing (Integrated Complex)

SURGICAL AND DISPOSABLE MEDICAL PRODUCTS

- Ayurvedic/Herbal Pharmacy
- Blood Bags
- Bandage Cloth Weaving On Power Loom
- Crepe Bandage
- Disposable Surgical Caps & Masks
- Dextrose Saline (I.V.Fluid) In Plastic Bottle
- Dextrose Saline (I.V.Fluid)
- Disposable Needles For Syringes
- Disposable Plastic Syringes
- Diagnostic Centre
- Electronics Blood Pressure Measuring Instument
- Hospital Cum Nursing Home
- Homeopathic Medicines
- I. V. Fluids (Ffs Technology)
- I.V. Set-Cannula
- Intravenous
- Medical College
- Plastic I.V. Bottles
- Plaster Of Paris Bandages
- Pharmaceuticals (Tablet, Capsule, Syrups And Ointments)
- Repacking Of Medicines
- Surgical Cotton & Bandage
- Surgical Examination Gloves
- Surgical Bandage
- Surgical Adhesive Tape On Cloth Surface
- Surgical Methylated Spirit
- Sodium Phosphate Enema
- Vetenary Medicines

ALCOHOL, BEER, IMFL, COUNTRY LIQUOR, WINE & OTHER RELATED PROJECTS

- Alcohol From Rice Straw
- Alcohol From Molasses
- Alcohol From Potatoes
- Alcoholic Beverages And Vinegar From Coconut Water
- Alcoholic Drinks From Ethyl Alcohol
  By Mixing Of Various Flavours (Flavoured Alcoholic Beverages)
- Beer Plant (E.O.U.)
- Country Liquor
- Cider Plant
- Ethanol (Biofuel)
- Grape Wine
- Herbal Beer
- Mineral Water (Packed In Bottles, Glasses, Jars)
- Rectified Spirit For Potable Alcohol
- Industrial Alcohol & Medical Alcohol
- Rectified Spirit From Rice/Paddy Straw
- Indian Made Foreign Liquor
- Imfl (Whisky) From Potatoes
- Octalol (Octyl Alcohol) From Molasses
- Potable Beer (Alcoholic) Based On Potato & Barley/Malt
- Vodka From Potatoes
- Whisky
- Wine From Dates

ENGINEERS INDIA RESEARCH INSTITUTE
EiRi

PULP, PAPER, STRAW/GREY BOARD, KRAFT PAPER,PACKAGING, PAPER CARRY BAG, PAPER FROM AGRO WASTE & STATIONERY ETC.

- Ammonia Paper
- Automatic Book Binding
- Adhesive (Fevicol Type)
- All Pin & Gem Clips
- Ball Pen
- Ball Pen Refill Ink
- Ball Pen Ink Remover
- Carbon Paper
- Card Board
- Carbon Less Paper
- Cellphane Paper
- Computer Continuous Stationery
- Computer Forms & Security Printing Press
- Corrugated Board & Box (Printed & Laminated)
- Corrugated Board And Boxes From From Card Boards
- Corrugated Cartons From Plain Papers
- Corrugated Paper
- Corrugatred Packing & Material (Bulb & Tubes Packing)
- Desk Top Publishing
- Defoaming Agent For Paper Plant
- Drinking Straw Paper
- D.T.P Cum Offset Press
- Egg Trays From Pulp
- Ecg Paper
- Exercise Note Book, Register And Pad
- Flexographic Ink
- Greeting Card By Offset Press
- Hand Made Paper Filter Paper
- Hard Board
- Hard Board From Bagasse
- Injection Ampoules Packaging Boxes
- Insulatiing Paper
- Kraft Paper
- Kraft Paper From Bagasse
- Laminated Packaging Paper With Printing
- Lamination & Coating On Paper
- M.G. Paper From Waste Paper
- Mill Paper From Waste Paper
- Mill Board From Rice & Wheat Straws
- Mill Board From Waste Paper
- Mini Paper Plant From Sisal
- Mini Paper Plant
- Multi Wall Paper Sacks
- News Paper For Children
- News Print Paper From Rice Straw/Bagasse
- News Paper Childrens
- News Print Paper

Market Survey Cum Detailed Techno Economic Feasibility Report on all Projects are available Contact.
"ENGINEERS INDIA RESEARCH INSTITUTE". 4449, Nai Sarak (D), Main Road, Delhi-110006 (India)
Ph. : 09811437895, 91-11-23918117, 23916431, 45626431, 64727385 Fax : 91-11-23916431
E-mail : eiriprojects@gmail.com, eiribooks@yahoo.com • website: www.eiri.in, www.eiriindia.org

PROCESS TECHNOLOGY BOOKS BY EIRI

07 Rotational Moulding Technology Hand Book
08 Plastic Compounding, Master Batches, Pet & Other Plastics
09 Synthetic Resins Technology With Formulations
10 Technology Of PVC Compounding And Its Applications
11 Hand Book of Polymer And Plastic Technology
12 Hand Book Of Fibre Glass Moulding
13 Technology of Reinforced Plastics
14 Plastic Additives Technology Hand Book
15 Technology of PET Bottles, Preform and Pet Recycling
16 Modern Technology of Extrusion & Extruded Products
17 Technology of Synthetic Resins & Emulsion Polymers
18 Technology of Plastic Additives with Processes and Packaging
19 Technology of Disposable Medical Products

Bakery, Confectionery & Breakfast, Pasta & Cereals

01 Hand Book Of Bakery Industries
02 Hand Book Of Confectionery With Formulations
03 Breakfast, Dietary Food, Pasta & Cereal Products Technology
04 Hand Book Of Modern Bakery Products
05 Modern Bakery Technology & Fermented Cereal Products With Formulae
06 Technology of Confectionery, Chocolates, Toffee, Candy, Chewing & Bubble Gums, Lollipop and Jelly Products with Formulations

Agro Cultivation, Animal Farming, Agro Plantation & Agro Chemical/ Pesticides/Floriculture & Bee Keeping

01 Poultry Farming & Feed Formulations
02 Hand Book Of Pig Farming
03 Agro Based H.B. Of Plantation, Cultivation & Farming
04 Agro Based Plantation Cultivation & Farming
05 Agro Chemical Industries (Insecticide & Pesticides)
06 Modern Bee Keeping & Honey Processing

ENGINEERS INDIA RESEARCH INSTITUTE
4449 Nai Sarak, Main Road, Delhi - 110006 (INDIA)
Ph : 91- 11- 23916431, 23918117, 45120361, 64727385, 23947058
E-Mail : eiriprojects@gmail.com Website: www.eiriindia.org

PROCESS TECHNOLOGY BOOKS BY EIRI

Mineral And Minerals

01 Hand Book Of Minerals And Minerals Based Industries

Rubber Chemicals, Compound & Rubber Industries

01 Rubber Chemicals & Processing Industries
02 Modern Rubber Chemicals, Compounds & Rubber Goods Technology
03 Technology Of Rubber & Rubber Goods Industries

Ayurvedic & Herbal Medicines

01 Ayurvedic & Herbal Medicines With Formulaes
02 Hand Book Of Ayurvedic Medicines With Formulations (A Complete Hand Book Of Ayurvedic & Herbal Medicines)

Steel & Stainless Steel, Non Ferrous Metals, Metal Extraction, Rolling Mill & Steel Wire

01 Modern Technology of Non Ferrous Metals & Metal Extraction
02 Processing Technology of Steels and Stainless Steels
03 Modern Technology of Rolling Mill, Billets, Steel Wire, Galvanized Sheet, Forging & Castings
04 Manufacturing Technology of Non-Ferrous Metal Products

Wood, Veneer, Plywood, Particle, Board, Fibreboard, Bamboo & Forest Products

01 Modern Technology Of Wood, Veneer, Plywood, Particle Board, Fibreboard, Bamboo & Forest Products

Products form Waste

01 Technology Of Products From Wastes Industrial, Agriculture, Medical, Municipality, Organic & Biological

ENGINEERS INDIA RESEARCH INSTITUTE
4449 Nai Sarak, Main Road, Delhi - 110006 (INDIA)
Ph : 91- 11- 23916431, 23918117, 45120361, 64727385, 23947058
E-Mail : eiriprojects@gmail.com Website: www.eiriindia.org